Classical Archaeology of Ancient Greece and Rome
Part III: A View from the Trenches

Professor John R. Hale

THE TEACHING COMPANY ®

PUBLISHED BY:

THE TEACHING COMPANY
4151 Lafayette Center Drive, Suite 100
Chantilly, Virginia 20151-1232
1-800-TEACH-12
Fax—703-378-3819
www.teach12.com

ISBN 1-59803-214-3

John R. Hale, Ph.D.
Director of Liberal Studies, University of Louisville

John R. Hale, Director of Liberal Studies at the University of Louisville in Kentucky, is an archaeologist with fieldwork experience in England, Scandinavia, Portugal, Greece, and Turkey, as well as in the Ohio River valley. At the University of Louisville, Dr. Hale teaches introductory courses on archaeology, as well as more specialized courses on the Bronze Age, the ancient Greeks, the Roman world, Celtic cultures, Vikings, and on nautical and underwater archaeology. He has received awards for distinguished teaching, including the Panhellenic Teacher of the Year Award and the Delphi Center Award. He has toured the United States and Canada as a lecturer for the Archaeological Institute of America and has presented lecture series at museums and universities in Finland, South Africa, Australia, and New Zealand.

Archaeology has been the focus of Dr. Hale's academic career from his B.A. studies at Yale University to his doctoral research at Cambridge University in England, where he received his Ph.D. degree. The subject of his dissertation was the Bronze Age ancestry of the Viking longship, a study that involved field surveys of ship designs in prehistoric rock art in southern Norway and Sweden. During more than thirty years of archaeological work, Dr. Hale has excavated at a Romano-British town in Lincolnshire and a Roman villa in Portugal and carried out interdisciplinary studies of ancient oracle sites in Greece and Turkey, including the famous Delphic Oracle. Currently he is participating in an undersea search in Greek waters for lost fleets from the time of the Persian Wars. In addition, Dr Hale is a member of a scientific team seeking to develop and refine a method for dating mortar, concrete, and plaster from ancient buildings—a method employing radiocarbon analysis with an Accelerator Mass Spectrometer.

Most of Dr. Hale's work is interdisciplinary and involves collaborations with geologists, chemists, nuclear physicists, historians, zoologists, botanists, physical anthropologists, geographers, and art historians. He has published his work in *Antiquity*, the *Journal of Roman Archaeology*, the *Classical Bulletin*, and *Scientific American*. He has written a book on the ancient Athenian navy, *Lords of the Sea*, for Viking/Penguin (2006).

Beyond archaeology, Dr. Hale's interests include rowing and music. A veteran of the Yale-Harvard boat race (the oldest intercollegiate sporting event in America!), he was a founder of the Louisville Rowing Club. Dr. Hale also serves as director of education for the Louisville Bach Society.

Table of Contents

Classical Archaeology of Ancient Greece and Rome
Part III: A View from the Trenches
Part III

Classical Archaeology of Ancient Greece and Rome

Scope:

The field of archaeology, which today covers all periods of the human past in all parts of the world, began as an investigation into the lost civilizations of Greece and Rome. The discipline takes its name from two Greek words meaning "ancient things" and "studies." Archaeology may be defined as the study of cultures through their material remains. Those remains may range in size from a grain of pollen in a wine jar to an entire buried city.

"Classical" archaeologists are researchers who continue the quest for an understanding of Greek and Roman antiquity. Although their discoveries include written records on clay tablets or papyrus scrolls, classical archaeologists devote most of their efforts to locating, recovering, and interpreting the seemingly mute remains of ancient sites—marble and mudbrick, bronze and concrete, industrial debris and great works of art, grave goods, cargoes lost at sea, pottery, coins, bones, and the very dirt that encloses them all.

What can you expect to learn from this course? By the end of the 36th lecture, you should have a clear idea of the scope of the field and of the methods that archaeologists use to find, map, and excavate ancient sites. You should be able to follow the process of conserving and restoring artifacts and understand the laboratory methods used to determine the age and provenance of artifacts and materials. Your "archaeological literacy" should embrace the accomplishments of pioneers in the field, the locations of important sites, and the archaeological terms for different time periods, cultures, and classes of artifacts. You should grasp the archaeological evidence relating to myths and legends and to historical events ranging from the trial of Socrates to the massacre of a Roman army. And you should see that no area of Classical archaeology is exempt from controversy, conflict of opinion, and a residue of doubt, uncertainty, and enduring mystery.

Above all, my hope is that this course will enable you to view the world of the Greeks and Romans, not as a sequence of historical events, but as an immense living organism, a system in which society, culture, and the natural environment interact in dynamic, creative, and sometime destructive ways. Out of this matrix came major religious, political, and philosophical concepts that continue to influence modern thought. As for the rich historical record of ancient literature and inscriptions, we are fortunate that these texts allow us to put names and faces to the long-dead individuals who participated in this extraordinary drama.

In terms of chronology, the course will span approximately 2,000 years. Most of the sites and discoveries fall within the "Classical" millennium from the 8th century B.C.—the traditional date for the first Olympic Games and the founding of Rome—to the reigns of the Roman emperors Hadrian and Marcus Aurelius in A.D. 2nd century, when Greco-Roman civilization achieved its fullest integration and widest impact. But to set Classical civilization in context, our survey must reach back in time to the 17th century B.C. and the great Bronze Age centers on the islands of Crete and the Cyclades. We will end at about 400 A.D., with the recall of the Roman legions from the western provinces and the imperial Roman edict that outlawed traditional religious cults in favor of Christianity.

The geographical scope of the course will also be wide-ranging. Archaeologists have excavated Greek cities from Spain to Afghanistan and from the Black Sea to the shores of North Africa. Long after the founding of these Greek colonies, the Roman Empire drew into a single administrative unit the territories of some 40 modern countries, from Britain and Morocco in the west to Romania and Iraq in the east. For both Greeks and Romans, sites on the periphery proved important for commerce and cultural change.

Like Caesar's Gaul, our course will be divided into three parts. In the first 12 lectures, we will trace the evolution of Classical archaeology from a pastime for collectors and antiquarians to a mature science. This epic story is marked by encounters with great archaeologists, their landmark discoveries, and the techniques they developed to bring the buried past back to life. Classical archaeologists have made many contributions to the field of archaeology in general, ranging from the grid system of excavation to the first scientific underwater "dig." Today, Classical archaeology is a multidisciplinary team effort that involves not only traditional diggers but geologists, geographers, chemists, physicists, biologists, physical anthropologists, historians, and linguists.

The second part of the course comprises a series of case studies that will take us to the sites of 12 important excavations. These ancient cities, trading emporia, frontier fortifications, religious sanctuaries, and other sites (a shipwreck, a Roman farm, a civic center, a battlefield, and even the interiors of a pair of bronze statues) have been chosen to illustrate the broad range of research in Classical archaeology. Each also features some particular problem, issue, or technical innovation.

The third part will present an overview of Classical civilization from an archaeologist's perspective, with focus on the detailed reconstruction of ancient life made possible by archaeological discoveries. Here, we will continually ask the question: What can archaeology reveal that written historical sources cannot? This part opens with the controversies concerning the origins of Classical civilization and closes with an examination of the evidence for the fall of the western Roman Empire and the end of the Classical world. Our approach for the most part, however, will be thematic rather than chronological. Important themes include the economic underpinnings of ancient society, the lives of those—particularly women and slaves—whose voices are almost entirely excluded from the written record, the technical achievements of ancient engineers and builders, the impact of imperial power and religion, and the vital importance of a common cultural tradition among the lands and communities of Classical antiquity. We will close by considering how the legacy of Greek and Roman civilization has helped to shape our own modern world.

Lecture Twenty-Five
Roots of Classical Culture

Scope:

With this lecture, we embark on the final leg of our voyage through the world of Classical archaeology. As you remember, we began in Part I by looking at the origins of archaeology at Pompeii and Herculaneum. We saw archaeology grow into a mature science concerned with recovering and interpreting material remains of the past. In Part II, we took an archaeologist's casebook tour of 12 sites or discoveries from the Bronze Age, the world of the Greeks, and the world of the Romans. In this final part of our course, our mission is to ask some larger questions about Classical civilization to see what answers archaeology can give us.

We'll begin in this lecture with the following question: Where did Classical civilization originate, and what does it owe to the older civilizations of Egypt and the Near East? When archaeology was born, in the 18th century, there was a belief that the Greeks stood as a fountainhead at the beginnings of Western civilization; that view has been challenged, especially in the 20th century. In this lecture, we will look at the archaeological evidence for the origins of Greek civilization and the later civilizations that grew out of it, including the Roman culture that spread over the Mediterranean basin and beyond. In each of these last 12 lectures, as we take up a topic, we will look at a specific site in the Classical world to see how that site can help us answer larger questions. For this lecture, our site is a tell called Sesklo.

Outline

I. The tell site of Sesklo is similar to Troy but on the other side of the Aegean. About 10 miles away from this hilltop site is the Gulf of Volos, across which Jason and his Argonauts sailed in the quest for the Golden Fleece.

   A. In the Bronze and Neolithic Ages, the Gulf of Volos was a heavily populated center of developing Greek culture. At Sesklo, one of the first Greek archaeologists, Christos Tsountas (1857–1934), discovered a village going back thousands of years before the time of Classical Greece. This village shows us in embryo some of the features that would set the Greeks apart from other Neolithic peoples.

B. In 1901, Tsountas came to Sesklo, having earlier worked with Schliemann at Mycenae. At Sesklo, he used a technique that was the reverse of Mortimer Wheeler's grid system. He left behind, in the middle of the site, a square column of sediment consisting of built-up layers of the tell. Such a column is called an *archaeological martyr*, in this case, *martyr* meaning "witness."

    1. This column of earth preserves in layers what Tsountas and his successors dug through and maintains a record for future archaeologists.

    2. The martyr reveals layers of burning, which can be seen where the soil changes color. Sherds of pottery and acorns—millennia old—are also preserved inside the mix.

II. What did Tsountas find at Sesklo that gives us a window on some of the differences in Greek civilization?

    A. Sesklo was a farming village, and we know from what they raised that its inhabitants were migrants to Greece.

        1. In fact, after the Ice Age, Greece was temporarily depopulated. We do not have any sign of human habitation for about 1,000 years at the beginning of the modern era. In the Mesolithic Age, we begin to find light evidence of habitation in such sites as Franchthi Cave.

        2. Some centuries after that, the first farmers seem to have arrived in Greece. They brought with them domesticated plants and animals, such as wheat, sheep, goats, and pigs, that do not have their origins in Europe or on the Greek mainland.

        3. These plants and animals come from the east—Anatolia, Turkey, the Zagros Mountains—where these species occur wild and seem to have been domesticated.

    B. Among the differences between the tell at Sesklo and those in the Near East is that, at Sesklo, the houses did not have party walls.

    C. Inside the houses has been found some of the most beautiful pottery ever created in the Neolithic Age. This pottery has a pallet of black, red, yellow, and white, mixed together in geometric patterns.

    1. The pottery has no visible practical purpose in terms of storage or cooking. An American archaeologist, Curtis Runnels, has offered the opinion that the pottery was for display.

    2. It is possible that these pots reveal the origins of a Greek tradition that spread across the Classical world: the *symposium*, a wine-drinking ceremony of friends gathered around a central container and served their drinks in cups.

III. From Sesklo, Tsountas went into the Cyclades. His work there is important because he discovered early Neolithic life there—not on the mainland, where scholars had focused, but on these small rocky islands in the Aegean.

    A. On such islands as Malta, Madagascar, Easter Island, or New Zealand, unique forms of life emerged that are quite different from those on the mainland. Islanders feel much safer than mainlanders and are able to achieve cultural developments more quickly. The fact that the archipelago of the Aegean was shown by Tsountas to be one of the hearts of Greek civilization explains some of the unusual features that set it apart from its Near Eastern antecedents.

    B. What does the Classical world owe to the Near East and Egypt? A Latin phrase sums up one way of answering this question: *Ex oriente lux; ex occidente lex*: "Out of the Orient, light; out of the Occident, law." In this view, creativity and inspiration are attributed to the Near East. Law and order, engineering, and the practicalities of life would come from the Greeks and Romans.

        1. The Greeks themselves were aware of this division. They had myths about borrowing their traditions from Phoenicia and Egypt, and were proud of the fact they could trace both their customs and individual bloodlines to places far outside the borders of Greece.

        2. Plato expressed Greek cultural jingoism by asserting that the Greeks had perfected everything they borrowed.

C. In the 18th century, when the modern view of the Greek world was solidified around the idealizing work of Winckelmann and others, the earlier part of the equation—the idea that the Greeks owed so much to Egypt and to the Near East—was forgotten. The Greeks were presented to the scholarly world as the originators of civilization.

D. A modern scholar, Martin Bernal, from Cornell, has written a long meditation on this process, including both the ancient Greek practice of borrowing and transforming cultural impulses from the East and Africa, specifically Egypt, and the modern forgetfulness of this debt.

    1. Bernal believes that our forgetfulness is, at heart, racist—Europeans claiming for ancestral Europeans the credit for being the prime force behind civilization.

    2. Bernal's book, *Black Athena*, has stimulated tremendous scholarly debate because it makes a double-pronged attack, first on the Greeks themselves—how little of their cultural baggage they actually manufactured—then on those scholars who suppressed the record of what is owed to the Egyptians, the Sumerians, and other pre-Greek peoples.

E. In looking at the evidence of Classical civilization, we can see that the Greeks are not the originators, nor did they claim to be. Temples with columns; the *kouroi*, those beautiful statues of young men; mathematics; science; metallurgy; the world of art and architecture; epic poetry—all these originated outside of Greece.

IV. Why were the Greeks successful, and what was it about their civilization that they truly originated?

A. A few cultural innovations are foreshadowed at Sesklo, including a sense of individualism that we find much less in the Egyptian and Near Eastern societies than in the Greek world—the idea of the individual as a measure of society.

    1. We see this idea develop in the Classical world into a great respect for the individual. The fact that writing became common in everyday life in the Greek and Roman worlds attests to the pride of individuals.

2. We have names of thousands of individual Greek and Roman citizens. We find artists—and even ordinary craftspeople—who sign their works, something that is not seen in Egypt and the Near East. We even see rivalries between craftspeople.

B. This sense of personal worth leads to two additional cornerstones of the Classical tradition that were new to the Greek world and, perhaps, inherited from the Cycladic civilization that Tsountas first illuminated.

1. One of these was the interest in giving ordinary people a place to speak in public. As you recall, in the heart of Athens was the Agora, open to all citizens to come and share in their government.

2. Above the Agora was the rock called the Pnyx ("the place of the crowd"). On this ancient stone, speakers would stand to address their fellow citizens.

3. In the Forum in Rome was the Rostrum, the speakers' platform where ordinary citizens could stand up and be heard.

4. If we look at Classical civilization from Scotland to Arabia, in every community, we see public meeting places, theaters, odeons (covered halls for musical performances)—all used for speechmaking—as well as schools of rhetoric.

5. The idea of proclaiming things in public and establishing one's identity as a citizen was an essential and unique innovation in Greek civilization. We can also see this idea in the archaeological record in the way ancient people laid out their communities.

C. The second important innovation of Classical civilization was competition, which we noted at Olympia. No earlier civilization had its most important religious sanctuary dedicated to contests between individuals.

1. This aspect of ancient life would grow into the Roman love of sports, which involved blood sports, heavy betting, and professionals. But in its beginning, Olympia was a place where people could test themselves against each other, one on one. Except for the rowing races, team sports played no part. Competition was focused on the individual.

2. Even the dialectic form that Socrates used is a contest of words. The philosopher who sits down in a study to write down thoughts gets nowhere. Progress in thought is made only when individuals are face to face, challenging and arguing with each other.

D. From this sense of the individual, we get, first of all, the idea of public responsibility, the onus of the individual to speak. Socrates himself said that the point of an education is so that a young man who goes to the theater will not be merely one block of stone sitting on another.

1. The individual must participate in public affairs, and archaeology shows that communities were set up for that purpose. We see a decreasing interest in private homes and the decoration of private homes.

2. Life was experienced outdoors, and wealthy people contributed beautiful things to the community.

V. What made Greek civilization successful? I believe that the answer to this question can be found in a new kind of militarism.

A. On display in the museum in the town of Nafplio in the Peloponnese is a suit of armor from Dendra, found inside a warrior's tomb. It has a conical helmet, with boars' tusks glittering on its sides in rows.

B. The body armor suggests that this warrior was one of the earliest heavily armed infantrymen, who could operate only in a line with many other infantrymen, each protecting the rest of the line with a shield held on the left arm.

C. Such a fighting unit, the *phalanx*, would develop into the Roman legions. The phalanx downplays the aristocratic cavalry or chariots and light-armed mobile troops and puts all its stock in a line of heavily armed men—equals, all depending on the others.

D. In this suit of armor, we see the beginnings of a tradition that will carry this Classical civilization through time and around the world. Those armed men will preserve and spread their own culture and bring new cultural impulses and wealth back to their world.

Suggested Reading:

Powell, *Homer and the Origin of the Greek Alphabet.*

Runnels and Murray, *Greece Before History: An Archaeological Companion and Guide.*

Questions to Consider:

1. How important is the study of prehistoric cultures in the Mediterranean for an understanding of Greeks and Romans in the historical period?

2. To what extent do the "high" achievements of Classical Greek and Roman culture—art, architecture, engineering, philosophy, literature, drama, science, medicine—seem to be part of its original "cultural DNA"?

Lecture Twenty-Five—Transcript
Roots of Classical Culture

Welcome back. Today, we embark on the third and final leg on our voyage through the world of classical archaeology. As you remember, we began in Part I by looking at the origins of archaeology itself at Pompeii and Herculaneum; its development right up to modern times as it grew into a mature science, of trying to recover material remains of the past, interpret and analyze them to understand things that the written texts of history just don't tell us. Then in our middle section, which we just completed, we did an archaeologist's casebook tour of 12 important archaeological sites or discoveries from the Bronze Age, the world of the Greeks, and the world of the Romans.

It's our mission in this final part to try to ask some big questions about classical civilization and see what archaeology has to tell us about the answers.

We'll begin today with the great question: Where did classical civilization originate, and what does it owe to the older civilizations of Egypt and the Near East? There was certainly a belief in the time that archaeology was born, back in the 18th century, that the Greeks somehow stood as a sort of fountainhead at the beginnings of Western civilization. They were the source.

People like Winckelmann shed a radiance over the Greeks, especially, as being superhumans who had called into existence forms of government, philosophy, religious belief—and above all, art—that had never existed before. That view has been challenged, especially in the 20th century, and we want to look at the archaeological evidence, the origins, of Greek civilization and the later civilizations that grew out of it, including the Roman culture that was spread all over the Mediterranean basin and beyond.

In each of these 12 lectures, as we take up our topic, we're going to start by going, through the magic of imagination, to a specific site somewhere in the classical world, and see what that site can do to lead us into the labyrinth of meanings and questions that are involved in these big issues.

Our site today, as we launch this part of our voyage, is a place called Sesklo. It is a tell (one of those artificial hills with a layer cake of villages or cities inside) just like Troy, but on the other side of the Aegean. About 10 miles away from this hilltop where we are standing at Sesklo, we can see a shining sheet of water, the beautiful blue stretch of sea that is the Gulf of Volos. This is the water across which Jason and his Argonauts, in that first ship, the *Argo*, rode away on their great and epic voyage, across the Aegean Sea, through the Hellespont and the Bosphorus to the end of the Black Sea, in their quest for the Golden Fleece.

Back in the Bronze Age, back in the Neolithic Age (the New Stone Age), this Gulf of Volos, up in the northern part of Greece—you can almost see Mount Olympus from one end of it—it was a center of developing Greek culture. But it got left behind in the classical period and we don't hear much about it during the great golden age of Pericles and Socrates and the more familiar classical Greeks.

Nonetheless, this was one of the most heavily populated areas. On this hilltop of Sesklo, one of the first great Greek archaeologists, a man named Christos Tsountas discovered a village going back thousands of years before the time of classical Greece which nonetheless shows us in embryo some of the features that are going to set the Greeks apart from other Neolithic peoples.

Tsountas came to the site in 1901. He was, at that time, in his middle 40s, but he was already a veteran of a couple of decades in having worked on archaeological sites in Greece. Schliemann had dug through those royal shaft graves at Mycenae and pulled out the famous mask of Agamemnon in beaten gold. His wife, Sophie, had explored other royal tombs at Mycenae. After this, it was Tsountas, as a young man in his 20s, who went there and did the hard, backbreaking work to get beyond the tombs and the easy finds and into the habitation area where the people actually lived, uncovering the vast complex of palace and associated rooms up on top of the hill at Mycenae.

He also got off the Greek mainland and out into the islands. He was one of the first people to take an interest in those Cyclades, little places like Syros and Sifnos, where he discovered hilltop communities, often with big fortification walls, where early farmers had lived millennia before the period of classical Greece.

When he came to Sesklo in 1901, he was already a very seasoned and very serious archaeologist. He's also—as an aside—one of a trio of archaeologists in my personal pantheon of greats. Also in this pantheon is the Italian, Giuseppe Fiorelli, whom we met bringing order to some chaos at Pompeii back in the 1860s, and trying to show that Neophyte, Heinrich Schliemann, how a dig ought to be done. And also, the American, Harriet Boyd, the discoverer and excavator of that intriguing little Minoan town of Gournia on the north shore of Crete.

Tsountas, like them, was very serious, very self-effacing, very non-promoting of himself. But of what he was discovering, he was a tireless promoter, and spent the rest of his life, until the 1930s, teaching at the University of Athens, trying to spread the word to the world about the roots of Greek civilization.

Tsountas was the most honest archaeologist whose work I've ever read. He did an early underwater exploration in the Straits of Salamis that combined battlefield archaeology, which we talked about for the Teutoburg Forest massacre site, along with the first attempt at an underwater archaeological survey on scientific principles—this was way back in the 1880s. He hired sponge divers, with their gray helmets, to go down and look for the remains of the Greek and the Persian battleships that should have sunk to the bottom during the great battle of Salamis in 480 B.C.

They had to do it in mid-winter and nobody had ever tried this before. The bottom is mud and whenever they disturbed anything, a column drum or a pot—of which they brought back a few—they stirred up such clouds of sediment that you couldn't see. Everything was blurred, as he said.

So he left a report for the scientific society that had funded the work saying, "We must regard this expedition as a total failure." I have to say I don't know when I would have ever had the moral courage to say this was a failure to the body that had granted the funds, so my hat is off to Tsountas.

At Sesklo, we are one the site of one of his great triumphs. We can see there an unusual archaeological thing. You remember Mortimer Wheeler, that man who devised the grid system for digging a checkerboard of pits over a site in well-organized, laid-out squares.

Tsountas used a reversed technique, which started by him and continued by archaeologists again reviving work on the site in the '50s and up to the present. This technique is to leave behind, in the middle of the site, a great square column of sediment, sediment that built up layers of the tell.

This is called an archaeological martyr, not because it has suffered—that's not what *martyr* means in Greek—but it means witness. This block, this column of earth that is left behind after the rest is stripped down to the levels of a village of the 4th or 5th millennium B.C., this preserves in it, layer after layer, what Tsountas and his successors dug through, and maintains a record, then, for future archaeologists to observe and to test as they also try to get the secrets out of this amazing site.

It's an extraordinary thing to look at this martyr because you can see layers of burning. You can see layers where the soil colors change. You can even see sherds of pottery and acorns—millennia old—preserved inside the mix.

What did he find at Sesklo which gives us a little window on some of the differences about Greece? It was a farming village, and we know from what they were raising that these people were migrants to Greece. In fact, after the Ice Age, Greece was temporarily depopulated. We do not have any sign of human habitation for about 1,000 years at the beginning of the modern era, when the ice sheets have gone, the Paleolithic is ending.

Then here and there in Greece, in the Mesolithic (the Middle Stone Age), we get some light evidence of habitation, places like Franchthi cave, down in the Argolid in the Peloponnese, where the archaeologists from Indiana University, whom we've already talked about, discovered obsidian that showed way back 8,000–10,000 years ago, Greek seafarers were leaving the mainland and going out in boats to the volcanic island of Melos to get that obsidian.

Some centuries after that, new people seem to have arrived in Greece, the first farmers. We feel that they're new because they brought with them domesticated plants and animals that do not have their origin in Europe or on the Greek mainland. They already had dogs in the Paleolithic for hunting, but along with that come sheep and goat, pig, and crops, like wheat, that were not domesticated in

Greece. The origins are from the East, from Anatolia, from Turkey, from the Zagros Mountains where these species occur wild and seem to have been domesticated.

There are tells all over the Near East, places where early farmers had their mudbrick homes, and when the rains eventually caused the walls to slump, they leveled them and built a new home on top, raising the mound higher and higher and higher. Tells are common.

What's different about Sesklo? First thing is, the houses don't have party walls. Instead of all being joined together in one enormous hive—as one sees at places like Çatalhöyük and many of the Anatolian and Near Eastern tells—each house is separate. Each house has its own identity. They all interface nicely by maintaining little alleyways between them. There are walls straight and parallel with each other; but every household is separate; every household is individual.

One thing that's found inside the houses is very intriguing to me. That is some of the most beautiful pottery ever created in the Neolithic. The potters of Sesklo became virtuosos. We don't know yet whether they were the men or the women or both, but they created a pottery that was so sophisticated that it had a pallet of four different colors—black, red, yellow, white—all mixed together in beautiful geometric patterns. It looks a lot like the pueblo patterns of the American southwest. It sometimes took two or three additional firings to get all of those minerals that had been applied to the outside of the pot, to take their final form and glossy color.

This pottery, the finest stuff, has no visible, practical purpose in terms of storage or cooking of food. Yet, it's got these beautiful patterns on it so it has to have been out and on display. There's a great American archaeologist, Curtis Runnels, who has offered the opinion that it was exactly for that. It was a sense of display, status symbols put up in homes.

There's nothing the anthropological mind likes better than a status symbol. But I would like to think that if we look at the likely function of these little pots—which can't have held lids, can't have been for storage and don't show the marks of cooking—that we can see the origins of a great Greek tradition, a tradition that spread all over the classical world (and that we will explore in depth when we have our session on ancient wine), and that is the symposium, the wine-drinking ceremony. A little cognate, perhaps, with the Japanese tea-drinking ceremony where a group of friends will get together, and there's wine in that large central bowl or vase and it's dipped out in little cups and served to the guests.

Just as on 18th-century teacups, there were intriguing patterns and colors to stimulate conversation, we know that the Greeks of the classical period loved to adorn the cups for that symposium, that wine-drinking ceremony, with scenes of myth or scenes of daily life that would stir up conversation.

I like to think of the sociability of Sesklo, of those house parties where people would come together, drink their wine and talk communally—not in a religious context, not in a political context, not in a context of militarism or necessity, but just sociability, as the start of something that is going to climax with the symposia described by Plato and Xenophon where Socrates himself is one of the drinkers. The flow of wine and the easy sociability around that circle led on to some of the greatest achievements in human thought and philosophy.

I mentioned that from Sesklo, Tsountas went on out into the Cyclades and studied those islands. In fact, he'd been out there in the 19th century as well. It's very important that he did that work on the islands because he found that some of that early Neolithic life was going on not on the mainland—where everyone's focus had been—but out on these small rocky islands in the Aegean.

This, in and of itself, is of great interest to me. I don't think archaeology has even begun to plumb the depths of what this all means—that it may have begun as an island culture. We know what the people who started agriculture on Crete, who came over from modern day Turkey with their livestock and their families and their seed crops, they had to have come in boats; they have to have been seafarers. Seafaring islands, these build a unique kind of civilization.

If we look at islands like Malta, Madagascar, Easter Island, New Zealand, unique forms of life can grow up on islands very different from those on the mainland where you never know who's going to come over the hill next, what army, what marauders, what danger. Islanders feel much safer. Islanders are able to develop forms quickly and in stranger ways than is possible on the mainland. I think the fact that the archipelago of the Aegean was shown by Tsountas to be one of the hearts of Greek civilization explains some of the unusual features that set it apart from its Near Eastern antecedents.

This is a great question. What does the classical world owe to the Near East and to Egypt? There is a saying that I was told I could have an A in Chinese History for, if I could just find the originator. We were all told this by our professor of Chinese History, Arthur Wright. He would start each semester by saying, "Anyone who can find the origin of the saying '*Ex oriente lux, ex occidente lex*' will get an A in this course. No one ever did. As far as I know, the original source of that little Latin phrase has never been found, but it means "Out of the Orient," or the East, "light." Inspiration. "Out of the occident," the West, "*lex*," law, order.

This is a way of looking at the world which put all of the creativity, the inspiration, coming from the Near East, the land that provided the Bible and the *Epic of Gilgamesh* and so on. The law, the order, the engineering, the practical side of things, would be the Greeks and the Romans.

Already, whoever thought of this—and this goes back certainly at least a millennium and a half, this saying, was trying to divide the world into these two polarized camps. The Greeks themselves were aware of this issue. They had many myths about how they got their traditions from Phoenicia, which did indeed, as we can tell, give them the alphabet. Or from Egypt. They were proud of the fact that they could trace not only customs, but individual bloodlines, genealogies of families back to these places far outside the borders of Greece.

Along with that was a great cultural jingoism, which is best expressed by Plato who said, yes, we Greeks borrowed a great deal from all these other peoples, but we perfected everything that we borrowed. So there you have the pride of the Greeks—almost the arrogance of the Greeks—about the perfection of their civilization and yet, at the same time, the debt that it owed to the Near East and Egypt.

In the 18th century, when the modern view of the Greek world came to be solidified around the works, the idealizing works of people like

Winckelmann, that earlier part of the equation, that they owed so much to Egypt and to the Near East—Samaria, Babylon, Assyria—that was forgotten. The Greeks were presented to the scholarly world as the originators of civilization. How anybody could have done this is beyond me.

A modern scholar, Martin Bernal, who taught at Cornell, has written a long meditation on this process. This includes both the ancient Greek process of borrowing and transforming cultural impulses from the East and from Africa and specifically Egypt; and the modern forgetfulness of this debt, and wishing to put on these first Europeans the mantle of credit for having invented all these things.

The fact that we still call the Pythagorean Theorem by the name of a Greek philosopher who, in fact, lived at least 1,000 years after the first recorded use of the Pythagorean geometric theorem in the Near East shows some of that cultural jingoism on our part. Bernal believed that it was basically a racist thing—Europeans trying to claim for ancestral Europeans this credit of being the prime civilizing force.

He wrote a book, more than one volume, very thick, entitled *Black Athena*, a real in-your-face title. If he had just called it *Reflections on Afro-Asian Influences on Classical Civilization*, it would have been bought by a handful of people and quickly forgotten. Instead, with that title, *Black Athena*, it has remained in print for 20 years. It passes my ultimate test of being a success: you can still see it sometimes in airport bookstores.

It has stimulated tremendous scholarly debate because he took a double-pronged attack first on the Greeks themselves—how little of their cultural baggage they actually manufactured from the start; and then on those scholars starting in the 18th century who suppressed the record of what we owe to the Egyptians, the Sumerians and those other pre-Greek peoples.

It's true that if you look at a lot of the spectacular evidence—and including the archaeological evidence of classical civilization—the Greeks are not the originators and, for the most part, never claimed that they were. Temples with columns; those kouroi, those first beautiful Greek statues of those young men, which are so reminiscent of contemporary statues in Egypt; mathematics; science; metallurgy; the whole world of art and architecture; epic poetry.

As far as the Greeks perfecting things that the Near Easterners and Egyptians had just gropingly moved toward, as Plato would have us believe, can we really say that the Parthenon is a perfected form of Karnac in Egypt? Or that the *Iliad* is the perfected form of the *Epic of Gilgamesh*? Certainly not. They are separate, but equal; they were trying to achieve different things and they are achieving greatness in different ways.

What can we see back there in the classical world—and in its origins—which does seem to be the distinctive core that not only made classical civilization, but made it a success? Let's be a little bit Darwinian about this. It's not just a matter of coming up with something new, an innovation, a mutation—it's got to be successful. There's got to be something that will carry that forward through time, produce offspring, new civilizations, in the case of a cultural innovation.

Why were the Greeks successful and what was it about their civilization that they truly did originate? We just had a couple of things adumbrated, foreshadowed, there at Sesklo. It's that sense of individualism that we get in the Greek world that we find much less of in the Egyptian and Near Eastern societies, the individual as the measure of society. That sociability, people in groups—independent of a king or a priest or a temple or a higher order—households getting together.

We're going to see this develop in the classical world into a great respect for the individual. The fact that writing became common and casual in everyday life in the Greek and Roman world lets us see how proud individuals were of themselves. We have names of thousands of individual Greek and Roman citizens. We find artists— and even just ordinary craftspeople—who sign their works, something you don't find that in Egypt and the Near East, and even show rivalry with other craftspeople.

There's a beautiful amphora by Euthymides, a potter of ancient Athens who worked down near that ancient Agora that we visited with John Camp. He wrote on his amphora not just his own name, Euthymides, but "as never Euphronios," who was a rival potter, just to show that he had produced one here which he was convinced would stand at the very top of all the pots that had been produced at Athens at the time.

That sense of rivalry, that sense of personal worth and value, I think then leads us to two other important cornerstones of the classical tradition which are new with the Greek world and perhaps inherited from that Cycladic civilization that Tsountas first opened the door to.

One of these is the interest in giving ordinary people a place to speak in public. If you go to the heart of Athens, what do you find? The Agora, the open space, open to all citizens to come and share in their government. Above it, the rock called the Pnyx ("the place of the crowd"). There's an ancient stone on the Pnyx where speakers would stand to address the crowds, to address their fellow citizens.

If you go to Rome down in the Forum, you've got the place called Rostrum. We still use that word today. Rostrum comes from the rostra, the beaks of captured warships, mainly Punic warships, which were set up there as war trophies around this place, the speaker's platform in the Forum, where ordinary citizens could stand up and be heard.

Let's pull back and get a macro view of classical civilization, from Scotland all the way to Arabia. In every community, we see public meeting places, theaters, odeons, those covered halls for musical performances, but also for speechmaking. We see schools of rhetoric where people are learning to talk. The idea of speaking in public, proclaiming things in public, establishing your identity as a citizen to that public of which you belong is an essential—and, I believe, uniquely new—thing in Greek civilization. We can see it in the archaeological record, in the way they lay out their communities.

The second thing is that "never Euphronios" element: competition. We spent an entire session at Olympia. What earlier civilization had not just an entire site, but their most important religious sanctuary dedicated to games, to contests, to rivalry between people, between individuals? This is going to grow into the Roman love of sports, which was a slightly different thing—chariots, blood sports, heavy betting, and professionals. In its beginning, it was a place where people could test themselves against each other, one on one. Except for the rowing races. Team sports played no part. It was all about the individual.

This emphasis on the individual and rivalry—I think we mentioned when we were down in the Agora, even the dialectic that Socrates used is a contest in words. It's the idea that a philosopher sitting down in a study and writing down thoughts gets nowhere. It's only when you're out there face to face with an interlocutor, another person, bouncing ideas off, challenging, arguing—then you move forward.

From that idea of the individual, we get first of all the idea of the public responsibility, the onus of the individual to speak. Socrates himself said the point of an education is so that when a young man goes to the theater, he will not be one block of stone sitting on another. You need to be an educated person. Pericles said that the definition of an idiot, someone who keeps to themselves, is a person who doesn't take part in pubic affairs.

The individual must participate in the public affairs and the archaeology shows this community set up to make that happen, and shows us a tremendous downgrading of interest in private homes. No fancy mosaics, no beautiful friezes or frescos in the private homes. The life was led outdoors and people contributed—if they were rich—beautiful things to the whole community. Then on that other side, the competition, the rivalry, the contests that make something unique of that Greek world that leads into the whole world of classical civilization.

What made it successful? You can have a model, but if it's not going to be perpetuated, if it's going to be wiped out, it doesn't matter how beautiful or interesting it may have been. I believe that it was a new kind of militarism that made it successful.

Go down to the museum in the beautiful little town of Nafplio in the Peloponnese, climb the stairs, and ask to see the suit of armor from Dendra. This was found in a warrior's tomb. It has a helmet, a conical type, with boars' tusks glittering on its sides in these rows, showing all of the boars that the warrior or hunter had killed.

What's really interesting is the body armor. It looks like the Michelin man, only in bronze—ring after ring after ring, expanding to a big one down at thigh level, to cover his whole body with this bronze armor. He's one of our earliest heavy-armed infantrymen and he can only operate in a line with lots of other heavy-armed infantrymen, each protecting the rest of the line with the shield held on the left arm.

Here we have a fighting unit, a phalanx, which we can trace back into the Bronze Age, which is going to develop into the Roman legions, which puts off to one side aristocratic cavalry or chariots, which had been so important to the Egyptians and the Near Easterners, and also the light-armed mobile troops, the slingers, the archers. Instead, puts all of its stock in a line of heavily-armed men, equals, all depending on each other. This is sort of a negation of the individuality that we saw in the rest of the society. In that suit of armor, we are seeing the very beginnings of a tradition that will carry this classical civilization—I would hesitate to call it a classical ideal—down through time.

It's easy it idealize that hoplite phalanx, to think of them all as Jeffersonian small farmers who grab the armor out of the back room when they're threatened, and assemble on a nearby field and fight it out. Our evidence suggests far from it. Those armed men are not only something that will preserve their own culture; they are the means of spreading it and they are the means of bringing new impulses back.

We find on the monuments of Egypt, monuments of the pharaohs, graffiti scrawled in the 6th century B.C. by visiting Ionian mercenaries, the heavy-armed troops who had a skill nobody else in the Mediterranean had. These were heavy-armed troops hired as mercenaries by the kings of Persia, the kings of Egypt, the kings of those Eastern lands, to be their armed forces. We know they went the other way all the way to Spain and served the kings out there.

So a sort of Viking-like group of people based on those islands and the mainland of Greece with a great tradition of individuality, enabled to travel and be successful and desired everywhere because of their skill at fighting as heavily-armed troops, and thus, perpetuating their tradition, bringing back wealth, bringing back new ideas, and ensuring that they will be consistently on the winning side in that great sweepstakes that we call the evolution of civilizations.

Lecture Twenty-Six
The Texture of Everyday Life

Scope:

In this lecture, we explore everyday life in the ancient world, examining archaeological evidence that tells us what went on in the streets, the public places, and the homes of ordinary people in ancient Greece and Rome. Our type site for everyday life is Pompeii. This was the city buried by the eruption of Mount Vesuvius which, in a single day, sealed in the city's inhabitants, their clothing, their pets, their domestic arrangements, their graffiti, all the humble moments and activities of the everyday. This is the place that captured the imagination of the world and convinced people that, over and above the great questions of art and philosophy, there might be something valuable in the idea of looking at the ancient world through its material remains.

Outline

I. In one of our earlier discussions of Pompeii, we briefly mentioned the estate of a woman named Julia Felix. Her property spanned more than two city blocks, with gardens, dining areas, porticos, and so on; one of her buildings was decorated with an extraordinary fresco, more than 100 feet long.

    A. This fresco was adorned with scenes of everyday life from the forum at Pompeii: shopkeepers selling their wares, people making speeches, a religious procession. It was not just a testimony of everyday life, but it shows an interest in everyday life as something to glorify.

        1. Throughout Pompeii and Herculaneum, we also find frescos that include graphic representations of sex, which were shocking for 18th-century visitors. In fact, there were so many frescos of sexual activity dotted around Pompeii and Herculaneum that, originally, people assumed many of these buildings were brothels.

        2. However, these depictions weren't pornographic. To the Greeks and Romans, they were a life-enhancing part of everyday existence.

B. The Athenians, to the east, had their own way of glorifying everyday life; they celebrated it by depicting ordinary scenes on pottery.

    1. Along with mythological scenes and scenes from dramas were scenes that show, for example, olive pickers going about their work in an olive grove. They're shown without any exaggeration—just ordinary people doing an ordinary job.

    2. There are also pictures of pottery makers, bronze workers, and fishmongers. One scene shows a young man after drinking too much, with a kindly prostitute, the *hetaera*, holding his head.

C. In the last lecture, we were searching for features that set the Classical world apart from the grand, older civilizations of the Near East and Egypt. This glorification of everyday life found in Roman frescos and Athenian pottery designs is just such a signifier.

D. Over the hills to the north of Athens, in the flat cattle country of Boeotia, is a place called Tanagra that had wonderful clay. Artists at Tanagra made terracotta figurines out of the clay, showing actors, musicians, women making bread, children playing games, carpenters working with wood, and so on. This array of themes is not typical of most artists. It's characteristic of the Greeks and Romans that they put a high value on everyday activities.

E. Even in their borrowings from the East, the Greeks and Romans introduced a homey touch. The griffin, for example, was borrowed by the ancient Greeks from the Near East. This magical beast had the body of a lion, the wings and head of an eagle, and the tall ears of a horse.

    1. Griffins are found across the Near East, often around treasures and temples, and they appear at Delphi and Olympia.

    2. It took a Greek artist to show a griffin family at home, in a scene with a nest, young griffins and their parents on either side. The foreleg of one of the parents is lovingly raised, touching the leg of the other parent on the other side of the nest.

3. This kind of lighthearted domesticity is part of our "big picture" of the Greek and Roman world. It's a feature that often eludes the net of historical writings and texts that have come down to us from the ancient world.

II. Let's consider leisure activities or activities that embody the element of choice in everyday life.

   A. Whenever we find artifacts of a certain kind proliferating in a specific area, we know that activities associated with those artifacts were increasing in importance for that culture. In our own world, we might think, for example, of the many different kinds of balls we have, implying an interest in ball games.

   B. In the same way, the Greeks and Romans were also interested in games. We find many images of games in stone, in paintings, and on frescoed walls, as well as actual artifacts from games. There is even an area in Ephesus where a checkerboard is carved into almost every marble step leading to that city's agora.

   C. On the other end of the Mediterranean, on the island of Sicily, is an emperor's hunting lodge called Piazza Armerina. The lodge is decorated with beautiful mosaics, showing people working out, trying to enhance their physical conditioning.

   D. Children were also a big part of everyday life. The Classical world does not bear out the current idea that children were treated as little adults. We have a huge array of toys, pacifiers, and other artifacts that relate to children. We even have a potty chair from the Athenian Agora.

III. This toilet seat leads us to basic bodily functions of ancient peoples.

   A. Where did ancients take care of the needs for urination and defecation?

      1. Greek houses are not known for having a separate room for these functions, which often were performed in public.

2. In the Roman world, public latrines were developed, large U-shaped rooms with benches around three walls. The benches were made of marble with holes cut in it, spaced about 18 inches apart. There were no partitions, doors, or locks and, perhaps, 5 inches of personal space between the users.

3. Directly under the hole was a flow of water from an aqueduct, rushing through to carry the waste away to the nearest river.

B. As mentioned earlier, sex was also of great interest to the ancients.

1. Young men were initiated into sex in formal ways by *hetaerae*, young women who were engaged to show them the art of love.

2. Brothels were available, but banquets were also held during which young women were brought into the home to entertain men. Couples would then go off to private rooms or participate in an orgy amidst the tables of the banquet hall.

3. Both heterosexual and homosexual activities are shown in art. Erect male sexual organs were fashioned in bronze and gold as amulets to hang around the neck and as pottery.

IV. In an earlier lecture, we touched briefly on the daily routine of the ancients, who were quite specific about when certain things should happen throughout the day.

A. The day began with sunup, making for a short day in winter and a longer one in summer. Months were usually lunar. The calendar was so arranged that the festivals that were assigned to certain days of the month fell on the night of the full moon. The Mediterranean has fair weather almost every day from May to September. The ancients took advantage of this for their summer festivals and all-night revels.

B. Ancient people generally rose at dawn to start the day. The markets would open shortly after dawn and close shortly after noon. People then went home, had a midday meal and a nap, and were ready for social activities in the evening.

C. Cities were filled with banqueting halls, where small groups of friends could gather together for an evening of conversation, food, and wine. We have many lamps to show that people extended their daily activities well into the nighttime.

D. Reading also became part of everyday life. Books were written to be read for pleasure. The great works of Homer might still be recited by a specialist at a dinner party, but scrolls also proliferated so that individuals could take home the works of Thucydides or Aristophanes or just a good novel in the Hellenistic and Roman periods.

  1. Romantic novels, featuring young lovers, were popular, as were novels telling of daring escapes, pirates, long voyages, and long-lost parents being rediscovered.

  2. Ancient people interacted with the written word, whether casual letters to friends or longer works to be read for entertainment.

E. These different hours of the day—the morning work period, the midday meal, and the evening social hours—were marked off by timepieces. Many communities had some sort of sundial with a *gnomon*. The Agora in Athens had water clocks, in which the level of water in a tank decreased, and a floating object marked the passing hours of the day.

  1. The ancients had two ideas about hours. We, of course, think of an hour as a fixed time span, but they were much more flexible. Some water clocks were marked with lines, reflecting the idea of a fixed period of time.

  2. Typically, however, hours were not thought of as fixed. The first hour of the day began at dawn, and the day ended at sunset. Thus, the hours were long in summer and short in winter, because every day had 12 hours and every night had 12 hours.

  3. We don't know of any way that the Greeks and Romans had to measure minutes and seconds. The shortest measures we know of are the water clocks that were used in the law courts in Athens to time speeches.

   a. Trials took place quickly in the ancient world, especially in Athens, perhaps because this ancient society was so litigious. The timer used for speakers in a trial was a jar of water with a hole in the bottom, with another jar below to catch the water flowing out.

    b. Sets of these timers were kept for each of the 10 tribes that would rotate through the administration of Athenian government, and they apparently came in different sizes.

    c. The only such timer that has been discovered gives the speaker about six minutes. This timer was probably used for minor witnesses. We know from the lengths of recorded speeches that a defendant justifying himself in a murder case, for example, would have been given more time.

V. The Greeks and Romans put a premium on filling one's life with agreeable activities.

    A. We have some interesting graffiti that attest to this outlook on life. In a city designed for retired soldiers called Timgad, in what is today North Africa, we find two sayings: "Hunting, bathing, banqueting, drinking, laughing; that's what life is about" and "Baths, wine, sex; they'll shorten your life. But what's life all about except baths, wine, and sex?"

    B. This seems to be a casual, secular view of the purpose of people on Earth. In many societies, individuals didn't (and still don't) have choices about their activities. With religious rituals, the economic necessities of making a living, the social customs and traditions of the community, and the political and military demands of the city, other societies didn't have free time. Greeks and Romans not only had free time, but they treasured it, and they invented many activities to fill it.

    C. We've been through a crisis in this country with the 9/11 attacks, but after these attacks, we were all urged to return to normal life. Our world owes much of its "cultural DNA" to the Greek and Roman world, where "normal life" was also the essence of society. To many people, unconstrained freedom of choice in everyday life seems more important than freedom of political action or decision-making.

D. Like the Greeks and the Romans, we have created entire building complexes to deal with casual, everyday life choices.

   1. For the Romans, one of these complexes was the baths, where men would go in the morning and women in the afternoon. People, including many slaves, would relax in the vaulted interiors of a bath complex, surrounded by lapping water.

   2. This leisure time extended beyond people to their pets. At Pompeii, the 18th-century excavators discovered a tag from a dog collar that read, "Greetings. I belong to Viventius. If you find me, please return me to my master." This dog was out on the loose, trotting around town, not a chained watchdog on duty. Like his master, this dog had the leisure and the choice to enjoy life exactly as he saw fit.

Suggested Reading:

Liversidge, *Everyday Life in the Roman Empire.*

Camp and Fisher, *The World of the Ancient Greeks.*

Questions to Consider:

1. To what extent do everyday pursuits and customs define a culture or provide an alternative view to its large-scale monuments?

2. What evidence will the modern world yield for future archaeologists about our own "everyday life"?

Lecture Twenty-Six—Transcript
The Texture of Everyday Life

Welcome back. It's the day of days. It's time for everyday life in the ancient world. We're going to be looking at the archaeological evidence for what went on in the streets, the public places, and the homes, of ordinary people in the world of ancient Greece and Rome. I promised you that in this final series of 12 presentations, we would be starting each time at a type-site, a place that introduces us to the theme and maybe exemplifies it.

For everyday life, you have to go back to Pompeii. After all, it was that city buried by the eruption of Mount Vesuvius which, in a single day, sealed in an entire city, its inhabitants, their clothing, their pets, their domestic arrangements, their graffiti, all of the humble little moments and the activities of the everyday. That's the place that really captured the imagination of the entire world. That's what convinced people that, over and above the great questions of art and philosophy, there might really be something to the idea of looking at the ancient world through its material remains.

At Pompeii, we've got to make a selection. We've already talked about some of the extraordinary visions that we get of everyday life at Pompeii. We remember Mark Twain visiting Pompeii as the tourist in the middle of the 19th century, getting ready to write *Innocence Aboard*. He was standing next to that podium of a temple where there were steps at a street corner. He saw the worn path of the pedestrians across the steps as they cut the corner from one street to the other, rather than go all the way around the edge of the temple.

That moment of everyday life—just like the ruts in the road from the chariot wheels that ran up and down the streets of Pompeii—captured his imagination more than all of the extravagant statues and frescos that he saw in the Naples museum.

At Pompeii, there is a house that we have cause to mention briefly. It was the property of a woman named Julia Felix. Julia Felix, at this big property spanning more than two city blocks, gardens, outdoor dining areas, porticos and so on, had one of her buildings decorated with an extraordinary fresco, more than 100 feet long.

What scenes had she asked the fresco painters to adorn that wall with? Scenes of everyday life from the forum at Pompeii: shopkeepers selling their wares; people standing up and making speeches; bits of a religious procession. It was not just a testimony of everyday life; but it shows an interest in everyday life as something to glorify, something to put up there with the high and the mighty and the gods and the heroes. Everyday life was something that the Romans and the Greeks were obsessed with.

All over Pompeii and Herculaneum, we find frescos that show ordinary people in ordinary situations. We're going to come back to some of those because in the 18th century, which was a pretty ribald age, these shocked the world to see sex, for instance, so graphically represented; scene after scene; position after position; body part after body part; choice of partner after choice of partner. It made people's hair stand on end.

That sex was another thing that intrigued the public and captured people's imaginations. In fact, there were so many frescos of sexual activity dotted around Pompeii and Herculaneum that originally people assumed every such building had to be a brothel. It was assumed that the houses of prostitution numbered in the dozens in these small cities. Now we know that's not so. There's one bona fide brothel that's got little cubicles, small beds, an upstairs and a downstairs, obviously a place of business. Of course, we get our word "pornography" from those ancients. *Porne* were prostitutes, and *graphē* means to write about them so that's the etymology of pornography.

But these aren't pornographic. They are to us; they were to our 18th-century forbearers who snickered and make smutty jokes about them. But to the Greeks and Romans, they were a life-enhancing part of everyday existence, not only to take an active part in the sexual activity, but also to have pictures of it around the walls of your own home, sometimes even in the entrance hall.

There's a famous one at Pompeii that shows a Priapus figure, a man, an adult male, with an extremely enlarged sexual apparatus, weighing his phallus on a little scale just to see how much this 3-foot-long thing weighs. It's in the entry hall of a grand Pompeian house.

Along with Julia Felix's beautiful fresco, we've got scenes of everyday life all over Pompeii. This was a house, remember, uncovered by Karl Weber back in the 1750s; this was one of the houses that first drew the world's attention to Pompeii.

The Athenians, to the east, had their own way of glorifying everyday life, showing that it loomed large in their consciousness, that it was something to be cherished and celebrated. Their form of honoring everyday life was to put it on their pots, on their bowls, on their vases, on their cups, along with the mythological scenes, along with scenes from the dramas that showed gods and heroes along with mythical beasts. There were scenes that would show, for example, olive pickers out in an olive grove, with long sticks to strike the branches and let the olives drop down on other blankets or nets they've spread on the ground. The month must be some time October, November, December; it's an early winter/late fall crop. But they're shown without any exaggeration, without any heroization, just ordinary people doing an ordinary job.

We've got pictures of pottery makers; bronze workers; fishmongers cutting the heads off fish; young men are parties throwing up after having one too many cups of wine; and the kindly prostitute, or a little bit more like a geisha, the *hetaerae*, who was there to entertain them, holding the kid's head so that he'll throw up in the right place.

This is everyday life with a vengeance. We are being invited into every corner of these people's lives. It's blended right in with the religious ceremonies, the young girls in procession carrying the sacred objects and so on. The very next pot may be a sign of a doctor examining a patient.

We were searching last time for things that set the classical world apart from those grand, older civilizations of the Near East and Egypt.

There's something unusual here, this glorification of everyday life found in Roman frescos and Athenian pottery designs. Also, if we go over the hills to the north of Athens, to the flat cattle country of Boeotia, we come to a little place called Tanagra that had wonderful clay. There were artists at Tanagra who loved to make little figurines out of the clay, terra cotta. These show actors, musicians, women making bread, children playing games, carpenters working with wood. This is not the typical array of themes that are chosen by the world's artists. It's something characteristic about the Greeks and Romans that they put this high value on what they did every day.

Even when they borrowed things from the glorious East, they would introduce a homey touch. One of the things that was borrowed by the ancient Greeks from the Near East was the idea of the griffin, a magical beast that had the body of a lion, the wings of an eagle, the head of an eagle, but also tall ears like a horse. It was one of those jumbles of animal anatomy, such as we also find in the chimera. You find griffins all over the Near East and they're often around treasures and temples, and they appear also at Delphi and Olympia, those great holy sites of the Greeks. But way back in the Bronze Age, when early impulses from the Near East were coming to Greece with religious ideas and artistic motifs, somebody brought along the idea of the griffin.

It took a Greek artist to think of showing a griffin family at home, in a little scene where there's a nest and you see the young griffins sticking their heads out of the nest and the mother and father are on either side, getting ready to feed the babies. The foreleg—whether we call it a hand or a paw or a hoof—of one of the parents is lovingly raised and put on the leg of the other parent on the other side of the nest.

This kind of domestiticity, this kind of glorification of everyday life, in a very lighthearted way, is part of our big picture of the Greek and Roman world. It's something that often eludes the net of the historical writings and the texts that have come down to us from the ancient world.

Let's pursue some of these different aspects of antiquity. Let's think first about the whole idea of public and private. Everyday life. Everyday life is, for us, divided very much into what you do in your own home—sometimes activities no one ever sees—and what you do out in public. If you buy a book on everyday life, I have to say they're awfully wide-ranging. They will include arts, crafts, the army, and miners.

I'd like to limit this concept of everyday life to more what we would call leisure activities, or at least things that you choose to do, rather than all the things to do with your job and your obligatory roles as a citizen or a member of a community or a worshiper that you have to do.

Let's look at the element of choice. Casual life. Casual has that element of choice—you weren't compelled to do it. That's our everyday life.

One great area for everyday life is pastimes. You're not working, you want to pass the time, have something to do. Whenever we find a culture that is proliferating artifacts in a certain area, we know that that area's increasing in importance.

So, for instance, in our own world, we go back to the 18th century, there aren't many forms of ball because there weren't many different games of balls. Now there are dozens. There's a different kind of ball for every game. That's a clue to future archaeologists, to whom our scripts may be unreadable, that we got real interested in ballgames. I'm sure they'll have many interesting speculations about why and what it all means.

The same way the Greeks and the Romans got interested in games. We find lots and lots of images in stone, paintings, frescoed walls, and actual artifacts from games. Games took over so much that there's even an area of Ephesus downtown—that great Hellenic city, Greek city on the western coast of Asia Minor—where you're trying to get down the steps of the main agora and there's a checkerboard carved into the marble steps, almost every step you take.

It's as if these loungers in the public space—you can picture them propped on one elbow and moving their drafts around the checkerboard as they compete with somebody on the other side—have taken over the public. We have the people, those grand agoras now with casual game players who come to the public place in order to play games.

From the other end of the Mediterranean, on the island of Sicily, there's a wonderful hunting lodge of an emperor—we don't know which one—called Piazza Armerina, decorated with beautiful mosaics. We see people working out. We see young women wearing bikinis and holding barbells, who are obviously doing some sort of ancient aerobics, getting carried on into physical conditioning.

There's a beautiful passage to support this in Xenophon's symposium, the story of Socrates at a drinking party where he tells all the guests that he's going to take up dancing because it's such a good exercise for all parts of the body.

This is everyday life, beginning to move through the hours of the day, taking over more and more of those hours, more and more of people's thoughts, and more and more of the material culture.

Children are a big part of everyday life. There's a current belief in intellectual circles that children weren't invented until very recent times, culturally speaking, that before that, they were just little adults. The classical world certainly does not bear out that idea. There's a huge array of artifacts that have to do with children, toys, pacifiers, little models of adult things for the child to play with.

And—my favorite artifact for the everyday life of the child—a potty chair from the Athenian Agora. It was two vases, more or less, one turned upside-down so the child can sit on it, and the other one fused to the top of that vase with a pair of leg holes so you can put the child in the vase. The child's legs would stick out, and there's a little hole through to the lower vase so that you don't have to remove the child as it answers the call of nature. This was part of everyday life. The child had to be catered for.

That child and its little toilet seat leads us to the big question of urination and defecation throughout the day. Where did it happen? Greek houses certainly are not notable for having a separate room for these functions. It happened in public, often. The Romans were the ones who developed this to an extremely high degree—public latrines. We have strong ideas about privacy, on all levels, many serious, some less serious. One of the less serious ones is answering the call of nature in a public place. We think that should be private.

We would need to shed that very quickly in the Roman world. The public latrines are large U-shaped rooms with benches around three walls. The benches are made of marble and they have holes cut in them, spaced about 18 inches apart. There were no partitions; there were no doors; no locks; there was maybe 5 inches of personal space between you and your neighbor. Everyone was in there together, answering the call of nature. Instead of toilet paper there was a sponge on the stick.

Running down the front of your little section of the marble bench, directly under the hole that you're sitting on is a flow of water that the Roman hydraulic engineers have ensured is filled with water from an aqueduct, rushing through to carry all of the material away to the nearest river and out to sea. You never wanted to go swimming in a river downstream from a Roman town.

So you're seated there, you finished up, you need to wipe yourself. Instead of toilet paper, there was a sponge on a stick. Here's the stick, there's the sponge, and there's a slot down the front of the seat so that you can insert the stick on the sponge, clean yourself, and then there's a little basin of water out there so you can wash the sponge and leave it in its basket for the next person to use.

Among the many humorous graffiti that we have from the ancient world is one from a bath from one irate customer to all the people who proceeded them, saying, "Use the sponge."

They were very frank and open about these bodily functions. We know that back at Pompeii, there was a man who was medic to Caesar, to the emperor, who wanted you to know—or at least wanted everybody else who came to the latrine to know that he, on a certain day, had sat there and "*cacavit bene.*" It sounds much nicer in Latin than it would in English, but it means he enjoyed a really good bowel movement at that spot. Here's the doctor of the emperor telling you about it.

Sex—which wasn't entirely linked with this world of bodily functions, but we're going to move on to it—was also of great interest to the ancients. It was a part of daily life and it was something that young men were initiated into in formal ways by these *hetaerae*, these girls, who were brought in to show them the arts of love. It was a skill; you were expected to be good at it. How were you going to figure it out by yourself?

There were places to go for sex, but also, sex was brought was into the home. Banquets were held with that central space open so that the hetaerae, the entertaining girls, the dancing girls, the prostitutes, could come in, entertain people and then go off to private rooms or just have an orgy right there amidst the tables with all the revelers taking part together. Of course, it's not limited to heterosexual sex. The ancients had a much more open-minded attitude, to some extent, than we do about who you would choose as a partner for your sexual activity.

They loved to put this into art. All sorts of sexual activities are shown in the art. Also, something that really amazed those 18th-century people who were looking at what was dug up at Pompeii and Herculaneum—sexual parts, especially erect male sexual organs, in bronze, in gold; little amulets to hang around your neck; pottery things to keep in the kitchen.

What were these? They were good-luck charms. We can't look at these and simply think the same thoughts we would have as looking at a rabbit's foot, but that's about all that it was. The fact that some of them are so large that we need a basket to carry them from the place they were made back to your house doesn't get around the fact that they are filling a very different function in that ancient society than such objects would fulfill in ours.

The shape of the day is something we've already had cause to refer to. The ancients were very specific about when certain things should happen throughout the day. The day began with sunup, so it was a short day in the winter and it was a long day in the summer. All available light is taken advantage of. Months were usually lunar. It was so arranged that the festivals that were assigned to certain days of the month fell on the night of the full moon. So you go out and revel all night long in that beautiful moonlight.

The Mediterranean is, of course, a place where from about May to about September, you can count on having fair weather every day. They took advantage of this for their big summer festivals and those all-night revels.

Whatever you've done the night before, you're going to get up at dawn and you're going to start your day. The markets would open shortly after dawn and extend until shortly after high noon, when it just gets too hot to be outdoors. That's the working day in the Mediterranean. It's left its imprint on things like the Spanish siesta, which still calls for going home, having a midday meal, and taking a good, long nap in the heat of the afternoon, before rousing yourself again. Nowadays, stores open again. That would not have happened in the ancient world. Instead, once you roused yourself from your afternoon torpor, the works is over, the public meetings are over; now it's time for the sociability, getting together with friends.

Cities are filled with little banqueting halls, where small groups of friends can get together—clubs, as it were—for an evening of conversation, little bit of food, and a lot of wine. The entertainment of life is all in those evening hours.

We have lots of little lamps that show that people extended their daily activities well into the nighttime, otherwise they wouldn't need these. In Romans lamps, some of them come in arrays with half a dozen spouts, each one of which would have a little wick. You probably read a book by such a light.

That has become another part of everyday life, reading. More than any other people before them—and more than a lot of people since—reading and writing were parts of casual everyday life. Books were written to be read just for pleasure. You would still get the great works of Homer recited by a specialist at a dinner party; but the proliferation of the scrolls so that you could take home the works of Thucydides or Aristophanes, or just a good novel in the Hellenistic and Roman periods.

There were novels with romantic young lovers, daring escapes, pirates, long voyages, long-lost parents being rediscovered—all of these were very popular. There was this interaction with the word. It could be graffiti, or a casual letter from a friend. We talked about all those letters found up at Vindolanda fort in northern England where the legionary folk and their wife are writing back and forth to each other on little wooden tablets. All of these contribute to a world of casual words, a sort of virtual reality into which you could immerse yourself alongside that pleasurable daily routine of the here and the now.

These different hours of the day—the morning work period, the afternoon, the midday meal and then the evening sociability—they were marked off by timepieces. Many communities had some sort of a sundial with a big gnomon. You may remember that Augustus put one up in Rome and we actually saw the archaeologist who figured out where it was under the pavements of modern Rome and dug down to it.

In Athens, in the Agora, there were water clocks, where water would spill out of a container at a fixed rate and something floating in the container would gradually sink as the water spilled out, marking the passing hours of the day.

They had two ideas about hours. We, of course, think of an hour as a fixed time span. They were a lot more flexible. Some of these marked gauges for the old water clocks. If you go out to the oracle site of Amphiaraus, north of Athens, a place called Oropos, you'll see a water clock. There were fixed lines, showing the idea of a fixed hour. But normal hours didn't work that way. The first hour of the day began at dawn and it ended at sunset. So the hours were long in summer, of the day, and the hours were short in winter because every day had 12 hours and every night had 12 hours.

This is alien to us, but the Greeks and Romans weren't worried about minutes and seconds. In fact, we don't know of any way that they had to gauge them. About the shortest measures we know of are the water clocks that were used in the law courts in Athens, to time speeches.

Let me say that I do feel that, of the many innovations introduced by the ancient world, this is one that could be renewed with value in our own time. Trials happened fast in the ancient world, especially in Athens, but there were a lot of trials. They were a very litigious society. They didn't want speakers, witnesses or defendants, to run on forever. So you were timed by a clock. The clock was a jar of water with a hole in the bottom, and another jar below to catch the water coming up. One of these has actually been found.

There were sets of these kept for each of the 10 tribes that would rotate through the administration of Athenian government and justice. It would have the tribe's name on the vase. They came in different sizes. The only one that's been discovered, by the Americans working in the Agora, gives you about six minutes of talking. This is probably a minor witness, maybe a respondent in a divorce proceeding or something like that. You would have gotten a lot more time from that, as we can tell from the lengths of the speeches, if you had been the defendant justifying yourself in a case of murder.

But nonetheless, even in those speeches, it's a common think to read, "I can see that my water has almost run out," or, "Even if I had twice as many jars of water, I would not be able to say all of the terrible things that this person has done to me."

In this way, you could measure brief periods of time. But one reason that we don't know the athletic records of those ancient athletes is there was no way to measure minutes and seconds; and the hours of the day themselves, as I told you, could expand and contract, depending on winter and summer.

All of this everyday life put a premium on filling one's life up in an agreeable way, with agreeable activities. This was something that the Greeks and Romans really prized. We have some interesting graffiti that bear upon this. In a city that was designed for retired soldiers, members of the legions, called Timgad in the modern world in North Africa, we find graffiti. One of them says, "Hunting, bathing, banqueting, drinking, laughing, that's what life is about." We have another graffiti, "Baths, wine, sex, they'll shorten your life. But what's life all about except baths, wine, and sex?"

This is a very casual, very secular view of why we are here, of what the purpose is of that expanse of time that each of us has to fill in this world. In many societies, you don't have choices. Between the religious rituals, the economic necessities of your job, the social customs and traditions of your community, and the political and military demands of the city or the region that you live in, you don't have any corners of your life to call your own. You don't have casual time, downtime.

One of the things that I think should really resonate with modern people about those ancient Greeks and Romans, they not only had it, but they treasured it and they invented a huge mass of activities. All of those activities matched with artifacts to fill it up.

We've been through the great crisis in this country of the 9/11 attacks. What were most people disturbed by? The disruption of everyday, casual life. You couldn't be casual anymore. What were we all asked to do? Go shopping. Please, be normal again. Imagine that happening in Assyria or Egypt. I don't think that would have been the appeal.

In this world, which owes so much of its nature, its cultural DNA, to that Greek and Roman world, that was what seemed the essence of that society—everyday life. It was that unconstrained freedom of choice, which, to many people, seems more important than freedom of political action or decision.

Like the Greeks—and especially like the Romans—we have created entire building complexes to deal with the casual, everyday life choices. For the Romans, it was the baths, where men would go in the morning and women would go in the afternoon. Everybody got to go. It's clear that many slaves were allowed to go to the baths. There, you would just relax in those vaulted interiors, surrounding by the lapping water, the controlled temperatures, the massages, the graffiti of those who'd gone before you, in a world apart from the world of the temple, the forum or the agora, the workplace—a place that was just for living; a place that was just for everyday.

This extended—and I'll close with this—beyond people, to their pets. There at Pompeii, the 18th-century excavators discovered a tag from a dog collar which said, "Greetings. I belong to Viventius. If you find me, please return me to my master." This was a dog that was out on the loose, trotting around the town, not one of the chained watchdogs at the door, doing a job all the time. It was a dog, which, like its master, had the leisure and the choice to enjoy life exactly as he saw fit.

Lecture Twenty-Seven
Their Daily Bread

Scope:

This lecture takes as its theme one component that might be thought of as the foundation of everyday life—daily bread. For the Greeks and Romans, a loaf of bread, usually made from wheat flour, was essential. Armies needed massive amounts of wheat to provide the daily bread for soldiers. Cities were founded in remote parts of the Mediterranean to channel grain imports to Athens or to Rome. Trade networks were set up. Barbarian chiefs and kings were bribed. Vast parts of each city's economy were devoted to that essential substance, the daily bread. Bread became more than just the staff of life. It spread, as wine would also do in its way, into religious thought and became, in fact, the basis of one of the most emotionally meaningful aspects of ancient Greek religion. The archaeological site that will lead us into this aspect of Classical antiquity is Eleusis, on the shores of a bay to the west of the city of Athens, looking across the water to the island of Salamis.

Outline

I. Eleusis is the Greek community that was most closely associated with the goddess of grain, Demeter.

   A. Several natural products were so important to the ancient economy that they were associated with gods: Demeter for grain and bread, Dionysus for grapes and wine, and Athena for olives and olive oil.

   B. As we saw in a previous lecture, wheat came from Asia. Greek myth, however, retained no memory of a time when grain did not grow in Greece. Thus, it was associated with Demeter, a sister of Zeus, who was present from the beginnings of human life in Greece.

   C. Eleusis was an important site for the myth of Demeter. She had a daughter, whom we call Proserpina or Persephone, but the Greeks generally called the daughter Kore, "the maiden."

      1. Demeter's brother, god of the underworld, Hades or Pluto, saw this radiant young girl picking springtime

flowers, back in the time when there was no winter and the Earth was abundant and fruitful throughout the year.

2. Hades carried the girl away to the underworld, leaving her mother, Demeter, desolate on the Earth's surface. In her grief, Demeter allowed all living things on Earth to go into a state of death, decay, or hibernation—this was the world's first winter.

3. At Eleusis, Demeter learned what had happened to her daughter, and Kore was restored to her mother through a fissure in the Earth. As we know, however, Kore had eaten a few seeds from a pomegranate in the underworld. The Fates decreed that for every seed she had eaten, the Earth would experience a month of winter in the annual cycle, during which Kore would return to the underworld.

4. Eleusis became a cult center for Demeter, a place where grain was celebrated, but also a place where one came face to face with the ultimate mystery: life coming out of death. The seed must be planted under the earth, just as Kore went down into the Earth; both seem to be lost to the sight of mortals, but both ultimately return to the land of the living.

5. For the Greeks, this was the ultimate mystery, and they celebrated elaborate pagan festivals each year at Eleusis to be initiated into the secrets of new life brought out of death.

II. In its original form, the wheat that came out of Asia was called *einkorn*. It's one of the clusters of wild grasses that have basically made human civilization possible.

A. From the perspective of the far future, we can imagine archaeologists looking back at millennia of human history and debating the most important change or invention or transformation.

1. The answer is almost certainly the transformation of certain wild grasses—wheat, barley, rye, millet, rice, and corn—into food crops and the development of a system of agriculture and food preparation that turned these into the basis of life for burgeoning populations all over the planet.

2. These developments transformed our species from wanderers on the Earth, hunters and gatherers, to sedentary people with large populations and the settled food supply that allowed cities and civilizations to emerge.

3. This is one reason that Demeter was honored, in recognition that the grain of which she was the goddess was an essential component of civilization.

B. The grain itself was given an identity in a relief at Eleusis. The relief shows a trinity of divine figures: the mother, the maiden, and a little boy called Triptolemus. The boy is the grain, and he never grows up to become a man. He is continually what Frazer called "the dying god," the sacrifice, the young man who must perish so that the next generation can grow.

C. In America, planting season is in the spring and harvest season is in the fall. The reverse is true in the Mediterranean world. Grain would be planted in the fall, grow throughout the winter, come up in spring, and be harvested in roughly the month we call June. This cycle gave a shape to the year in the same way that the day was shaped by the Sun.

1. In years that the Greeks were involved in warfare, the fighting stopped in June, and the warriors returned home, got the harvest in, and went back to fight a second season in the late summer and fall.

2. The Romans, by professionalizing the military and using legionnaires who were not tied to home farms, were able to station forces on permanent duty on the fringes of the empire.

D. Within that cycle, of course, different tools and methods were used to prepare the soil, nurse the grain to maturity, harvest it, and process it.

1. The plow was needed to break the soil in Greece, unlike in the river valleys of the Nile, the Tigris, and the Euphrates, where the soil was generally soft and rich. Part of the point of domesticating animals, such as the donkey and the ox, was to pull the plows. By the end of the Roman Empire, we read about wheeled plows.

2. After plowing, farmers had to sow the seed. This was done by hand, by boys carrying skins or baskets and casting seed over the plowed field.

3. Continual hoeing and tending of the fields was required to discourage weeds and deter birds and animals from eating the crop.

4. At harvest time, the people of the ancient Near East had used sickles, originally those with obsidian chips in the blades. The Greeks used iron sickles, which was a great innovation. Iron was abundant and cheap and came into use for all farming implements.

5. The Romans established a tradition of improving agricultural practices. In Gaul, we find reliefs showing mechanical harvesters being dragged by draft animals through fields and scything through stands of grain.

6. Once the grain was gathered in, it would be tied into sheaths and allowed to dry, after which it would be ground into flour. Related crops, such as emmer or oats, will stand up to freezes and cold winters but must be parched or roasted before they can be ground into flour.

7. Of course, the wheat must be separated from the chaff, and for this, every community had a threshing floor. These were broad, circular, paved areas of stone. Around this, draft animals would tow a contraption called a *sledge*, with pieces of flint in the bottom to break up the grain and loosen the seed from the surrounding bits of the plant.

8. Finally, on a breezy day, the grain and chaff would be thrown into the air, and the wind would carry away the lightweight chaff, leaving behind the hard, heavy kernels of grain. These would be scooped up and stored in a granary.

E. We see granaries everywhere in the Classical world. The footers of these are characterized by tiny walls, closely spaced. A large timber structure would have rested on top. The walls on the bottom lift the structure clear of the ground, away from the dampness of winter so that the grain doesn't rot. The small passages in the footer also provide ventilation and access for ferrets, cats, or dogs to track down vermin that might otherwise get into the precious grain supply.

F. One of the well-known threshing floors (*haloa*) in Greece is at Delphi. These facilities also provided early societies with natural places to hold dances and theatrical performances, and the one at Delphi became the site of an annual pageant.

III. After harvesting and storing the grain, the next step was to mill it into flour, and we find a range of technologies for milling grain in all communities.

    A. Such technologies may be as simple as a *metate*, a grinding stone, and a handheld pestle, the *mano*, which would be rolled or rotated over the grain every day for hours, to create enough flour for the day's bread. This task was horribly tedious, and people quickly sought ways to perform it more efficiently.

    B. In the Classical world, gritty volcanic rock was often crafted into a device similar to a double funnel with an hourglass shape. This would be placed on top of another stone that had a conical top. The grain would be poured into the top of the funnel while a slave or a donkey rotated the device. This action would grind the grain, and the flour would spill out the bottom.

    C. As a result of this process, Classical bread contains a certain measure of grit, for which archaeologists are thankful because it has provided us with one of the only ways we have to determine how old adults were at death.

        1. Up until the time that the wisdom teeth come in—traditionally age 18—the teeth are not very worn. The eruption of the teeth gives an almost year-by-year sequence for human beings during the first part of their lives. Physical anthropologists can, thus, be very precise about the age of a child, based on dentition.

        2. After the wisdom teeth come in, however, the human body doesn't give many chronological clues to its age, except in countries where stone-ground flour was baked into tough, chewy bread, which had the effect of grinding away at the teeth. Physical anthropologists now have tables that identify how much tooth wear from grit is associated with various ages.

D. The early millstones were quickly seen to be insufficient. Roman engineers turned their ingenuity to finding better and faster methods for grinding grain.

   1. We are familiar with the harnessing of water for gristmills in our own colonial period. The Romans did the same thing. The most amazing work of Roman agricultural technology is a watermill at Barbegal, in southern France, where the flour was ground for the city of Nîmes.

   2. The Romans found a hillside with a water source at the top, brought in by an aqueduct from a distant spring. The aqueduct channel divided into two and spilled down two millraces, and as it did so, it passed through individual houses on the slope (all connected inside).

   3. In each house was a mill wheel, 8 on one side, 8 on the other side—16 mill wheels at once—turning day and night to grind grain into flour to feed the city of Nîmes.

E. Communal ovens were used in almost every Roman settlement. Each household would work its flour into dough and shape it into loaves. Some people had ovens in their homes, but that arrangement was costly in terms of space and fuel. In many communities, loaves were taken to the bakery, then retrieved after they had been baked. Small wooden stamps found in some houses in Pompeii were probably used to identify the loaves of bread for each household.

IV. These means of providing for the cities were not sufficient for long. In Athens, for example, by the 5th century, the city could no longer feed itself from its own fields. In the case of Rome, already by the time of the republic, people couldn't feed themselves from the farms of Latium or Campania.

A. Grain had to be imported, and the Greeks and Romans became dependent on distant growers in a way that Near Eastern societies never did. In fact, the Egyptians became great exporters of wheat to both the Greeks and the Romans.

B. It was a great moment in the Roman year when the watchers on the capes of southern Italy would spot the immense grain freighters appearing in the annual fleet, coming over the sea from Egypt and bringing tons of grain from the Nile Delta and its farms for Rome to feed its million inhabitants.

C. Docks were constructed to receive these gigantic ships. We can get an idea of what the ships looked like from the two big barges found in Lake Nemi, south of Rome, that we discussed in one of our first lectures.

D. The Athenian response to the lack of grain was to establish colonies or trading posts or take over areas that could provide the city with grain. One impetus behind the growth of the Athenian maritime empire was the desire to secure grain-producing regions and make them part of the Athenian power network.

V. We started this lecture at Eleusis, where Demeter lost her daughter. At this site a cult of spiritual rebirth grew up, the closest we get in ancient societies to the charismatic personal communion with the other world that we take for granted in most religions today.

A. The Athenians built a huge square hall at Eleusis called the Telesterion, where people gathered every year. In September, mystery celebrations were held there. Initiates came, and after sacrificing a pig and washing themselves in the waters of the sea, they went into the dark hall and were shown things that changed their lives.

B. Seated on bleachers around three sides of the hall, up to 3,000 people crowded into the interior space for this annual life-changing experience. The priestesses and priests would enter a structure called a *palace* on the stage area in the center, then come out and pronounce revelations. People left the hall feeling that they had been reborn.

C. What was revealed? There is not a single question about antiquity that we would more like to have answered than that one, but each participant took an oath of silence, and we don't know of anyone who ever broke that vow.

D. What was a mystery then remains a mystery to us and is tied in with the ultimate mystery of these plants; unlike the fruits of trees, which can be plucked and leave the tree behind, or the olive trees or the grapes on the vine, with grain, life had to come from death.

Suggested Reading:

Liversidge, *Everyday Life in the Roman Empire.*

Wilkins, *Food in Antiquity.*

Questions to Consider:

1. Argue for or against the idea that the transformation of wild grasses into food crops enabled the spread of civilization more so than, say, the harnessing of fire.

2. To what extent can the militarism of the ancient Greeks and Romans be traced to the need to feed their populations?

Lecture Twenty-Seven—Transcript
Their Daily Bread

Welcome back. Our theme last time—everyday life—has a component that might be thought to be the foundation of everyday life, and that is people's daily bread. For the Greeks and for the Romans, a loaf of bread, usually made from wheat flour, was something that they couldn't do without. Armies needed massive amounts of wheat to provide the daily bread for the soldiers. Cities were founded in remote parts of the Mediterranean to channel grain imports to Athens or to Rome. Trade networks were set up. Barbarian chiefs and kings were bribed. Vast parts of each city's economy were devoted to that essential substance, the daily bread.

It became more than just the staff of life, of food. Daily bread—as wine was to do also in its way—spread itself into religious thought and became, in fact, the basis of one of the most emotionally meaningful aspects of ancient Greek religion. This is our theme, their daily bread.

The archaeological site that will lead us into this particular aspect of classical antiquity is Eleusis, or as it's said in modern Greek, Eleusis on the shores of a bay to the west of the city of Athens, looking across the water to the great island of Salamis. Eleusis is the Greek community that was most closely associated with the Goddess of Grain, Demeter.

There were several natural products that were so important to the ancient economy that gods were associated with them: Demeter, for grain and for bread; Dionysus, for the grape and the wine; and Athena for the olive and the olive oil.

Athena is in charge of the only one that can claim to be homegrown in the classical world. As far as we can tell, the Minoans on Crete may have been the first to domesticate the olive tree, which they found growing wild as the oleaster on the island of Crete, and then spread it on to other Greek lands, throughout the Aegean area and finally, to all corners of the Mediterranean and anywhere that has a Mediterranean climate where these trees can grow.

But wheat was different. Wheat had come from Asia, as we saw last time when we were at Sesklo, a little farming town of the Neolithic, where those earliest farmers put their wheat and their sheep and their goats and had settled down in Greece.

Greek myth retained no tradition of this. They knew that wine had come from somewhere else because Dionysus was a god who comes to Greece in a ship, from overseas. So the myth remembered the foreign origins of the grape, but it had lost sight of the fact that there was ever a time when there was no grain growing in Greece. So the goddess, Demeter, was one of those great Olympian gods, a sister of Zeus, who was there from the very beginnings of human life in Greece, according to Greek myth.

Eleusis was an important site for her myth. She had a daughter. We think of her by the names of Proserpina for the Latin name, Persephone for the Greek name. But the Greeks generally just called her the daughter Kore, "the maiden." So we have the mother, Demeter, and the maiden, Kore.

It happened that Demeter's own brother, God of the Underworld, Hades or Pluto, looking up from his underworld realm, saw this radiant young girl walking around, picking springtime flowers, back in the ages when there was no winter, there was no bad weather; everything was abundant and fruitful throughout the year, with no annual cycles of growth and decay.

He had the earth open and he drove his chariot up and he grabbed the girl, knowing or not knowing whether it was his own niece and not sure whether he would have cared if he had known. Down into the underworld he went, leaving Demeter desolate on the earth's surface, not knowing where her daughter went, roaming over the earth. In her grief, she allowed all living things to go into a state of death or decay or hibernation—the world's first winter.

It was at Eleusis that she learned what happened to her daughter. It was through a cave at Eleusis that you could still see, as an ancient Greek tourist, and you can still see today, that a fissure opened up and the girl was restored to her mother.

But something had happened while Kore, the maiden, was in the underworld. She'd been persuaded to eat a few seeds from a pomegranate. It was decreed by the fates that for every little fleshy seed of the pomegranate she had eaten, there would be a month of winter in each annual cycle, where she must once again go back down to her husband in the underworld.

Eleusis thus became the place for a cult of Demeter, a place where the grain was celebrated, but also a place where one came face to face with that ultimate mystery, that in the case of the grain, life can only come out of death. The seed must be planted under the earth, as Kore went down into the earth, seemed to die, seemed to be lost to the sight of mortals, if it's going to sprout again and grow and come back to the land of the living.

The Greeks called this the mystery, the ultimate mystery of death bringing about new life. We will be ending our time with daily bread today, back here at Eleusis, seeing that that little cleft in that little cave which they venerated as the place where Hades or Pluto restored the girl to her mother, became the centerpiece for a gigantic religious complex, where some of the most elaborate pagan festivals of all are celebrated each year, for thousands of years, involving Greeks, Romans, from all over the Mediterranean, who came to be initiated into these mysteries.

About this wheat. It came out of Asia and, in its original form, it was called einkorn. You get just one little grain to each spikelet. It's one of the clusters of wild grasses that have basically made human civilization possible. From the perspective of the far future, we can imagine archaeologists looking back at millennia of human history and debating about what was the most important change or invention or transformation.

When I was a kid, people would have said fire or the wheel, or some benighted books, the bow and arrow. None of those things. I think it will be—hands down—the transformation of certain wild grasses into food crops, and the development of a system of agriculture and food preparation—because these grasses aren't normally something that our digestive systems can make much of—that turn wheat, barley, rye, millet, rice, and corn into the staffs of life for gigantic burgeoning populations all over this planet. These transformed our race, our species, from wanderers on the earth, moving around after the season of available life forms that hunters and gatherers have to pursue, to sedentary people with the big populations and the settled food supply that allowed cities and civilizations to happen.

This is one reason that Demeter was so celebrated, so honored. It was recognize that this grain of which she was the goddess was an essential component of civilization. The grain itself was given a little identity. We've got a trinity of divine figures here: the mother; the maiden; and as we see in a relief at Eleusis, a little boy who's called Triptolemus. He's the grain. He never grows up because he's never going to be a man. He is continually what Frazer called "the dying god," that sacrifice, that young man who must perish in order that the next generation can grow up.

He, it was recognized, came from across the sea. There are lovely pictures of him on Greek vases, on little winged chariots, drawn across the waves to Greece as he spreads the cult and the culture of the grain.

We're used to thinking, in America, of a planting season in the spring and a harvest season in the fall. We have our Thanksgiving celebrations late in the fall (we have it in November, which is truly crazy).

It's the other way around in the Mediterranean world. The grain would be planted in the fall. It would grow and sprout and send down its roots during the wet, chilly winter, and then come up with the bright sunshine of spring and come to harvest in roughly the month that we would call June. This had a huge impact on the entire year. The year had a shape to it the way a day had a shape to it. June was the time of the harvest and the harvest involved almost everyone. Even Spartans, who didn't do their own farming, still had to go back home and make sure that the helots and the serfs were getting in the crop.

So most years that the Greeks were involved in warfare, everybody stopped whatever they were doing in June, went home, got the harvest in, and then went back and fought a second season in the late summer and autumn.

The Romans, by professionalizing the military and having legionnaires who were not tied to home farms, were able to have these forces on permanent duty out at the fringes of the empire, fighting wars that lasted for years. I'm sure one of the things that really disturbed the army of Alexander the Great, when he led them all the way from Macedon to the borders of India, the Indus River, was, "What's going on back on the farm?" They finally did refuse to go any further east when he wanted to press on to the Genghis and the Bay of Bengal; they turned around and went home.

Within that cycle, of course, there have to be different tools and different activities to prepare the soil, nurse the grain to its maturity, harvest it, and process it. The plow was needed in order to break the soil in Greece. Some areas are very lucky when it comes to planting. River valleys—the Nile, the Tigris, the Euphrates—the annual flooding puts down a layer of rich, soft silt that you can generally get your seed into before weeds have a chance to sprout or before it has time to harden into a firm crust.

The Greeks didn't have that luxury. They had to use plows. Part of the point of domesticating animals like the donkey and the ox were to get draft animals to pull those plows along. Ultimately, by the end of the Roman Empire, we read about wheeled plows. They are trying to mechanize the whole process, make it easier to plow more. This was worked into the consciousness; their life grew out of a farming background in Greece. They have a funny name for early writing. *Boustrophedon*, they called it, "as the ox plows," which meant that the writing went along from left to right on the top line, then turned the corner and came back from right to left on the second line and so on, back and forth across the stone, just as an ox would plow.

The plowing is only the beginning. You then have to go out and sew. This was done by hand, boys carrying skins or baskets, casting out that seed, broad casts over the plowed field. Then there was continual hoeing and tending of the field, keeping down the weeds, keeping away the deer, the wild animals, the crows that might come in to take the crop. You couldn't rest for a moment. Farming is, of course—as anybody who knows from a farming family—a year without casual days and days off and holidays and everyday life. There is always something to do.

When it came to harvest time, the ancient Near East had used sickles, starting with obsidian chips in the blades. The Greeks moved into iron sickles. Of course, iron was a great transformation. Iron was abundant, was cheap, and became used for all farming implements, from plowshares to the sickles, the scythes for cutting the hay.

The Romans established a tradition of trying to improve on agricultural practices. They had greatly improved sickles for harvesting the wheat. They even, in Gaul, which was one of their breadbaskets, modern France, they developed mechanical harvesters on a very large scale that we see in reliefs being dragged by draft animals through fields and scything through vast stands of this golden grain.

At any rate, once the stuff was gathered in, it would be tied into sheaths and allowed to dry. One good thing about wheat is that it's ready to be ground into flour once it dries. But there are other crops, related, that had the benefit that you could grow them further north, in hilly country, or outside the Mediterranean area altogether, crops like emmer or oats, which will stand up to freezes and cold winters. These are great, except you've got to parch them or roast them before you can grind them into the flour.

However, it did allow for people from the Mediterranean to take their agriculture north, all the way up into, for instance, Britain. In fact, Scotch oats were introduced by Roman legionnaires, who were fighting campaigns up there in the north of England and then Scotland, just as the bagpipe was probably borrowed from the legionary pipers who would play those double-reed instruments to keep the legionnaires in step.

But wheat was the basis of it all. One thing that had to be done to the wheat was to separate it from the chaff and the little husks and the stems. For this, every community had a threshing floor. These were broad, circular, paved areas of stone. If you had a flat, level stone surface that nature had provided, that was fine. Most communities had to construct their own. Around this, draft animals would tow some such contraption as a sledge with little flint stuck into the bottom—you can still see these in rural Greek farming areas—to break up the grain, loosen the seed from all the surrounding bits of the plant. Then it would be thrown up in the air and the wind, on a breezy day, would carry away the lightweight chaff and the hard, heavy kernels of grain would fall right back onto the threshing floor, be scooped up, and then stored in a granary.

We see granaries everywhere in the classical world. Wherever you see lots of tiny little walls closely spaced and can't imagine anything being able to get in-between them, you're looking at the footers of a granary. It would have been a big timber structure set on top. The walls on the bottom lift it clear of the ground so that the damps of the winter that's going to come between you and the next harvest aren't going to get in and rot the grain.

Also, the little passages in there give ventilation and at the same time, access for ferrets or cats or dogs to get in and track down the vermin, the mice and the rats who might be otherwise getting up into your precious life-ensuring grain supply.

One of the famous threshing floors in Greece was at Delphi. The Greek name for a threshing floor is transliterated as a *haloa*. These provided early societies with a very natural place for dances and theatrical performances. The one at Delphi became the site of an annual pageant in which a little boy would dress up as Apollo, with his bow and arrow. Somebody would construct a mock cave and the person dressed as the dragon python would hide inside, and the little boy would come up and shoot the python inside there on the threshing floor, kill the python, and then they'd set fire to the cave and it would go up in a big bonfire and a great time would be had by all.

This was the kind of thing that would be on these threshing floors, and give us a background for the development of Greek drama, all those tragedies and comedies about the gods and the heroes.

Once it's been put in the granaries, the next step is to mill it so it's flour. We find the different range of technologies for milling the grain in all communities. It may be as simple as a little *metate*, a grinding stone, and a handheld pestle, the *mano*, which would be rolled or rotated over the grain every day for hours, in order to create enough flour for that day's bread.

There's a very moving part of the *Odyssey* by Homer in which Odysseus, lying in disguise in his courtyard, having returned to his palace, hears before dawn the lament and the prayer of one of the flour-making women, one of the slaves of his own palace, who has spent the whole night grinding flour. It's like the poor girl in the Rumpelstiltskin story; she's been given a task and she's just got to do it. This woman was assigned a certain amount of grain to grind into flour. It's taken her all night to do it and she's raising up a prayer to Zeus to release her from this bondage, this horrible task.

It is a horrible task and quickly, people tried to find ways to get around it, to do it more efficiently. In the Mediterranean world, the classical world, they used often that fine volcanic rock that was so gritty—found around Rome and Pompeii—and would shape it into things that were like double funnels of an hourglass shape, and set these on top of other stones that had a conical top. If you poured the grain in the top and had a slave or a donkey to rotate that hourglass-shaped piece of volcanic stone, you would grind away the grain and out through the bottom would spill the pure, white flour, ready for mixing with water and yeast, and for baking.

The result of this was that in all classical bread, there was a certain measure of grit. Archaeologists are kind of thankful for this because it has provided us with one of the only ways we have to tell how old adults were at death.

The Greek and Roman traditions for bread baking endured down to modern times. They endured down to the time where we get dates on tombstones and we can tell how old people were. Physical anthropologists have gotten in and checked out the teeth and have seen how much wear is on the teeth of a 60-year-old, a 50-year-old, the 40-year-old.

Up until the time that you are getting your wisdom teeth in—which is traditionally age 18 (they're sometimes called 18-year molars)—your teeth are not very worn. Certainly, the wisdom teeth that are coming in at 18, they're not worn at all. The eruption of the teeth is giving you an almost year-by-year sequence for human beings during the first part of their life. Physical anthropologists can thus be very precise about a child being 14 to 16 years old, based on the dentition, or seven to eight years old.

But once we get past the 18-year molars, the human body doesn't give us that many chronological clues to its age, except in countries where—as with the Greeks and Romans—this stone-ground flour was turned into tough, chewy bread, and you had to chew it and grind away at your teeth. The teeth were gradually worn down until they looked like ivory piano keys. I have seen sets of teeth from old people in the Roman world. They don't have a cavity because they had almost no sugars, except for honey, which was nothing tooth-rotting to put in your mouth. But they have been worn down by the constant grit and there are nice little tables that tell you how much wear from grit is associated with various ages.

If you read these estimates, 30 to 40 years old, check and see what it was that the archaeologist was using. If it's a Greco-Roman situation, I would imagine it's probably the wear on the teeth from the bread.

Very quickly, even the potential of these little things that are found at Pompeii and Herculaneum and Ostia, the port of Rome, those millstones that were worked by the draft animals or by slave labor, they were insufficient. They couldn't grind enough grain for the needs. So the Romans turned their ingenuity—they were great engineers—to ways to do it better and faster, grind the grain.

We, of course, are familiar with our own colonial period when waterpower was harnessed for these gristmills. They did the same thing. The most amazing work of Roman agricultural technology is a watermill at a place called Barbegal, in southern France, where the flour was ground for the city of Arles, which was a great Roman center there in southern France.

They'd found a hillside with a water source at the top, brought in by an aqueduct from a distant spring. The aqueduct channel divided into two, and came spilling down two millraces. As it spilled down the millraces, it was passing through houses, individual little houses, on the slope (they were all connected inside). In each house was a mill wheel, eight on one side, eight on the other side—16 mill wheels at once—turning day and night to grind the grain into flour to feed that city.

It may be also that a lot of that flour was then exported, although you don't usually export flour very far from the source because it's not going to keep as well as the grain. So it was probably all just for that one town.

We have to imagine that what was preserved at Barbegal may have existed all over the empire and we just haven't been lucky enough to find the remains or identify them, specifically these hill slope kind of arrangements, as mass production applied to the question of how you produce flour for people's daily bread.

There were ovens in every Roman community. Households would take their flour, work up their dough, and shape it into the loaves.

Some places had their own ovens in the house, but that's expensive of space. It's also expensive of fuel. Many communities did what is done in modern Morocco, for instance. You took your loaves down to the corner bakery, turned them in there, and after they were baked, you went back and got the loaves and took them home. This raises the question of how do you determine your loaf is that one?

I believe that these little wooden stamps that have been found in some houses in Pompeii, which have a person's name on the stamp were actually stamped into the loaves of bread in the same way that, in modern Morocco, each house has its own little stamp to put on its bread, so as they're sent away to the baker, there can be no confusion when they come back to the house.

These means of providing the cities only went so far. It wasn't long before, in the case of Athens, back in the 5th century, the city could no longer feed itself from its own fields. In the case of Rome, already by the republic, people couldn't feed themselves from the farms of Latium, or the farms of Campania, those central plains of Italy.

So they had to import the grain to make their daily bread. They became dependent on distant growers in a way that Egyptians, the great Near Eastern societies just weren't. They lived on those river valleys; they lived at the source of supply. The Egyptians became, in fact, great exporters of wheat to both the Athenians in the Greek world (and to other Greeks) and to the Romans.

It was a great moment in the Roman year when the watchers down there on the capes of southern Italy would spot the immense grain freighters appearing in that annual fleet, over the sea from Egypt, bringing the tons upon tons of grain from the Nile delta and its farms that Rome depended on to feed its million inhabitants.

There were huge docks for the reception of these gigantic ships. If we want to know what they looked like, we can probably take pictures of what those two big barges looked like that were found in Lake Nemi, south of Rome. Remember, this is the lake which the dictator Mussolini drained so that his engineers could get these great monuments of Roman engineering out of the lake, which had preserved their fine wooden structures through the centuries. They were burned, of course, in the end of World War II during enemy action (it's hard to know which enemy was involved).

At any rate, they're not there anymore, but we know how complicated, how heavy, how sophisticated these giant ships were for the transport of this grain, and what a big event it was for Rome and how impossible the life of Rome would have been if there hadn't been these fleets of gigantic ships, bringing not, in this case, luxuries from far distant places, not exotic goods, but the very staff of life. They had to import their grain, just as they had to work for their water in both Greek cities and Roman cities, with massive engineering projects to pipe the water in from great distances.

It gives a different kind of nature to life when you have to make such effort to get the basic necessities. It's certainly not true of all civilizations that this is required of them.

The Athenian response to not having enough grain in their hinterland to feed themselves was to establish colonies or trading posts or just take over places that could provide them with the grain. One of the impetuses behind the growth of the Athenian maritime empire was the desire to secure the grain-producing regions and make them part of the Athenian power network, the Athenian empire.

So we find Athenian fleets and troops down in Egypt during a time when there's a local ruler trying to get free of the Persian king of kings and his rule, fomenting the rebellion, actually ruling in Egypt for six years, jointly with the Egyptian ruler, funneling Egyptian grain and Egyptian wealth back to Athens. We find the Athenians trying to take over Syracuse and the island of Sicily because that's a great grain-producing region.

Finally, way up in the Crimea, that peninsula that projects into the northern edge of the Black Sea from Russia, Athenians and other Greeks established cities, forts, garrisons, and trading posts. It is an extraordinary fact that more of their grain came from the fields of the Ukraine than came from Greece. It was more likely that if Socrates broke a loaf of bread, smeared a little fish paste on top and ate it, it's more likely he was eating Russian-grown grain than anything that was produced within Attica itself. So this need for the wheat, this need for the imported grain, drove the economies at a very fundamental level of both Athens and Rome.

We started at Eleusis. That was where Demeter lost her daughter. That was where a cult grew up of spiritual rebirth, the closest we get to in ancient societies to the charismatic personal communion with the other world—the spirit world, the divine—that we take for granted in most religions today.

The Athenians built a huge square hall at Eleusis called the Telesterion where people come every year. In September, in the year of the battle of Salamis, during the days when the Persians and the Greeks were facing each other there on the straits of Salamis, they had the mysteries. Initiates came, and after sacrificing a pig and washing themselves in the waters of the sea, they went into that dark hall and they were shown things that changed their lives.

Seated on these bleachers around three sides of the hall, up to 3,000 people crowded into that interior space for this annual life-changing experience. It was a little thing called the palace that was down in what would have been the stage area in the center. The priestesses and priests would go inside and then come out and reveal things in the dark hall. Torches must have played some part. Maybe some sort of a window facing the rising sun played some part. They revealed things. People came out feeling they were reborn.

What did they reveal? There is not a single question about antiquity that we would more like to know and to have answered than that. But they all took an oath of silence. Just like any other initiation, you swear that you won't tell what secrets were revealed and what objects were shown. In the thousands of people and in the centuries of passing years, that involved each year an Eleusinian mystery celebration, we don't know of a single person who ever broke that vow.

What was a mystery to them remains a mystery to us, and is tied in with that ultimate mystery of these plants which, unlike the fruits of trees which can be plucked and leave the tree behind—or the olive trees or the grapes on the vine—here, life had to come out of death.

Lecture Twenty-Eight
Voyaging on a Dark Sea of Wine

Scope:

We devoted the last lecture to bread and all the artifacts and systems that grew up around grain, flour, and bread. In this lecture, we'll look at its counterpart, wine. Just as bread had as its goddess Demeter, wine, too, had a god, Dionysus. He is sometimes thought of as the inventor of the process of distilling wine from grapes and sometimes as the wine itself; ancient people were, thus, drinking the god as they drank wine. Our site to represent wine in this lecture is far from the main centers of Classical society, up the River Rhône from Marseilles, in a region of Burgundy whose modern name is Vix.

Outline

I. Everyone drank wine in the ancient world, including children.

   A. We have from Athens tiny vases called *oinochoe*, which were used in the wine festivals of springtime specifically for children. These vases have scenes on them of children at play.

   B. Wine was always diluted, not just for children, but also for adults. The typical proportion of Greek and Roman wine served at the table was one part wine and three parts water. Wine was also flavored with a number of additions, such as spices or tree resin.

   C. Wine was extraordinarily important in the Greek world and even included a formal religious dimension. It was not just an economic, agricultural, or social item in the baggage of Greek and Roman civilization but was wrapped up with the Olympian gods. Dionysus was sometimes called the 13th Olympian and was exalted. His purpose was to cause forgetfulness of cares, intoxication, liberation of the spirit, joy, and sexual mayhem, all of which makes him a strange god in our eyes.

   D. Dionysus is the god not only of drinking wine and the agriculture of the wine but of certain festivals that spun off into forms that we wouldn't necessarily link to wine drinking and intoxication. All the theatrical performances in Athens, for example, were done at the theater of Dionysus, in front of the god's own statue. His image was carried from the temple to the theater, and his high priests sat next to the statue to affirm that the performance was a religious contest.

II. In 1952, archaeologists in Vix discovered, at the tomb of an Iron Age Celtic queen or princess, a great tumulus, many meters tall, with a chamber in which the royal person had been buried.

    A. Inside the chamber were found the partial remains of a tall and robust occupant. This person probably would have been classified as a male by modern physical anthropological tables, except that all her belongings were found along with her, including jewelry and other feminine possessions. A four-wheeled cart was in the grave, in which she must have ridden around the countryside during the time that she presided over that corner of the Celtic world.

    B. The artifact found in the tomb that most surprised archaeologists was a *krater*, a ceremonial vessel in which wine and water would have been mixed in the Greek and Roman world.

        1. Made of bronze and 5 feet tall, this krater was the largest ever discovered. In addition, it was ornamented in a lavish style for which there was no precedent in any monumental Greek bronze vessel. It had *volute* handles, beautiful spiral forms coming up the side of the vase to its rim, with Classical mythological figures worked into the handles.

        2. Around the rim of the krater were many plaques of bronze, showing horsemen and charioteers in an archaic style of the art of around 500 B.C. These had probably been assembled onsite because they were detachable. On the back of each one was inscribed a Greek letter that matched a letter on the rim of the body of the pot where that appliqué was intended to be fixed.

        3. The size, beauty, and level of workmanship of this vessel were unique. It was the single most spectacular find of apparatus associated with the *symposium*, the wine-drinking ceremony from Greece, found hundreds of miles outside the Greek world in the tomb of a Celtic princess.

C. It now seems that the monarchs of the Celtic tribes who inhabited central Europe were approached by traders from the Mediterranean world. These traders wanted to lure out of central Europe things of great economic value: amber, slaves, furs, timber, metals, and salt. Because the Celts were the ironworkers of the world, the Greeks and Romans obviously wanted Celtic iron expertise, as well.

    1. Their method was neither to incorporate those Celtic lands into their orbit through political takeover or military conquest nor to trade as equals with the Celtic people.

    2. Instead, the Greeks and Romans attempted to find the leaders of these remote regions and buy them with gifts. It's a measure of the value placed on wine that the gift with which this particular family had been bought was the most spectacular wine-related artifact that we know of from the entire Greek world.

D. Why was the site of Vix, lying between the Rhône and the Seine, so important?

    1. The Greeks were interested in tin from the region for producing bronze. They traded through Celtic countries for tin that came from the Atlantic seaboard, from Cornwall and other sites along the Atlantic.

    2. Greeks couldn't go out through Gibraltar and up to Cornwall on their own because the Phoenicians had a grip on that strait. Instead, a caravan route and a river transport route were developed by the Greeks to make an end run around the Phoenician stranglehold at Gibraltar and through France.

E. The vessel found at Vix tells us something about the Celts and their love of wine and something about the global market as the Greeks and Romans saw it.

    1. The Greeks and Romans would send items—perhaps items of great value, such as the krater, perhaps items of minimal value, such as simple amphorae of wine—to people who put a tremendous premium on these goods.

2. Once the royal family's goodwill had been bought, the goods that the Greeks and Romans needed would flow through the Celtic or Thracian or Scythian realm to the Mediterranean. The wine was the lubricant that oiled the wheels of international trade.

III. Wine, under its god, Dionysus, also plays a leading role in Greek myth.

    A. Dionysus himself is supposed to have come from the sea. As mentioned in the last lecture, the Greeks retained a memory that grapes had come to them from Asia. They showed Dionysus, in some of their art, on his own ship, cruising through the Aegean. In one story, he transformed pirates who had kidnapped him into dolphins and caused their ship to become a floating vineyard. Thus, when Dionysus landed in Greece, he was already surrounded by the vine.

    B. Perhaps the most disturbing of the surviving Greek tragedies is the *Bacchae* of Euripides. It was written at the end of the playwright's life for performance before the king of Macedon, an ancestor of Alexander the Great. The *Bacchae* tells the story of how Dionysus came to Greece and of the disapproval from the establishment of his intoxicant.

    C. Given the late arrival of wine in mythical tradition in Greece, archaeologists who analyzed the set of tablets with Linear B inscriptions found at Pylos were surprised to find the name of Dionysus. It's possible that this reference is to an ordinary man, but it seems more likely that the tablet reveals the Bronze Age presence of wine and the cult of wine in Greece.

    D. Archaeology, with the assistance of chemistry, has been able to document wine being made and drunk in Greece at least since the early Bronze Age, in the 3rd millennium B.C.

        1. Patrick McGovern, a chemist and archaeological researcher at the University of Pennsylvania, has made it his life's work to conduct chemical analyses of residues found inside ancient pottery. At one point in his career, he was invited to analyze Minoan and Mycenaean pots from the Bronze Age.

        2. When Arthur Evans excavated in the palace of Minos at Knossos, he found what he called magazines, large storage areas, filled with gigantic pots called *pithoi*.

These pots would have been quite heavy when full, and ropes would have been wound around the pots to allow them to be hoisted and moved by cart or trolley.

3. McGovern and his team analyzed the inside of such pots and found that they had held wine. McGovern also found the residue of wine in pots from other ancient sites, including Myrtos on the south side of Crete and one from a building in Attica. Both of these sites dated back to the early Bronze Age, long before the myths of Minos and Dionysus.

4. The *pithoi* had an oddity of design, a hole near the base. If one were to try to tap the jar at that point, the *lees*, that is, the dregs of the wine, would, in theory, pour out along with the wine, making it less fit to drink. The usual way to get wine out of these jars would be to dip it from the top.

5. Thanks to ethnographic parallels discovered on the dig at Torre de Palma, we may understand what lies behind this early Bronze Age design. In antiquity (and in modern Portugal), the grape juice would have been "sealed" into the jar with a layer of olive oil, which would sit on top and prevent dust and air from reaching the juice. When the juice had fermented, the wine would be poured out of the hole at the base of the jar.

IV. Of course, the importance of wine continued through the Roman period, during which, if one were to take a count of the ships at sea at any given moment, most of them would have been carrying cargos of wine.

A. The Kyrenia ship that we discussed in Lecture Eighteen was a great freighter filled with amphorae of wine, quite typical of the wrecks we find from the Greco-Roman world on the bottom of the Mediterranean. Indeed, most of these shipwrecks are just piles of amphorae today.

B. For many years, scholars had questions about how the trade of the ancient world was carried out. One popular hypothesis was the "monopoly theory" of ancient history, in which ancient peoples were said to have started with nothing and gradually accumulated knowledge through experience. Under this theory, if a group of people started with no knowledge of the sea, they would be timid and hug the shore in their voyages; later, they would get bolder, until they were willing to use a compass and cross the open ocean.

1. With this theory, it was assumed that the Greeks and Romans typically didn't get much beyond the shore, although nothing could be more counter to common sense. The most dangerous place to be in a ship is near the shore.

2. Nonetheless, the idea that the ancients did not venture into open water bedeviled the study of ancient navigation and trade. Robert Ballard, the oceanographer and scientist who discovered the *Titanic*, formed a partnership with Anna Marguerite McCann to study the trade routes of the eastern Mediterranean by looking at the locations of amphora wrecks.

3. Specifically, this team decided to look at the route between Rome in central Italy and Carthage on the African coast in modern Tunisia. After the Romans defeated Carthage in the Punic Wars, they rebuilt the port as a Roman city and set up the business of importing wine and exporting olive oil. Amphorae would have been used on both sides of this trade.

4. What route did the trade take? Did the Romans creep along the coast of Italy, follow the coast of Sicily to the closest crossing point to Africa, cross over, and finally, creep along to Carthage? Or did they just cross the sea in a southwesterly direction from Rome, out of sight of land most of the time?

5. Starting in Sardinia, Ballard and McCann towed remote-operated vehicles (ROVs), equipped with cameras and lights, along the sea floor. Ultimately, they found a highway of discarded amphorae and shipwrecks that ran all the way from Carthage to Rome.

6. Ballard's theory is that these are the empties, that the crew, sailing these great ships filled with wine, would take the opportunity to crack open an amphora and drink it down. To get rid of the evidence, the amphora, now empty, would be tossed over and sink to the bottom, left to mark the ship's route.

7. This finding reaffirms for us the vital importance of wine— both as the blood of the ancient economy and of ancient life in general—and tells us something important about the technical skill of the Romans as navigators.

Suggested Reading:

Fleming, *Vinum: The Story of Roman Wine.*

McGovern, *Ancient Wine: The Search for the Origins of Viniculture.*

Questions to Consider:

1. Can you account for the Classical world's preference for wine over that even more venerable alcoholic beverage, beer?

2. How many modern commodities or substances overlap in our culture with the roles played by wine in antiquity?

Lecture Twenty-Eight—Transcript
Voyaging on a Dark Sea of Wine

Welcome back. Last time, we looked at bread—one of the staffs of life of the ancient world—and all of the artifacts and system that grew up around grain and flour and bread. This time, we are going to look at its counterpart: wine. Just as bread has a goddess, Demeter, wine has a god, Dionysus, sometimes thought of as the inventor of taking the grape and distilling the alcohol beverage from it, a sort of hero founder figure. Sometimes thought of as the wine himself so you would have a feeling of drinking the god himself as you were drinking the wine.

Everybody drank wine in the ancient world. Children were indoctrinated early on into wine drinking. We have from Athens little tiny vases called *oinochoe*, which were used in the wine festivals of springtime, specifically for the children. They have little scenes on them of children playing or swinging so that it was a big moment for a child when you got your first little wine pitcher and were allowed to drink your first wine officially at one of the festivals of Dionysus.

To relieve all of the parents listening at home, the wine was always cut, not just for the children, but for the adults. The typical proportion of Greek and Roman wine served at the table was one part one and—this is hard to believe—three parts water. One of the accusations of barbarism that the Greeks and Romans always leveled against the Celts, was they didn't cut their wine with water. Nonetheless, it would have been then flavored with lots of additions—spices, for instance, or tree resin, giving us the famous retsina that has endured down to the modern times in Greece.

Wine was extraordinarily important in the Greek world. If you were to take the fuss, the technology, the economic importance that we moderns assign to tea and coffee, plus hot chocolate, plus wine, beer, hard alcohol, a lot of the water that we drink (certainly the bottled water that we drink) and add some medicine, the salves that you would rub into open wounds as antibacterial treatments, add drugs—the whole world of drugs—you still wouldn't be getting to something as fundamental to the Greeks and Romans as that one substance of wine was, because you would be lacking the formal religious dimension. Wine is not just an economic, cultural, social item in the great baggage of Greek and Roman civilization—it's in there with the Olympian Gods.

Dionysus was sometimes called the 13th Olympian (I've never been able to get a clear idea of who were the exact 12). But he is someone who is very exalted. And the fact that his purpose is to cause forgetfulness of cares, intoxication, liberation of the spirit, mirth, joy, sexual mayhem, makes him a very strange god in our eyes.

He is the god not only of drinking and of the wine itself and of the agriculture of the wine, but of certain festivals that spun off into forms that we wouldn't necessarily link to wine drinking and intoxication. All the theatrical performances in Athens were done at the theater of Dionysus, in front of the god's own statue. His image was carried from him temple to the theater and his high priests were sitting right next to the statue to affirm that this is a religious contest of playwrights and actors and choruses, all serving the god Dionysus with their plays, with their spectacles, with their shows.

Each one of these lectures, we've tried to start at a site, an archaeological discovery that will lead us in to thinking about one of these big themes that runs through the classical world. For wine, I would like to take us far from the main centers of classical society, up the River Rhône, from Marseilles, which was already there by the 6th or 7th century B.C. Phocaean Greeks had founded a city they called Massalia, which has morphed into the modern city of Marseilles. We'll follow the Rhône River up. We'll come to the point where it's no longer navigable, but which is, as we know, a close point where you can portage over to the headwaters of the Seine.

In that region of Burgundy, we will come to a place whose modern name is Vix. In 1952, archaeologists discovered at the tomb of an Iron-Aged Celtic queen or princess, one of these great tumuli, many meters tall, with a chamber inside in which the royal person had been buried.

They excavated it in the winter. I've seen pictures of the excavation. It seems to have been done in a rainstorm. The chamber, when I saw it, was filled up with water and mud and they were fishing the stuff out. It must have been some sort of desperate rescue excavation to lead to this sort of situation.

At any rate, they found the partial remains of the occupant—a very tall and robust person. This person probably would have been classified as a male by modern physical anthropological tables, except that all of her belongings were found along with her, including all of her jewelry, some of her feminine possessions, the fibulae, the broaches that held her cloak in place. She had a four-wheel cart that was in the grave with her that she must have ridden around the countryside in, during the days when she was presiding over that corner of the Celtic world.

Then the artifact that made the jaws of the archaeologists drop: a krater. This is a ceremonial vessel in which wine and water would have been mixed in the Greek and Roman world, and they occur by the thousands in the Greek and Roman world. Sir William Hamilton found lots of kraters in those tombs in Etruria and in Campania when he was collecting his vases way back in the 1760s. There's a great krater by the Athenian vase painter Euphronios, a very controversial import to the United States in recent decades that was a centerpiece in the Metropolitan Museum of Arts' collection of Greek vases.

But this was a krater with a difference. It was not made of pottery. It was made of bronze, and it was 5 feet tall, the biggest one ever discovered. Not only that, but it was ornamented in a lavish style that there was no precedent for, in any sort of monumental Greek bronze vessel. It had volute handles, these beautiful spiral forms coming up the side of the vase to its rim, and there were classical mythological figures worked into the handles, medusas and other shapes.

Then around the rim, there were many plaques of bronze, showing horsemen and charioteers in an archaic style of the art of around 500 B.C. These had been assembled probably on-site because they were detachable, these little plaques of the horsemen and the chariots. On the back of each one was inscribed a Greek letter. There was a matching Greek letter on the rim of the main body of that pot where that appliqué was intended to be fixed.

It was of a size, of a beauty, of a level of workmanship that was unique. Here is the single most spectacular find of apparatus associated with the symposium, the wine-drinking ceremony from Greece, found hundreds of miles outside the Greek world in the tomb of a Celtic princess. Here was a mystery.

It now seems that the sheaths, the monarchs, the kings, queens, princesses of the Celtic tribes who inhabited central Europe were approached by traders from the Mediterranean world, by Greeks, by Romans. They wanted to lure out of those regions of Europe things of great economic value: amber, slaves, furs, timber, metals, salt, all sorts of raw materials. Since the Celts were the great ironworkers of the world, got onto the techniques of ironworking long before the Greeks and Romans did and certain technical tasks, they obviously wanted to get some Celtic expertise as well.

Their method was neither to incorporate those Celtic lands initially into their orbit through political takeover or military conquest, nor was it just to trade as equals with those people to find the miners in Cornwall who were producing the tin, or the people who lived on the beach in the Baltic who were collecting the amber. No, they took the more direct route, and typical throughout the ages, of all economic powers that want to suck resources out of remote regions. You find somebody who's in charge and you buy them. You buy them with gifts. It's a measure of the value placed on wine that the gift with which this particular family had been bought was the most spectacular piece of wine-related artifact that we know of from the entire Greek world.

Why was that spot so important, Vix? It lies between the Rhône and the Seine. The Greeks needed tin for all of their bronze. Whenever they mix bronze, they need nine parts copper to one part tin, and they did not have any access to tin mines anywhere in their own regions. So they would trade through Celtic countries for tin that came from the Atlantic seaboard, from Cornwall and other sites along the Atlantic.

They had to work their way through Celtic lands to get to the Greeks. Greeks couldn't go out through Gibraltar and up to Cornwall on their own because the Phoenicians had a grip on that strait. They had said that beyond the pillars of Hercules, there lay a sea boiling with monsters or a sea full of mudflats or—who knows, perhaps even a place where you fell off the edge of the world. But the Phoenicians had spread the alarm that you couldn't go that way, and they probably made sure that no Greek ship was ever allowed to sail out. So a caravan route and a river transport route were developed by the

Greeks to do an end run around this Phoenician stranglehold at Gibraltar, to go up through France.

That great vessel tells us something about the Celts and their love for wine. She only had a couple of cups in there with her. One was a black-figured Attic cup and another one was a silver cup. It tells us that the Celts were enamored of this aspect of the classical world. They couldn't, of course, grow the grapes themselves up there in central France; at least at that time, they were not doing so.

But it also tells us something about the global market as the Greeks and Romans saw it. They would take items—perhaps of great value like that krater, perhaps of minimal value like simple amphoras of wine—and send it to people who would put a tremendous premium on this. Once the royal family's good will had been bought then there would be a flow coming through that Celtic or Thracian or Scythian realm, as we work our way east, of all of those goods that the Greeks and Romans needed, but which lay outside their own domain. The wine was the lubricant which oiled the wheels of this international trade.

Wine, under its god Dionysus, plays a leading role in Greek myth. Dionysus himself is supposed to have come from the sea. As I mentioned last time, the Greeks retained a memory that grapes had come to them from the east, from Asia. They showed Dionysus, in some of their art, on his own ship, cruising through the Aegean. There's a story that this boy, this son of Zeus, had been kidnapped by pirates. As they were holding him there on the ship, he warned them to let him go. They mocked at him and laughed at him—this mere boy, what could he do against an entire shipload of pirates?

He showed what he could do. He cast a spell on them; he transformed the pirates into dolphins who then leapt overboard and threw themselves into the sea and swam away. He caused the ship itself to turn into a floating vineyard. A grapevine sprouted down near the keel, grew up the mast, spread out on the support for the sail, the yardarms, and bore fruit, magically, right there. When he landed, he was already surrounded by the vine itself and he was able to bring it to Greece and introduce that cult.

The most serious play—I think many would agree—that we have from this surviving Greek tragedy, certainly the most disturbing, is the *Bacchae* of Euripides. It was written at the very end of his life, for performance up in Macedon for the king of Macedon, who was an ancestor of Alexander the Great. The *Bacchae* tells the story of how Dionysus came to Greece. It was not an easy coming because according to the myth and according to Euripides' play, the establishment disapproved of this intoxicant. Parenthetically here, we should say this is something we can see throughout history.

I've had occasion to mention a great paleobotanist, Cheryl Ward, who discovered on the floor of the Red Sea a 16th-century or 17th-century shipwreck which had onboard coffee, black sludge that she was able to identify as coffee beans. By the way, this is 17th century A.D. This was an early shipment of coffee coming from the East. This was about the time it became popular in central Europe. By the early 1700s, most German towns had a coffeehouse and all of the fathers were angrily telling their children not to go down and drink coffee.

Johann Sebastian Bach, in Leipzig, actually performed at Zimmerman's Coffeehouse and wrote a comic skit and music about an angry father, warning his daughter that if she persists in drinking coffee, he will see to it she never marries at all in her life.

That's a comical view, but wine, according to this, had the same negative effect on the rulers of Greece at the time it was introduced. Euripides gives an introductory speech to Dionysus as he arrives on the scene.

> I am Dionysus, son of Zeus. I have come a long way from Lydia and Frigia [regions in modern Turkey], the lands of the golden rivers [Lydia is indeed a place where gold dust comes down in the river from the hinterland], across the steps of Persia, the cities of Bactria, Arabia, the Anatolian coast, where the salt waves beat on towered strongholds of Greek and Asiatic. I have made them all dance and they have learned to worship me and know me for what I am—a god. And now, I have come to Greece.

Given this late arrival in mythical tradition for wine in Greece, it was a surprise for archaeologists, who analyzed the set of tablets with Linear B inscriptions found at Pylos, to find the name of Dionysus on one of those tablets. It's still not 100% certain that that's the name of Dionysus the god. In classical times, Dionysus was the proper name of ordinary men. But it does occur along with names like Poseidon, who we know is a god, and Potnia Theron, the mistress of beasts, who we know is a goddess. So it seems quite likely that that Dionysus on the tablets shows us a Bronze-Age presence for wine and the cult of wine in Greece.

Way beyond that, archaeology, and specifically the study of chemistry, has been able to document that wine was being made and drunk in Greece at least since the early Bronze Age in the 3rd millennium B.C.

A great scientist, chemist, and archaeological researcher named Patrick McGovern at the University of Pennsylvania, has made it his lifework to develop chemical analyses to study the residues on the inside of ancient pottery that archaeologists find. Of course, you can do it even if you just had a single sherd of a pot, with that little bit of residue still adhering to it, and see what they were holding at the moment when they were broken and passed out of use.

He was invited by archaeologists who were working with the Minoan and Mycenaean Bronze Age pots to come and analyze those pots and see what they held. When Sir Arthur Evans excavated in the palace of Minos at Knossos on Crete, he found what he called magazines, big storage areas in what would have been the basements of the palace, filled with *pithoi*, those gigantic Ali-Baba-style pots. There were sometimes decorations of ropes worked around them in the clay to duplicate what would have been the ropes on the original that allowed it to be hoisted out of its place and shifted onto a cart or a trolley or something to move it because they would have weighed a tremendous amount when they were full.

What was in them? One thought they were olive oil because it's recorded in the ancient Linear B tablets that olive oil was very important. It was used, of course, for cooking and for anointing the body and as a lubricant and lamps for illumination, but also in the Bronze Age period, especially at Pylos, apparently, as a basis for perfumes. There was an ancient perfume industry.

Was that all that was in those pots? Patrick McGovern and his team analyzed the inside of the pots and found they had indeed held ancient wine. He was then given more pots from more ancient sites, including Myrtos, on the south side of Crete, and also a big *pithos* from a building in Attica. Both of these sites, Myrtos and the place in Attica, went right back to the early Bronze Age long before the myths of Minos; long before Dionysus is supposed to have found Minos' daughter, the Cretan princess Ariadne abandoned on the island of Naxos, and carried her away to be his consort. Long before this could ever have possibly been fitted into any historical scheme, people at Myrtos, people in Athens, were using great big jars to ferment wine.

These jars had an oddity of design. They had a hole near the base. Patrick McGovern said he didn't know why that hole was there. If you were to try to tap the jar at that point, the lees, the dregs of the wine, should, in theory, come pouring out along with the wine, make it cloudy, make it less fit to drink. The normal way, of course, would be to dip the wine from the top. We've got lots of pottery dippers that are used for lifting the wine out.

I think that, thanks to the ethnographic parallels that were showered upon us at the University of Louisville when we were working in the countryside of Portugal on the dig of Torre de Palma, we got to actually see what lies behind this early Bronze Age wine jar design. I've seen it in a little village north of the city of Estremoz in the Alto Alentejo region of Portugal. This is the last place, apparently, when you can still find a tavern owner who will invite everybody in at the time of the vintage (that is the autumn, a little before the olive harvest) and the grapes will be carried in in baskets, dropped on the floor of the tavern, the café in this town, and everybody gets to come in and tread the grapes.

As the juice runs out of the grapes, it slides over the slanting floor and into a little hole. Below the hole is a bucket and as the bucket fills up, the café owner picks up the bucket and walks over to one of these *pithoi*, one of these great big jars. I've seen his. They have the dates on them, the years in the 1600s when they were made, so they are, in themselves, great antiquities. He pours the grape juice in and when he finishes filling them up, he does not cover them, as they would be normally covered with some sort of solid top, or even with cloth. He pours in olive oil. The olive oil will not mix with the wine, just like salad dressing. You'll see what happens, unless you shake it.

The olive oil sits on top in an absolutely airtight seal that keeps out dust and air.

So the wine is transformed from the grape juice, below the olive oil, but you wouldn't want to dip down through it to get it. You, instead, have a little hole in the base of that big pot, that jar, just where those early Bronze Age vessels had it, and that café owner, when he's ready to get you a bottle of wine, which he charged me about $1.25 for, he pulls out the little stopper, fills up the bottle, and puts the stopper back in. The level of the wine in the pot comes down a little bit. The olive oil spreads out as it comes down that swelling form of the pot, but it's always keeping the airtight seal right to the bottom. This would be very confusing if this was happening in antiquity because now you would have residues of olive oil overlying the wine that may or may not have been picked up by the chemical techniques.

At any rate, it was an example of a form of pot from 5,000 years ago, which is still to be seen today, the 21st century, in use, in a rural setting of the Mediterranean civilization and which may show us its modern use and ethnographic parallel for that ancient pot.

It was interesting enough to McGovern that people on Crete and people in Attica, way off to the north, were using the same technology back there in the early Bronze Age.

So wine was important in the Bronze Age. It went on being important through the classical period, the Roman period, where I imagine if you were to take a count of ships at sea at any given moment, most of them were carrying cargos of wine.

The Kyrenia ship was discovered thanks to the work of George Bass and the Institute of Nautical Archaeology, working there in southwest Turkey, their headquarters at modern Bodrum. The ship was actually found outside a harbor on the north side of Cypress, and painstakingly pieced together from its remains found on the seafloor by Michael Katzev and his team, it was a great freighter filled with amphoras of wine.

It was typical of the wrecks we find from the Greco-Roman world on the bottom of the Mediterranean. Most of them are just piles of amphoras today. Sponge divers are so accustom to these they hardly take notice anymore.

Indeed, archaeologists themselves are a bit jaded with yet another amphora wreck because there's thousands of artifacts—including all those huge, heavy amphoras that you're going to have to clean and conserve and study and publish—and it may just be the 50th one that's been found from that particular century of the Hellenistic or Roman period.

They're very durable. Remember Jacques Cousteau excavated one at Grand Congloue, once he'd perfected the scuba technology. That was his first site to work on with Benoit, the French archaeologist. You may remember Benoit, watching his little monitor as the divers worked their way through the stacks of amphoras on these ships.

There was a great question about the trade of the ancient world and how it was carried out. For years, stay-at-home scholars had assumed that on the "Monopoly theory" of ancient history where you start with nothing and gradually accumulate things each time you go around the board, that if you start with no knowledge of the sea, you will be timid and hug the shore, and as you get bolder, up to modern times, you're willing to get hold of a compass and get out there and cross the open ocean or the open Mediterranean.

It was assumed that the Greeks and the Romans didn't typically get out of sight of shore. Nothing could have been more counter to common sense. The most dangerous place to be in a ship is near the shore. Most accidents happen near the shore. Most ships are wrecked near the shore. You want to be as far out as you can possibly be. For most of the Mediterranean, if you send somebody up to the masthead, they can see land anywhere.

At any rate, this dictum, that the ancients were not venturing into open water, was bedeviling the study of ancient navigation and ancient trade. Robert Ballard, an oceanographer and scientist who had made himself famous by discovering the *Titanic*, formed a partnership with Anna Marguerite McCann, (whom we've already met working at the Roman port of Cosa), in order to try to study the trade routes of eastern Mediterranean by looking at the location of these amphora wrecks on the bottom, or just stray amphoras.

Specifically, they decided to look at the route between Rome in central Italy and Carthage on the Africa coast in modern Tunisia. After the Romans defeated Carthage in the famous Punic wars, the wars that saw Hannibal, the Carthaginian general leading his elephants and his armies across the Alps and into Italy, in spite of that great feat, the Carthaginians lost. The Romans were angry with them so they tore down the city, sewed salt, and then some years later thought, it would be really good to have a port city there again.

So they rebuilt Carthage and if you go there today, you will a Roman city with fabulous mosaics, Roman buildings, Roman forum, and a Roman lifestyle. This called for a lot of wine, to be taken from Europe, and at the same time, olive oil was taken from North Africa back to Rome. Amphoras would have been used in both of these kinds of trade.

So what route they were taking? Were the Romans creeping along the coast of Italy then, following the coast of Sicily, then getting to the closest place to Africa, crossing over there and creeping along to Carthage? Were they doing that or were they just crossing the sea in a southwesterly direction from Rome, out of sight of land most of the time?

They started in Sardinia with Robert Ballard's research vessel and they towed these little ROVs, these remote-operated vehicles with cameras and lights, over the seafloor, looking at the featureless, muddy expanse day after day, people watching the monitors 24 hours, until suddenly the first amphora popped into view, then another and another and another. They were in amphora alley. They were on a highway of discarded amphoras and shipwrecks that they found later ran all the way from Carthage to Rome, and identified the line of the ships. When they got to the end of it—and it was not very wide—it was clear that the Romans knew exactly where to steer to get to Carthage on the sea over the southern horizon. The amphoras just stopped.

Robert Ballard's interesting theory is that these are empties, that the crew, sitting there on these great ships filled with wine would take the opportunity to crack open an amphora and drink it down. Jacque Cousteau had actually seen robber holes where people had poked tiny holes into the necks of amphoras and inserted straws to suck out the wine. But to get rid of the evidence, the amphora, the empty, would then be tossed over, sink to the bottom, and mark the line of the ships. Since this trade happened over centuries, and since it involved thousands of cargos—not just the ones that went to the bottom—the result was this very well-marked trail along the Mediterranean Sea.

This reaffirms for us both the vital importance of wine—the blood of the ancient economy and of ancient life in general—as well as telling us something very important about the technical skill of the Romans as navigators. Truly, a lovely marriage of different needs within archaeology for the economic side, questions about the technology of seafaring, and wine provided the answer.

Lecture Twenty-Nine
Shows and Circuses—Rome's "Virtual Reality"

Scope:

The theme of this lecture embraces the world of sport and entertainment among the ancient Greeks and Romans. In one sense, then, we are looking back to some of our previous themes, in which we've seen systems built around bread and wine that pervaded the agricultural, economic, social, and religious aspects of antiquity. At the same time, this topic of the ancient entertainment industry looks forward to some of our upcoming topics, including the infrastructure of technology and engineering in the ancient world, the roles of slaves and women, and general issues of economics and government. How did emperors manage to rule with the technology and communications available to them in the first centuries of our era, in an empire that embraced dozens of modern nations that could never get along today? They had tools other than the legions to make that a possibility. Juvenal, a Roman satirist, paid tribute to what he felt were the two obsessions of the people, cultivated by the Roman ruling elite and the emperors to ensure that the citizens would be obedient subjects. He said that, in olden times, the Roman people had been interested in governing and in bestowing consulships and offices on representatives who would then rule their empire. But in his day, the people desired only two things: *panem et circenses*, "bread and circuses." In this lecture, we look at a well-known site of one of the Roman circuses, the Colosseum itself.

Outline

I. Juvenal (A.D. 55–127) equated the public dole in Rome, a system under which citizens were given their daily bread, with the circus.

    A. The circus for Romans was the racetrack, especially where chariot races were held. The great one was the Circus Maximus in Rome, an entertainment facility that could accommodate probably a quarter of a million people.

    B. Instead of being an oval racetrack, the track at Circus Maximus was shaped like a paperclip, with a *spina*, a narrow wall that ran down the middle, around which the chariots would circle. The spina was ornamented with obelisks and statues of gods and emperors.

C. There was also a set of eggs and dolphins that were removed one by one to indicate the passage of the seven laps that were part of each race. The chariots probably took 8 to 10 minutes to complete a race.

D. The Circus Maximus has left minimal archaeological traces. The track can be seen, but most of the objects from the spina have long been taken away. Visitors must picture in their minds the slopes of the Circus Maximus, with wooden bleachers and the box for the emperor and his family, which led back to the imperial palace on the Palatine Hill.

II. One feature of the Roman entertainment complex that doesn't require our imagination is the Colosseum, the single most striking antiquity in Rome.

A. The Colosseum is located at one end of the Forum, over the site of an ancient lake. The site takes its name from the colossal statue installed there by the emperor Nero. In the year 71, the emperor Vespasian chose the earlier site of Nero's pleasure lake and palace for a grand amphitheater, an oval entertainment complex for gladiatorial combats and wild animal shows.

B. Throughout the centuries, the Colosseum was never buried; it was always the most visible landmark in Rome. For this reason, it has had a reverse appeal for archaeologists. The structure was built with hydraulic concrete and high-quality travertine. Archaeologists have been able to dig into its foundations and see some of the engineering involved to make possible the magical shows and transformations in the Colosseum.

C. When the Colosseum was inaugurated, 9,000 animals were killed in the opening days. Exotic animals brought from Africa or Europe—bears, bulls, elephants, zebras, camels, lions—all fought in the sands of the Colosseum. When the animals were cleared away, gladiators with various kinds of armor and weapons would fight to the death.

III. German archaeologists have been working inside the Colosseum to try to understand how these contests were managed and how magical transformations were performed, with animals appearing from nowhere and castles or forests seeming to rise up out of the floor.

A. Dotted around the oval of the Colosseum were almost 30 lifts, elevator shafts that descended below the floor. Ropes and pulleys would have been run down each of these shafts, and simple lifts could bring up, from different levels, wild animals in cages, stage sets, or gladiators, all ready to appear magically at the level of the performing arena.

B. The animals were brought up to a certain level, then released from their cages; they would run up a ramp and suddenly appear in the middle of the sand, without the audience being able to quite see where they came from. They would then fight, the day would wear on, and at the end, the carcasses were hauled off.

C. Below the sand, deep in the bowels of the Colosseum, slaves would move sets into place to prepare for the next day's performance. The shows had to be timed exactly so that the appearances and disappearances would take place in dramatic sequence.

IV. The Colosseum excavations show evidence of how the site was prepared, with massive hidden foundations under the outer ring; how the structure was built; and how all the theatrical contraptions worked. The investment in terms of human ingenuity and money is staggering.

A. One inscription about the source of the funds for building the Colosseum has been found and has been interpreted by many archaeologists to be the wealth of Judea, brought back to Rome after the suppression of the Jewish Revolt in the late 60s and early 70s.

B. We have images of the triumph of Titus, a future emperor and the general in charge of putting down the Jewish Revolt, surrounded by his troops as they carry the treasures of the temple of Solomon into Rome. The Romans looted Judea, and many people believe that's what made possible the huge expenditure to build the Colosseum.

V. The Colosseum is also the most obvious place where we can get a look at something that became a "virtual reality" for Greeks and Romans, an interest in the exploits of epic figures in the arena.

A. Charioteers were among the top members of the entertainment industry. Often, they were slaves and began their careers as teenagers. They learned the technique of wrapping the reins of the chariots around their waist and guiding the horses through the turns. Chariot racing was a risky endeavor, and many charioteers died in their 20s.

    1. The lives of the charioteers show us one of the ways that slaves could achieve upward mobility into the ranks of accepted Roman society. We will talk about slaves in the ancient world in a future lecture, and we will see that the arrival of freed slaves in society did for the Romans what immigration does for the modern United States, bringing in new people to the citizen body.

    2. In America, this process is lateral, coming from outside. In the Roman world, it was vertical, coming from below, from the ranks of the slaves. The charioteers are the most prominent examples of such people because they could make millions of *sesterces* through their winnings, buy their own freedom, and set themselves up as wealthy citizens.

B. The epitaph inscription for one of the most famous charioteers, Diocles, illustrates the extent to which the virtual reality of the Roman arena occupied the minds of the people. Diocles was a charioteer of the red faction, and the writer of his epitaph recounts in great detail the statistics of his career. The archaeological discovery of this inscription seems to tell us, much more than any historical record does, about the concerns on the mind of the average Roman.

VI. Of course, both the charioteers and gladiators were also involved with animals, and one of the developing areas of Classical archaeology is faunal analysis, especially the study of animal bones.

A. A young Canadian paleozoologist, Michael MacKinnon, has been one of the leaders in this area for Roman archaeology. MacKinnon worked with our team on the dig at Torre de Palma in Portugal and was able to tell us that many of our animal bones were red deer. Forests must have covered much of that part of Portugal, and people had gone out on horseback, hunting the deer. There had also been an industry in our villa of turning the deer bone into hairpins, fishhooks, and other tools.

B. Another aspect of MacKinnon's research as a zooarchaeologist is to understand what species were brought to the amphitheaters for the famous wild animal shows, in which, according to the literary sources, thousands of wild animals fought humans and each other for the entertainment of the crowd.

C. What were the mechanics of getting these animals out of their habitats, onto ships, and across the sea to Rome? The literary sources describe widespread destruction of habitat, a vast range of animals, and great reliance on African fauna. To what extent do these sources and the mosaics found at Piazza Armerina in Sicily and elsewhere tell us how these animals were captured in the wild?

    1. From the work of faunal experts and paleobotanists who reconstruct ancient ecologies of plants, we know that this quest for wild beasts at least partially brought on the destruction of the forests of North Africa.

    2. Today, the Sahara virtually reaches to the Mediterranean, but that wasn't true in Roman times. In antiquity, there was a strip of forests, rivers, lakes, wooded hills, and plains, filled with an abundance of wildlife. All that is gone because of the hunting and deforestation of the Romans.

VII. The Roman tradition of games began, of course, with the Greeks. Recall from our visit to Olympia that the games were sacred to the Greeks, contests in honor of the gods. Archaeology has been able to fill in some blanks and show us some interesting corners of the ancient games that we wouldn't suspect from historical texts alone.

A. At Olympia, we know the list of the official games: chariot races; races on the backs of horses; chariot races with mules; footraces of different lengths; track and field, represented by the pentathlon; wrestling; boxing; and "all-in boxing" (*pankration*), which is like modern kick-boxing and in which contestants sometimes died. In addition to the games for men, at other times, there were games for women in honor of the goddess Hera.

B. Not mentioned in historical texts about Olympia was a weightlifting contest that was not one of the official ancient games.

    1. A man named Bybon was said to have thrown over his head, with one hand, a stone weighing 315 pounds. We know this from the inscription on the stone itself, a reddish block of sandstone. This remarkable feat reminds us of those mysterious weights used by Greek long jumpers that enabled them to jump further than a modern Olympic athlete.

    2. In interpreting this inscription, we must keep in mind that the Greeks had centuries, even millennia, behind them, of intense emphasis on physical training. Remember the young athlete found in the tomb at Metapontum. Analysis of his bones revealed that his life had been devoted, since boyhood, to athletic training.

    3. Our tradition of sports on an intense amateur or professional level goes back only about 150 years. It's possible, although modern athletes would disagree, that the Greeks achieved some standard of strength that we have not yet reached.

VIII. It's not just individual objects but entire structures that help expand our knowledge of the ancient Greek athletics that lie behind the Roman obsession with sport and entertainment.

A. There were four sites for ancient games: Olympia; Delphi, site of the Pythian Games in honor of Apollo; the Isthmus near Corinth, where games were held in honor of Poseidon; and Nemea, in the Peloponnese, where, as in Olympia, games were held in honor of Zeus.

B. Since the early 1970s, American archaeologists from the University of California at Berkeley, led by Stephen Miller, have been digging at Nemea, studying the temple of Zeus and the sports complex there. One of the major discoveries was the tunnel through which the athletes walked from their changing area into the stadium. This tunnel, like the tunnel at Olympia, shows us that long before the Romans developed the vault, Greek architects had already done so.

C. This tunnel, built around the year 320 B.C., bears graffiti written by bored athletes, standing around waiting for their events. One read, "Akrotatos [a man's name] is beautiful." Below this, another person scratched, "To the one who wrote this."

D. At Nemea and Isthmia, the system of the starting gate was worked out. Runners lined up along a long stone sill in the ground that had grooves in it—one for the left foot and one for the right foot.

    1. Runners would crouch down in a position with their hands out front, ready for the starter's call. Postholes found in these stone sills obviously held upright wooden posts with rope strung between them to hold the runners at the start.

    2. Experimental archaeology has revealed that this system was effective for starting a race because the contest started when the poles fell over and the rope was taken down. Anyone who made a false start was simply tripped by the rope because it hadn't hit the ground yet and was automatically punished by falling down.

IX. These insights into ancient Greek athletics, along with all the material from almost 200 amphitheaters and countless hippodromes and circuses, have helped archaeologists build a complete picture of the sports and entertainment industry. However, we must always remember that the literary sources can show us aspects of attending these events that may not be captured in the archaeological record.

A. A wonderful example comes from Ovid's *Ars amatoria,* "*The Art of Making Love*," a series of poems in which the poet imagines men trying to enchant or charm women, one of which is set at the Circus Maximus.

    1. From this poem, we learn many things that archaeologists can't know. For example, the bleachers had painted divisions for each person's seat; we know this because the young woman keeps trying to edge away from the boor who is reciting the poem by Ovid.

    2. We know that printed programs were available because he fans her when she gets hot. No archaeological trace had survived of those. Finally, we know there must have been a grille in front of the seats, because he offers to tuck her toes up in the grille so that she can be more comfortable.

B. Through this combination of archaeological and literary evidence, we get a rich picture of this industry. But we should never forget that such activities were perpetuated by the Romans to distract the people from the fact that they were living in an autocracy, an oppressive empire in which they had virtually no control over their own destinies. It seems to have been enough for the Romans that they could go to the arena or the circus and watch life-and-death struggles in the lives of others.

Suggested Reading:

Futrell, *Blood in the Arena: The Spectacle of Roman Power.*
Valavanis, *Games and Sanctuaries in Ancient Greece: Olympia, Delphi, Isthmia, Nemea, Athens.*

Questions to Consider:

1. What parallels can we point to in our own society of the Romans' preoccupation with sports and entertainment?

2. How just is Juvenal's criticism of Rome's leaders, who consistently provided the people with *panem et circenses*, or "bread and circuses"?

Lecture Twenty-Nine—Transcript
Shows and Circuses—Rome's "Virtual Reality"

Welcome back. Today's theme embraces the entire world of sport and entertainment industry among the ancient Greeks and Romans. So we are, at the same time, looking back to some of our previous themes where we've seen systems built around things like bread and wine that pervaded the agricultural and economic and social and religious aspects of antiquity.

At the same time, this topic of the ancient entertainment industry looks forward to some of our upcoming topics, including the infrastructure of technology and engineering in the ancient world, the role of slaves and women in the ancient world, and general issues of economics and government. How did the emperors manage to rule with the technology and communications available to them back in the first centuries of our era, an empire that embraces dozens of modern nations which, by no stretch of the imagination, could ever get along today?

They had tools other than the legions to make that a possibility. Juvenal, a Roman satirist, paid tribute to what he felt were the two obsessions of the people, cultivated by the Roman ruling elite and the emperors than ensured that people would be obedient subjects. He said that in olden times, the Roman people had been interested in governing and in bestowing consulships and offices on representatives who would then rule their empire. But in his day, the people only desired two things: *panem et circenses*, "bread and circuses."

The bread, we've already talked about. There were a million people in Rome. Great fleets of grain ships came from Egypt and other grain producing areas. They came to the mouth of the Tiber and the grain was unloaded. There was a public dole so that the citizens of Rome didn't really have to work to have a minimum subsistence. They could go down to the great warehouses in the Forum and get their daily bread directly from the public dole.

This is obviously destructive in a sense of citizenship, independence, rights, responsibilities, being an active part in your community. So the dole on the one hand, the bread, was equated then by Juvenal, with the circuses. The circus was a very specific thing for the

Romans. It was not a ring with elephants and a ringmaster with a whip. The circus was the racetrack, especially for chariot races. The great one was called the Circus Maximus, in Rome, an entertainment facility that could provide seating, or at least places to stand and watch the show for probably a quarter of a million people.

It had a long spina running down the middle. Instead of being an oval racetrack like Churchill Downs in Louisville, or Hialeah, it was an up-and-down hairpin turn, sort of like the shape of a paperclip. The spina, the narrow little wall that ran down the middle, around which the chariots would circle, was ornamented with obelisks, statues of gods and of the emperors. There was also a set of eggs and dolphins which, when removed, indicated, one by one, the passage of the seven laps that were part of each race. So the chariots, racing around the Circus Maximus, in their seven laps, probably took 8 or 9 or 10 minutes to complete that race, much longer than horses have to compete today in a standard track.

The Circus Maximus has left minimal archaeological traces. It's been excavated. You can see the track; you can get down and run on the track if you want to. But most of the objects from the spina have long been taken away. You have to use a lot of your imagination to picture the slopes of the Circus Maximus with their wooden bleachers (which occasionally collapsed, killing a lot of the spectators), and the box for the emperor and his family, which led back to the imperial palaces on the Palatine Hill, and in which the emperors could display themselves to the crowds.

But there is one feature of the Roman entertainment complex which doesn't take that much imagination because it's the single most striking antiquity left in Rome. It's the poster child of Roman antiquities: the Colosseum.

The Colosseum is located at one end of the Forum, over the site of an ancient lake. The emperor Nero had decided to build a great palace for himself called the *domus aurea*, "the Golden House." He had a giant statue, 130 feet tall, of the Sun God, put up there. It was a colossal statue and because it was a colossus, it gave its name to the site and that's why we call the building itself the Colosseum. It's not because itself was a giant thing.

Nero was so hated that his buildings were dismantled after his death. A later emperor, Vespasian, that man who had suppressed the Jewish revolt, decided in the year 71 to put a grand amphitheater—an oval entertainment complex for gladiatorial combats and wild animal shows—on the spot of the pleasure lake that Nero had built. That was the spot that was chosen. It took a decade to build the thing. We're starting each time with an archaeological site. This is our archaeological site for our games and entertainment lecture, the Colosseum itself.

You might imagine that all that was necessary to do was clear off all of the greenery and ferns and things that had grown over the Colosseum through the centuries because it was never buried. The Colosseum was always above ground; it was always the most visible thing in Rome. There was a great English writer of the medieval period, the early medieval period, called the Venerable Bede who records what people of his day said about the Colosseum and Rome: "While the Colosseum stands, Rome shall stand. If the Colosseum falls, Rome shall fall, and if Rome falls, the world will fall." This is a good argument for historic preservation, at least in the case of the Colosseum.

Archaeologists have been interested in the Colosseum because so much of it is left. It's got the reverse appeal from a lot of the ruins we've been talking about. This was a structure built with good hydraulic concrete, with stone, travertine stone, very hard, of good quality. Archaeologists have been able to dig into its foundations, see how the site was prepared, and see what some of the engineering involved in order to make it possible to have these magical shows and transformations out there in the Colosseum.

It's a little bit like Hollywood today, where so much of our modern computer engineering and graphics engineering is applied to pure entertainment. That was what the Colosseum was. People would go there day after day when the games were being held. When it was inaugurated, 9,000 animals were killed in the opening days of the celebratory inauguration of the Colosseum. Exotic animals brought over from Africa, or down from Europe—bears, bulls, rhinoceros, elephants, zebras, camels, lions all poured out onto the sands of the Colosseum, fighting each other, fighting humans. Then the animals were cleared away and gladiators in various kinds of armor and armed with different kinds of weapons, would fight to the death. Thousands of gladiators would fight also.

These were places of blood and death out there on the sand. We have a microcosm of this left in the Iberian bullfight, which has survived down to our own time, where you buy a ticket to see a combat to the death. But the scale of it in the Roman age completely surpassed anything in our modern world.

German archaeologists have been working inside the Colosseum to try to understand how all this was done. They have uncovered evidence in that great oval (it's not a perfect circle) of how they worked their transformations and their sleight of hand, which would make castles rise up out of the floor, or forests suddenly appear.

There were almost 30 lifts, elevator shafts, dotted around the oval that descended deep into the earth below the Colosseum floor. Ropes and pulleys would have been run down each of these shafts, and elevators, or just simple lifts, could bring up, from different levels, wild animals in cages, the stage sets, or the gladiators, ready to suddenly appear magically at the level of the performing arena.

The animals came up to a certain level, were then released from their cages, and would run up a ramp and suddenly appear in the middle of the sand, without the audience being able to quite see where they came from. They would then fight, the day would wear on, and at the end, the carcasses were hauled off.

Down below the sand, deep in the bowels of the Colosseum, the slaves would get ready then for the next day's performance, moving the sets into place. The whole thing had to be timed exactly so that, as with the best theatrical shows, it was a dramatic sequence of these appearances and disappearances.

The Colosseum excavations show great evidence of how it was built, how the site was prepared, with the massive hidden foundations under the outer ring, and how all the contraptions work that got the animals up into the Colosseum. Think of the investment here in terms of human power, human ingenuity, money for all the animals to be shipped into Rome and maintained until the day of the fight, and money for all those gladiators who were going to be fighting also. This is one of the biggest areas of the Roman economy into which money was funneled.

One thing that appeared was an inscription about how the Colosseum was built, where the money came from, and many archaeologists interpret this as meaning that the emperor took the spoils of Jerusalem, the spoils of the temple of Solomon that had been sacked during the Roman crushing of the Jewish revolt in the late 60s and early 70s. That wealth had been brought from Judea to Rome. There was nothing like a boost to the Roman economy from the taking over or the punishing of a rebellious province because then the looting could be wholesale and all the wealth of that province could be carried back to Rome.

We have images of the triumph of Titus, a future emperor who was the general in charge of putting down a Jewish revolt, being surrounded by his troops as they carry the treasures of the temple of Solomon into Rome, the great seven-branched candelabra, the Menorah, from the temple, the shofars, the trumpets, and other gold and silver treasures from that temple. This is just the tip of the iceberg. They looted Judea and many people believe that's what flowed into the Colosseum. That's what made this huge expenditure, initial expenditure of the building possible.

Then we have *panem et circenses* with a vengeance, the bread, the circuses, the crowd entertained. This was the most obvious place where we can get a look at something that became a virtual reality for Greeks and Romans, an interest in the doings of epic figures down there in the arena or at the circus, the racetrack.

In other words, you're not thinking anymore about your war heroes. In fact, under some emperors, it was illegal to write a biography in praise of a great general other than the emperor because that could be politically dangerous. But there was no political danger about praising a charioteer, a gladiator, a boxer, an actor, or a singer. These are safe targets for popular obsessions and for hero worship.

So a strange situation came about where we get emperors actually being part of the entertainment complex. The best-known figures in the empire being not war heroes, scientists and inventors, great public speakers like Cicero—no, they're members of the entertainment industry.

Charioteers are at the top of this list. Often they were slaves. They started in their teens. They learned the technique of wrapping the reigns of the chariots around their waist, guiding the horses around the turns. It's a very complicated, very tricky, and very risky endeavor. Many of them die in their 20s, as their tombstones tell us.

The poet Martial wrote a beautiful epigram, which is also an epitaph for one of these young charioteers:

> I am Scorpus. I was the glory of the roaring circus, the darling of Rome, much applauded and short-lived. The envious Fates counted my victories instead of my years and made the mistake of thinking I must have been a very old man to have won so many. They took me when I was 26 years old.

That's a poetic epigram, but these charioteers show us one of the ways that slaves could achieve upward mobility into the ranks of accepted Roman society. We'll be talking about slaves in the ancient world two sessions from now, and we'll be seeing that the arrival of freed slaves in society did for the Romans what immigration does for the modern United States, bringing in new people to the citizen body.

In America, it's lateral, from outside. In the Roman world, it was vertical, from below, from the ranks of the slaves. The charioteers are the most prominent exhibit of such people because they could make millions of sesterces, through their winnings, buy their own freedom, and set themselves up as men so rich, they could actually create little temples to the gods as thank offerings, and endow those temples and provide for their children and grandchildren and generations to come.

I want to read you the inscription, the epitaph inscription for one of the most famous of these charioteers, a man named Diocles, charioteer of the red faction. I sometimes give lectures at Louisville (we're in a big horseracing area, the Bluegrass of Kentucky) to the Equine Industry program because track stewards from all over the United States are interested in the problem of how do you support a racing industry without lots of gambling going on. That was the motive for most Americans to go to the track. Now it's much easier to win your money online or at a casino. How are horseracing establishments going to compete?

They're interested in the Roman method, where the betting was never the driving force. The Romans had worked out a series of teams—red, white, blue, and green, and under some of the crazier emperors, purple and gold would be added—and you had somebody to cheer for in every race. It was more like NASCAR or the NBA, where you are cheering for and supporting a team. This guy, Diocles, drove chariots for lots of teams. They're all recorded, and how many wins.

One thing that we can see about this idea of creating this virtual reality, you've got to have something to absorb people, to occupy their minds. They're not controlling their own destiny anymore. Let's fill up their mind with statistics about athletes. So they memorize the stats. This archaeological discovery of this inscription tells us, I think, much more than any historical record does, about what the mind of the average Roman was filled up with.

> Gaius Appuleius Diocles, charioteer of the red faction, a Lusitanian by birth. [So he's from that same corner of the ancient Roman Empire that is today modern Portugal, and the site of our dig at Torre de Palma at that Roman stud farm where horses were bred for the chariot races.] He lived for 42 years, 7 months, and 23 days.

> He first raced for the white faction [and the consuls under whom he first race], and he won his first race for the white faction in the consulship of [another set of government officials]. He raced for the first time for the green faction [more consuls], he won for the first time for the red faction and the consulship of [more consuls]. [Remember they don't have a simple numbering system for years at this stage and that's why I'm sparing you all of the names of the consuls that identify the years in this kind of inscription.]

> Diocles won the following totals. He raced four-horse chariots for 24 years. He started in 4,257 races and he won 1,463 times. [Given that there can be up to a dozen chariots in any race, this is a pretty incredible 25 percent performance rate, or better.]

In the first race, after the procession (that's the premier race of the day, the *pompa*, the procession, the parade at the beginning of the day at the races) was an occasion when all the chariots would come out on other track (this is very beautifully rendered for you in the movie *Ben-Hur*), along with images of the gods being pulled on parade floats and other parts of the spectacle.

The most prestigious race of the day was the first one after the *pompa*, the first one after the procession. He won that 110 times. In single combat (like a duel with other chariot), 1,064 times. He won 92 major prizes. Of these, 32 were of 30,000 sesterces; 3 of them with six-horse teams; 28 races in the 40,000 sesterces category.

And on and on and on through the numbers of chariots, where he finished, how many times he took second place, how many times he took third place, how many times he came from behind and won, how many times he was out front from the beginning and nobody ever passed him. Statistics, statistics, statistics. This was his life. He wanted you to remember it.

If you go to cities like Aphrodisias, way out in Turkey, you will see the tombs of charioteers with the dozens of victory wreaths that they received as their prizes, carved in stone onto the tombs so that you can tell, from how many of these are draping their monuments, how successful they were in their lives.

These charioteers, these gladiators, these people of the Roman world, are also involved with animals—the charioteers with the horses of the teams and gladiators and those who were thrown into the arena with all those wild animals. One of the great developing areas of classical archaeology is a study of animals, what we called faunal analysis of bones from a site, looking at the animal bones rather than just the bones of human beings.

One of the people who's been leading the charge for Roman archaeology in this area, the young Canadian zooarchaeologist named Michael MacKinnon. I had the very good fortune to work with Michael MacKinnon in the dig at Torre de Palma in Portugal, where the chief of the operation, Stephanie Maloney, invited him to come and analyze the hundreds of animal bones that we had found on this working farm from the Roman Empire. He had a lot of surprises for us. He is one of those people who can pick up a bone and tell you that this is the left back lower leg of a juvenile female sheep.

He found for us that very surprising and what had seemed a very civilized, tame landscape, many of our animal bone were red deer. There must have been forests all over this part of Portugal. People had gone out on horseback hunting the deer. All those mosaics that showed hunting parties were just showing a real slice of life. There had been an industry of our little villa of taking the deer bone and turning it into hairpins, needles and other kinds of tools.

Wild animals also played an important role at the Coliseum in Rome and at amphitheaters like it all over the empire. Another aspect of Michael MacKinnon's research as a zooarchaeologist is to understand what species were actually brought to the amphitheaters for these great and famous wild animal shows where, according to the literary sources, thousands of wild animals—many from Africa and of exotic species such as lions and leopards—were fighting humans and fighting each other for the entertainment of the crowd.

He wants to understand what condition they were brought in. What were the mechanics of getting these animals out of their wild habitats, onto ships, across the sea to Rome? Pliny claims that a leopardess once broke loose on the docks in Italy and attacked people there. It's of great interest to know how reliable the literary sources are, which describe widespread destruction of habitat, a vast range of animals, and great reliance on African fauna. To what extent are the pictures we find in mosaics at Piazza Armerina in Sicily and elsewhere really showing us how these animals were captured in the wild?

One thing that's clear to us from the work of the faunal experts and of the paleobotanists who reconstruct ancient ecologies of plants— and also just from the historical record—is this quest for wild beasts was one of the things that helped destroy the forests of North Africa. Today, the Sahara virtually comes to the Mediterranean. That wasn't true in Roman times. There was a grand strip of forests, rivers, lakes, wooded hills, and plains, filled then with this abundance of wildlife, sort of like equatorial Africa or the Serengeti Plain today. All of that is gone because of the hunting of the Romans, because of the deforestation of the Romans, and the pulling out of the environment all of these animals, thousands at a time, was just one impact, and a very unfavorable one of this great entertainment industry.

The Roman tradition began, of course, back with the Greeks. For the Greeks, as you'll remember from our visit to Olympia, the site of the original Olympic Games, all the games were sacred. They were contests in honor of one god or another. Archaeology has been able to fill in some blanks and show us some interesting corners of the ancient games that we wouldn't have suspected from the historical texts alone.

For instance, at Olympia, we know the list of the official games: chariot races; races on the backs of horses; chariot races with mules; footraces of different lengths; the track and field, represented by the pentathlon; the wrestling; the boxing; the all-in boxing which is like modern kick-boxing, along with wicked straps around the hands to protect the hand, but also increase the force of the punch (people sometimes died in that one, called the *pankration*). All these different games. Then in addition to the very famous games for the boys and the men, at other times, there were games for girls and women in honor of the Goddess Hera.

We knew all about that, but there was a real surprise found at Olympia, a game that hadn't been mentioned. It was something like a shot-put, apparently, or weightlifting, neither of which were part of the official ancient games. It was testified to by the find of a reddish sandstone block of stone that had an inscription on it, saying that some man named Bybon had thrown this over his head with one hand. The stone weighs 315 pounds. So this makes us pause, scratch our heads about either the reliability of these ancient inscriptions or the unbelievable prowess of these ancient weightlifters.

It may mean that he lifted the stone, got it over his head and then took one hand away so he was holding it with one hand. But even so, this is kind of incredible in the technical sense of the word incredible.

On the other hand, we have to face the fact that, as with those mysterious weights that we talked about the Greeks using in their long jumps that seemed to have allowed them to go even further, perhaps by dropping the weights behind them while they were in mid-jump, further than a modern Olympic athlete, perhaps that stone is representing for us something we need to remember.

The Greeks had centuries, or even millennia behind them, of intense emphasis on physical training. Remember our young athlete there at Metapontum who was found in that tomb. His bones were analyzed and showed a very specific diet, a lifetime devoted, from boyhood, to training, and we know he was part of a tradition of centuries.

Our tradition of sports on an intense amateur or professional level only goes back about 150 years. We are children compared to the Greeks in terms of this, and it may be that we're looking at this stone as a real testimony to some standard of strength and achievement that our athletes have not yet reached. No modern athlete would agree with that, but I like to try to believe ancient inscriptions until they have been absolutely proven impossible.

It's not just individual objects that have been found that help expand our knowledge of the ancient Greek athletics, which lie behind the Roman obsession with sport and entertainment. Entire structures have been discovered. There were four sites for these ancient games: Olympia; Delphi, where the Pythian Games, in honor of Apollo were held; the Isthmus near Corinth, held for Poseidon, the God of the Sea, where there was a shipway and ships could be pulled across from sea to sea and the great city of Corinth, for Poseidon, the God of the Sea; and then Nemea, down in the Peloponnese, also like Olympia, in honor of Zeus.

Since the early 1970s, American archaeologists from the University of California at Berkeley, led by Stephen Miller, have been digging at Nemea. They've studied the temple of Zeus and they've studied this incredible sports complex. One of the big excitements was to find the tunnel through which the athletes walked from their changing room area out into the stadium, the running track and the place for the track and field events. This tunnel, like the tunnel at Olympia, shows us that long before the Romans developed the vault, Greek architects had already done so.

Of course, I need to have an aside here and point out that this is another one of those things where early credit was given to Greeks and Romans that should have been given to earlier peoples—

Egyptians, Near Easterners—because their vaults predate those of Greece.

But back around the year 320 B.C., the Greeks at Nemea put up a beautiful vaulted stone tunnel which would allow the athletes to suddenly appear out of the hillside, onto the stadium, and then take their places for the run. Inside the tunnel were the graffiti of bored athletes standing around waiting for their event. There was one of them, "Akrotatos kalos," a man's name, "is beautiful." This is probably an example of that Greek homosexual interest that we talked about on another occasion. But the funny thing is, below this, some other person has scratched, in a different handwriting, "Yeah, to the one who wrote this." So we're editorializing on the graffiti.

At Nemea and at Isthmia, the system of the starting gate has been worked out. They lined up along a long stone sill in the ground that had groves in it—one for your left foot, one for your right foot, you set your toes in the grooves—and you crouch down in a position with your hands out front, ready for the starter's call. There were posts holes found in these stone sills that obviously held the upright wooden post that had a rope strung between them to hold the runners at the start.

It was found through experimental archaeology that this was a great way to start a race because the race started when the poles fell over and the rope was taken down. Anybody who made a false start was simply tripped by the rope because it hadn't hit the ground yet, and was automatically punished by falling down and then being unable to get back up and finish the race.

These insights into ancient Greek athletics, all of the material we have from the almost 200 amphitheaters and countless hippodromes and circuses, the racetracks, the theaters, have helped archaeologists build up a very complete picture of this racing and entertainment industry. But we always have to remember and we always have to be grateful for the literary sources, which show us that there are aspects to the attending of these events that are not capturable in the archaeological record.

The favorite for me comes from the poet Ovid's *Ars amatoria*, "*The Art of Making Love*"—or as I think of it, the art of picking up women—which is a series of poems in which he imagines men trying to enchant or charm women, one of which is set at the Circus Maximus.

We learn from this many things that the archaeologists can't know. The bleachers had painted divisions for each person's seat and we know that because the young woman keeps trying to edge away from this bore who's reciting the poem by Ovid. He keeps telling her, "You've got to stay in the lines," as he keeps edging nearer and nearer. We know there were printed programs because he fans her when she gets hot with the program of the day. No archaeological trace had survived of those. Finally, we know there must have been a grille in front of the seats because he offers to tuck her toes up in the grille so that she can be more comfortable seated where she is.

Through this combination of the archaeological evidence, the literary evidence, we get a very rich and very full picture of this industry. But we should never forget that the whole thing was started by the Romans in the republic and by the earlier Greeks—or taken over from the earlier Greeks—to be in the empire a mask. It's a beautiful, charming, fascinating mask that is a distraction from the fact that people whose lives now seem rich and full of incident are really living in an autocracy, in an oppressive empire where they have virtually no control over their own destinies. It seems to have been enough for the Romans that they could go to the arena or the circus and watch life-and-death struggles in the lives of others.

Lecture Thirty
Engineering and Technology

Scope:

In this lecture, we will devote ourselves to archaeological discoveries that have laid bare some unsuspected achievements of ancient Greek and Roman engineers and technical inventors. We've had occasion, throughout this course, to talk about the wonders of ancient engineering; the control these engineers had over their materials, including the famous hydraulic cement; the interest they took in moving water from one place to another through aqueducts; and their naval engineering, which created fabulous pleasure ships and freighters that brought grain from Egypt to Athens or to Rome. All these achievements are the bedrock of Classical Greek and Roman engineering, and they formed a foundation for those civilizations. It's impossible to think of those achievements without including the engineers, architects, and technical crews that created such buildings as the Parthenon. In this lecture, we will focus on two discoveries that exemplify these wonders and have given us glimpses of ancient technical achievements that we scarcely dreamed possible. The first of these discoveries is from a Roman fort called Aquincum in Austria; the second is the Antikythera device, a creation of Greek engineers, sometime in the 1st century B.C., that puts the lie to that conventional belief that the Greeks were not interested in engineering and technology.

Outline

I. In 1931, Lajos Nagy, director of the Aquincum museum, became interested in investigating the Roman fort's firehouse.

   A. In the lower level of this house, which had itself been burned, probably sometime in the 4th century, Nagy found a strange mass of bronze tubes and pipes, along with an inscription dating the find to A.D. 228. His discovery was hundreds of pieces of a pipe organ, an instrument with a long and honorable history.

   B. The pipe organ dates back to the time of the great Greek scholars and inventors at the library of Alexandria in Egypt and to one in particular, an inventor named Ktesibios (fl. 270 B.C.).

    1. Ktesibios applied water engineering to create a mechanical set of pipes constructed on the model of the panpipes.

    2. He made a number of bronze pipes of different lengths and set them on a wooden case with a water pump mechanism inside, allowing compressed air to be applied to the ends of the tubes. Specific tubes could be chosen by the instrumental performer by pushing down what amounts to a key, which would open the base of that tube and allow a rush of air to enter.

    3. This *hydraulos* operation probably required two people, one to operate the keyboard and another to pump to keep up the pressure between the water and the air inside the valves and pipes.

  C. To reconstruct the jumbled mass of pipes, Nagy first had to determine their original orientation. This, in turn, required reconstructing the layout of the original building to determine how the organ might have fallen when the building was burning. Once he worked all this out, Nagy had what looked like a modern portable pipe organ that has since been put to the test.

II. This *hydraulos* ties into one of the chief interests of Greek and Roman engineers: moving water.

  A. As we've said, the Mediterranean offered a challenging landscape to the Greeks and Romans, and the long stretches between rainfalls left an imprint on agriculture. Olive trees, for example, became a backbone of Mediterranean agriculture, because they could survive through the dry season. Further, the great estates took their shape from the availability of only widely scattered sources of water.

  B. One of the projects of the Athenian tyrants called the Pisistratids was the construction of an aqueduct to bring water to the Agora that they were developing to be the new town center.

    1. When the Athens metro was constructed, workers tunneling under the streets of the city hit the submerged aqueduct, a long pipe made up of sections of terracotta tubing. These sections, similar to miniature barrels with lips around the ends, led from the springs outside the city through the city wall.

2. Cutouts in the top of these pipe sections would have enabled inspectors to see obstructions blocking the flow of water.

3. At the Agora, a Y-shaped contraption was installed to divert the water flow into two different fountain houses.

C. The project in Athens is an infant of engineering compared to the achievement on the island of Samos by another Greek tyrant, Polycrates.

1. Among his other accomplishments, Polycrates built gigantic moles, or jetties, to enclose the harbor at Samos, along with ship sheds for his war fleet.

2. The water supply on Samos was insufficient for the expanding population of the capital city. Thus, Polycrates instructed his engineers to build a tunnel that would bring water from a source on the other side of a nearby mountain.

3. The engineer who designed this tunnel is known by name, Eupalinos. Remarkably, he chose a spot on one side of the mountain for the ingress of water, a matching spot on the other side for the water to flow out and be diverted to the town, and a method of driving tunnels from either end until they met in the middle. A jog in the middle of the tunnel attests to how close the workers were to meeting at the midpoint.

4. Distance, of course, was not the only issue; the angle for the flow of the water also had to be calculated accurately to take advantage of gravity. Miraculously, the difference in the height of the two tunnels working their way toward the center was only 1 meter.

5. Having linked up, the two crews then dug a new tunnel alongside the walkway as the actual channel for the water, with deep shafts reaching the surface and smaller airshafts for maintenance workers.

III. The Greek hydraulic systems were, of course, far surpassed by those of the Romans.

A. The Greeks knew how to use gravity to move water from its source to a different place, but the Romans realized that water could actually go far below the level of its destination and be brought back up, using the water's own pressure.

B. At a site in Aspendos, in southern Turkey, we find the remains of Roman aqueducts that lead water from an elevated source across an immense plain. Towers at intervals on the plain carry the water up and down, enabling it to gain enough pressure to reach the next tower.

IV. In addition to these waterworks, ancient Greeks and Romans also made achievements in building bridges, roads, and dams, some of them dating back to the Mycenaeans. Chief among the Greek achievements—and one known to us only through underwater archaeology—is a computer.

A. In 1900, a shipwreck was found by a group of Greek sponge divers who had been forced to take refuge from a storm behind a rocky islet off the southern coast of the Peloponnese called Antikythera.

B. Over the next couple of years, archaeologists went back to the site and sent divers down to retrieve much of the material from the wreck. They found complete bronze statues of great beauty, as well as a small concreted mass that obviously had some metal at its core.

C. When one archaeologist began to chip away at the mass, to his amazement, interlocking gears of various sizes began to appear. Eventually, the chunk was taken to a scientific lab and exposed to X-rays and gamma rays to pierce through the mass of corrosion.

D. What was seen on the inside was dozens of gears, of many sizes, all obviously made to interlock, because all the teeth on the gears had the same angle, notches of 60 degrees, and were the same size. On the surface of the device were inscribed the signs of the zodiac and some numbers.

1. To those who study ancient astronomy and astrology, these numbers, 76, 19, 223, were significant. The number 223, for example, is the cycle of lunar months that typically occurs between one eclipse and the next.

2. The number 19 was the cycle of years in the calendar system invented by an Athenian named Meton, who had worked out a way to reconcile the solar annual calendar with the lunar religious calendar of Athens.

3. The number 76 was from Callippus, an astronomer who had adapted Meton's 19-year cycle into a 4-year cycle that would have applied to the Olympic Games, for instance.

4. Clearly, this wasn't some sort of simple sighting device. Each of the gears represented a heavenly body and its motions. The Sun and the Moon, for example, were represented by small gears; Jupiter and Saturn, each describing slow cycles that span years, were represented by larger gears.

E. The Antikythera device is in the National Museum at Athens today, still encrusted in its lump, along with a beautiful reconstruction. It was apparently enclosed in a wooden box for portability.

1. Inside the box were bronze plates inscribed with all the information about the heavenly bodies that could be tracked.

2. A crank was turned to move all the gears one notch, enabling the movements of the planets to be synchronized and allowing users to predict eclipses and other phenomena.

3. Most remarkably, it was possible to determine the zero date, the year in which the device had been set up, by working back to the beginnings of the cycles represented. The year was pinpointed to 80 B.C.

F. This small treasure, of which there is no indication in any ancient text, completely surpasses all our previous ideas about the capabilities of ancient Greek scientists.

Suggested Reading:

American School of Classical Studies at Athens, *Waterworks in the Athenian Agora*.

De Camp, *The Ancient Engineers*.

Questions to Consider:

1. Individual gods presided over bread, wine, and olive oil. Why was there no single deity of water?

2. "Mediterranean" climates exist throughout the world. Do they breed a distinctive culture or lifestyle?

Lecture Thirty—Transcript
Engineering and Technology

Welcome back. We are devoting ourselves today to archaeological discoveries that have laid bare some unsuspected achievements of ancient Greek and Roman engineers and technical inventors. We've had occasion, throughout many of our times together, to talk about the wonders of ancient engineering, the control that these engineers had over their materials, including the famous hydraulic cement, the *pozzolana*, the concrete; the interest they took in moving water from one place to the other, through aqueducts, to feed the cities; their naval engineering that created these giant ships, such as brought the grain from Egypt to Athens or to Rome; or that created those fabulous pleasure ships out in the middle of Lake Nemi.

All of these things are the bedrock of classical Greek and Roman engineering, and they formed a bedrock for that civilization. It's impossible to think of those achievements without including the engineers, the architects, and the technical crews that created such things as the Parthenon—no mean feat. These people ensured that, embedded in the Parthenon, were incredible technical refinements, the famous entasis of the Parthenon where, through swellings and gentle curves, they enhanced the feeling of a perfect rectangular solid by minute adjustments that fooled the eye into thinking one was seeing a more perfect building than was actually there. This is actually distorting the positions and the shapes of the columns and of the podium on which the column stood, in order to make the thing look perfect. This shows us generations of technical study behind these achievements.

What I want to do today is just focus on two discoveries that exemplify for me the wonders that somehow slipped away from our attention in the corpus of literary works that survived from the ancient world, and have provided us the archaeological discoveries with glimpses of ancient technical achievements that we barely dreamed of. Particularly, this involves our second one at the end of the lecture, the Antikythera device, a creation of Greek engineers, sometime in the 1st century B.C., which very much puts the lie to that conventional belief that the Greeks were not much interested in engineering and technology.

Let's start in the Roman world with our starting site for today's lecture. We're going to go up to Hungary, to a little Roman fort called Aquincum, and a place where in 1931, the man in charge of the Aquincum museum, a man named Nagy, was investigating the area of the Roman fort's firehouse. Because with so many timber structures, there had to be a crew that would zip around and take buckets of water and put out burning buildings.

He found, down at the lower level of this house, which had, itself, been burned and destroyed probably by the barbarians who invaded that part of the Roman Empire sometime in the 4th century, he found a strange mass of bronze tubes and pipes, along with an inscription. The inscription said:

> Gaius Julius Viatorinus, consul of the colony-ranked city of Aquincum, and former *aedil* [a sort of police chief], out of his own pocket endows this pipe organ for the firefighters' command of the said organization in the time of the consulate of Modestus and Probus.

That dates it for us to 228 A.D.

What Nagy had found were hundreds of pieces of a little pipe organ dating to the 3rd century A.D. These pipe organs have an honorable history, stretching back to the time of the great Greek scholars and inventors at the library of Alexandria in Egypt, and to one in particular, an inventor whose name might be transliterated as Ktesibios. Ktesibios liked to use water power in order to create amazing and surprising effects.

That library of Alexandria was the sort of university of the ancient world, the technical and engineering research center. It was there that Eratosthenes, one of the librarians, figured out a way to measure the circumference of the world, simply using the shadows from obelisks and cast down through wells. I hope that's something you're familiar with. He got it within a few hundred miles correct and certainly knew all along that the Earth was a ball, a globe. He was typical, Eratosthenes, of the kind of focus on science, focus on mechanics, that was being carried out there at Alexandria.

Ktesibios took an interest in hydraulics that was already very strong in the Greek world with all of its water channels and aqueducts, and applied it to machinery. Our word "hydraulics" comes from this pipe organ because that was its named, a *hydraulos*. The "*hydr*" at the beginning is from the Greek word for water, *hudōr*. The "*aulos*" at the end is from the Greek word for "pipe."

Although an *aulos* can be any tube, it is particularly applied to pipes in the sense we will still use that word of a musical instrument, a pipe. The pipers, who are sometimes mistranslated as "flute girls" who played, for instance, when the Spartans had the walls of Athens torn down in order to celebrate the event, they were playing things that looked like the chanter of a bagpipe, with a double reed stuck into the ends and little contraptions, mouthpieces over that so you'd blow into it without touching the double reed—the same way you blow into a harmonica without touching the double reed—and you produced a very vibrant, pungent kind of sound.

Ktesibios got interested in the idea that he could apply water engineering to this problem of the *aulos* to create a mechanical set of pipes that could play all the notes and maybe, possibly, several notes together. His model was the famous panpipes where shepherds would take reeds of different lengths—you can still see these, sometimes called the syrinx—tie them together in a tablet form, and then run the mouth over the top of the reeds to produce a range of notes.

By making those out of bronze, by making lots and lots of the bronze pipes of different lengths, by setting them up on a wooden case and having a water pump mechanism inside the case, he could apply compressed air to the ends of different tubes. These tubes would be chosen by the instrumental performer, by the pushing down of what amounts of a key—and we still call them keyboards—which would open up the base of that tube and allow the rush of air to go in.

It required two people to do this hydraulos operation, as far as we can tell. There need to be a person at the keyboard, and another person pumping on the side to keep the pressure up between the water and the air that was inside the valves and the pipes, feeding into those tubes.

This instrument was wildly popular. We spent our last time together at the arena. We've got lots of mosaics that show the entertainments at the arena. My favorite one of all is showing a lot of leopards and wild animals running around and people tied to stakes, being mauled by these animals, and gladiators fighting. Out in the middle of it all is what looks to be a calliope player, a little fellow, a musician, sitting at one of these pipe organs, playing tunes for the crowd. It's like the organ at a ballpark that plays the sing-along numbers and the National Anthem. Here was somebody to entertain you—as if all of the mayhem wasn't enough, let's get some popular music in there also.

These hydraulos instruments showed up on coins; they showed up on reliefs. We have one from Egypt which shows a trumpet player standing next to the hydraulos. So the next time you're in a disc shop and have a chance to buy a CD of trumpet and organ, just do it. You will get a chance to hear, with your modern ear, the same kind of sonority that those ancient Romans and Greeks were enjoying with the hydraulos and those other brass instruments.

It was quite a task to put that jumbled mass of pipes back together. For one thing, all the wooden stuff had disappeared, and that meant the case and most of the mechanisms. It was only the bronze fittings that had to do with the pump, and then all those tubes.

Nagy first of all had to figure out their original orientation. So we had to do some reconstruction of what the original building would have looked like, how that organ would have fallen from the upper floor, where it was kept, down through the burning building, and then tipping on its back, spilled out its little bronze pipes. But once he'd worked all this out, he had what looked like a little modern portable pipe organ that has been put to the test, the reconstructions. There's a reconstruction now in a firefighter's museum in Budapest. They are very proud to have this relic of past technology that they can play and listen to and enjoy, thinking that they are hearing the sounds of these ancient firefighters that were enjoyed so long ago.

Our hydraulos, as I said, ties into one of the chief interests of those Greek and Roman engineers. We've remarked again and again, they were living in a challenging landscape. The world of the Mediterranean was a place with a specific climatic regime that put a premium on water. Any place where the last rains are happening in April, and it may not rain again until September or October, is a place where water is going to matter.

It left its imprint, of course, on agriculture. There weren't enough springs to go around so a crop like olive trees that could survive through the dry season without needing water became part of the backbone of Mediterranean agriculture. Also, there were great estates that took advantage of the fact that there's only one set of springs; we're going to build our big royal palatial manor house here, surrounded with our slave quarters, and then rule this vast expanse. It all depended on the availability of the water.

The direct ancestor of the modern hacienda, the modern ranch, the modern southern plantation of the antebellum period, is that Roman *latifundiae* system, the villa system, which had the big estates. Why were the big estates important and practical and a viable way to treat the landscape? Because water only was available at widely-scattered places, and small farms couldn't exist without some permanent water source on them.

Out of that need for water came this whole world of what we called hydraulics, using that word out of the water and the tube that applied to the little pipe organ. I'd like to look at some of the achievements of the ancient Greeks in terms of their hydraulic interests that take us all the way back to the 6th century B.C., and the time of those Greek leaders called tyrants, who seized control of cities like Athens and islands like Samos in the Aegean, and wrought incredible works of architecture and engineering.

Let's start with Athens. They had a set of tyrants called the Peisistratids. Peisistratus himself was the father who seized control of Athens, and his sons, Hippias and Hipparchus, carried on his rule. During their reign, they tried to make Athens a modern city. It would be a modern city even by the standards of the 18th century of our era, because of their engineering efforts and their interest in hydraulics.

When the Athens metro was put in and they were tunneling under the streets of Athens, they hit the submerged aqueduct, the long pipe, hundreds and hundreds of meters long, made up of sections of terra cotta tubing. It was like miniature barrels with lips around the ends, that led from the springs outside the city right through the city wall, down to the agora at the north side of the Acropolis that the Pisistratids were developing to be the new town center.

There it was, if you go to the Evangelismos tube station, you can see that in a really exemplary way, the Athenians have enshrined behind glass the bits of the Peisistratid aqueduct so that as you get out of your train and walk up to the naval hospital or the American School of Classical Studies, you are passing an aqueduct 2,600 years old, buried under the streets of Athens.

You can not only see the individual terra cotta sections of the great pipe; you can see that they wanted to inspect the pipe and have ways to get in if there were problems. So there were little cutouts in the top of the pipes where a section had been neatly cut around, a rectangular piece, that would open—you lifted it up—and you could then see if there was something blocking the water in that area, put your hand or some mechanical device in, and clean it out. It was a very sophisticated device.

When they got down to the agora, they wanted to feed different springs, different fountain houses, so we get a great "Y" contraption that will divert the water flow when it hits the agora itself into two areas and send it through two different fountain houses.

This is an infant of engineering compared to what was done on the island of Samos by another Greek tyrant, a famous fellow named Polycrates. Polycrates is one of those wonderful persons whose history was only written by his enemies and so we get a very negative view of Polycrates.

But he did all sorts of extraordinary things. He built out into the harbor of Samos gigantic moles, or jetties, by having stones placed in the water until they broke the surface, and enclosed a huge harbor. He built ship sheds for his war fleet, where the ships could be hauled up out of the water and kept under roofs to protect them from the rain. When his political enemies were getting after him, he locked up their wives and children in the ship sheds and threatened to burn it down. Maybe it's not entirely unjust that he gets a bad rap from history.

He's also someone who used triremes, those early three-level oared ships that we talked about before, as troop transports, to send mercenaries abroad to places like Egypt, to fight for Egyptian monarchs who were waging wars of freedom against the Persians.

He had a problem there on Samos of water supply. He was expanding his capital city, but the water supply couldn't keep up with the new population. Cisterns only go so far in an area where much of the year is without any rain. But he knew there was a very good source of water on the other side of the mountain, against which the city backed up.

So Polycrates had his engineers figure out a tunnel trajectory that would bring water through the mountain. Hundreds of meters would have to be cut through the mountain and then an aqueduct constructed from the springs on the far side that would lead the water in, through the long tunnel, and then down to his city.

This engineer, the designer of this tunnel of Polycrates, we actually know by name: Eupalinos. He was from the Greek city of Megara, right next to Athens, and he must have been an itinerant expert who would go around to different city-states and offer his services. We know that at times in the Greek world, city-states would have, on their payroll, and engineer to handle problems like this and allow the city to build new walls or structures or create new designs.

Eupalinos, in ways that we still can't figure out today, figured out how to pick a place on one side of the mountain for the ingress of the water, a matching place on the other side that it would flow out and then be diverted to the town, and a way of driving tunnels from either end until they met in the middle. As I said, it was hundreds and hundreds of meters. I've never walked all the way through Eupalinos' tunnel, but a long way is enough to make you marvel at the achievement.

The work was pretty slow because the tunnel wasn't going to be gigantic and couldn't have had more than about five workers up against the face of the rock, chipping away with their picks, and moving the work forward into the heart of the mountain as they went. Then the anxiety they must have felt the whole time that they were going to somehow miss each other in the middle after all this work.

You can still see the results of a final meeting of these two tunnels being driven towards each other. They got very close. Maybe they could hear each other, maybe just from measuring tapes from the ends of the tunnel and knowing how wide the mountain was, they knew that they were within range. They each turned toward each other and went the last little bit. So there's a jog in the middle of the tunnel of Eupalinos, there on the island of Samos.

Distance, of course, is not the only issue, but the angle because the angle for the flow of the water has to be accurately calculated so it will be drawn by gravity right down through the mountain. Miraculously, what was the difference in the height of the two tunnels working their way? One meter. That was all. The tunnel that was being driven from one side was just one meter of height off of the tunnel that had come all those hundreds of meters from the other side.

You can still see the marks of the picks of one crew pointing in this direction meeting the marks of the picks from the other crew on the walls of the tunnel. Having linked up, they then dug a completely new tunnel down alongside the walkway and that was the actual channel for the water, with deep shafts reaching the surface, and some shafts cut up through the tunnel to give air for people who would come in and do work and maintenance along this incredible feat of engineering.

In this way, Samos was then able to become one of the great Greek cities of the world because its water problems had been solved.

All these hydraulics of the Greeks, of course, were far surpassed by the Romans. We have, from the Roman period, books, manuals on aqueducts. The Romans were tremendously impressed by their own skills with aqueducts, and that word also has a simple meaning, *aqua*, "water," and *duct*, "to lead" water.

The Romans figured out something that the Greeks didn't. The Greeks knew how to use gravity to take water from its source down to a new place, a destination. The Romans realized that water behaved in a certain way so that it could actually go far below the level of its destination and be brought back up, if you could use the water's own pressure to push it first down and then back up a corresponding slope. Of course, we do this often when we need to drain a tank and put a hose in our mouth and get that little bit of suction going to get the water flow. Then it doesn't matter if some of the hose is below the level of the tub into which you're pouring the water.

Romans figured this out and at a place like Aspendos, down in southern Turkey, we can find the remains of Roman aqueducts where the source of the water is very high. It's going to cross an immense plain. They lead it right down to the level of the plain and periodically have these immense towers to carry the water up again and then get a head of steam up, a head of pressure, as it goes down the other side of the tower and shoots off to the next one. It goes up and down, up and down, right across the plain until it finally gets to the great city with its theater and its typical array of Roman amenities. This was all unthinkable without that water. Given the challenges of the terrain, they had to figure out a way to get things from a high place, through a low place, and back to a semi-high place, or the Roman achievements just would not have been possible.

In addition to all of these waterworks, there were Greek and Roman achievements in bridge building, road building, dam building, and many other aspects of ancient life. In fact, some of these go right back to the Mycenaeans. You can see Mycenaean bridges and Mycenaean dams that were marvels to the classical Greeks who didn't go much in for roads and dams and bridges. As I've said before, the ancient Greeks of the classical period were so impressed by these that they attributed to them to giants called Cyclops, who must have come in an used these huge stones to create the fortification walls of the bridges of the dams of the Mycenaean world that they could really only dream of.

But those classical Greeks, once they got into that think-tank mindset that we find at the library at Alexandria, with all of those great experts working together, did some remarkable achievements of their own. Not on this super scale of the Mycenaean or the Roman tradition, but working on a very small scale.

Chief among their achievements—and one only known to us because of underwater archaeology—is a computer. The year was 1900 of our era, and we've already briefly described the scenario. A group of Greek sponge divers was coming back from a trip to the far end of the western Mediterranean when they were hit by storms and had to take refuge behind a rocky little islet off the southern coast of the Peloponnese called Antikythera.

Bored with their forced inactivity, they decided to put on their suits and dive. If this has been scuba, they probably wouldn't have done this because it was 200 feet down to the bottom and that's beyond comfortable range for scuba diving, and we're still 45–47 years from the first commercially-available scuba diving equipment.

So they took the famous copper helmets and the body suits. A sponge diver went down and he came back up, very shaken. He'd had an experience like Stefano Mariottini, the experience of a man who's gone down to the seafloor in the Mediterranean and has seen body parts. But he realized he was looking at statues.

He had, in fact, found the remains of a great wreck, with bronze statues and treasures on it and lots of other things. Over the next couple of years, archaeologists went back to the site, stayed on the surface, sent the sponge divers down, and got as much of the material from the bottom as they could from the Antikythera wreck. We don't have any wood from the wreck; it was all eaten up by those teredo worms.

The stuff from the bottom included this concreted mass that obviously had some metal at its core, but they were dealing with complete bronze statues, body parts of statues of great beauty, things that they'd never dreamed of finding. Remember at this time, one of the very few bronze statues available was that little charioteer, the statue of the boy found at Delphi. So to find an abundance of bronze statues, the great striding Zeus or Poseidon, that had not yet been found in the sea off Artemision. It's hard for us to imagine the impact that this chance discovery by these sponge divers had on the imagination of Greeks and art lovers around the world.

So the little chunk, the concreted mass, did not get a lot of attention to begin with. But once they'd worked through the identifiable bits of ancient art, one of the scholars turned his attention to this mass that obviously had iron, or more likely, bronze stuff inside of it.

He began to chip it away, and to his amazement, gears began to appear, interlocking gears of various sizes, one of them a great big thing with four spokes across it, flat spokes like a wheel. But he couldn't clean it off enough to see all the details. Eventually, the chunk was taken to a scientific lab and exposed to X-rays and gamma rays to pierce through the mass of corrosion and concretions on the outside, and see what was within.

What was inside was just amazing to them. They'd already known it was gears. In fact, one idea was it had been some sort of primitive astrolabe, a ship's instrument for navigation because after all, it had been found on a ship and we're used to thinking that if you're out there at sea and you don't have navigational devices, you're probably lost, which is far from true. That had been the natural assumption.

What they found was dozens of gears, many different sizes, but all made to interlock because all the teeth on other gears had the same angle, notches of 60 degrees, and the teeth were the same size so they could all interlock. But some of the gears were very small, some very large.

They kept working away at cleaning the device and they began to find inscriptions. The signs of the zodiac were inscribed by name on one of the plates. The Moon, the Sun, the planet Venus, and then some numbers, 76, 19, 223.

To those who studied ancient astronomy and astrology, these were very significant numbers. Two hundred twenty-three is the cycle of lunar months that typical occurs between one eclipse and the next. Nineteen was the cycle of years in the calendar system invented by an Athenian named Meton, who, back at the time of the Peloponnesian War in the 430s B.C. had worked out a way that the Athenians could reconcile their solar annual calendar with their lunar religious festival calendar. So every 19 years, it would cycle back to the beginning point and all of the festivals would fall at the same point of the solar year, as well as on the fixed days of the lunar months. Seventy-six was from Callippus, an astronomer who had taken Meton's 19 and made it a quadrennial, a 4-year cycle, that would have applied to the Olympic Games, for instance.

This was huge. It was clear now that this wasn't some sort of simple sighting device. This was a device where the dozens of gears inside, each one represented a heavenly body and its motions, some of them, of course, in very rapid motion. The Sun, the Moon, those would be the small gears; Others in very slow motion, to the naked eye. Venus and Mars moving fairly rapidly; Jupiter and Saturn, way out there, still quite visible to the naked eye of those ancient astronomers, but describing very slow cycles that span years. But each one represented by its gear.

If you go to the National Museum at Athens today, for me, their greatest exhibit at all is the Antikythera device, still encrusted in its lump, the X-rays that show what's inside, and then a beautiful reconstruction of the entire thing. It was apparently enclosed within a wooden box so you could carry it around under your arm. It was only 1 foot long by about 9 inches x 3 inches thick, so a small thing.

But inside, if you open the door, you saw first bronze plates inscribed with the instructions, inscribed with all of the information about the heavenly bodies that could be tracked, and you found a place where you could turn a crank so all the gears moved one notch. For the little ones, that was a great part of their circumference; for the great big ones, the one notch wasn't making much of an impact. But it meant that you could synchronize the movements of all of those heavenly bodies; predict eclipses; predict conjunctions of the planets; the risings of the planets; their first appearance at different times of the year.

The old Farmers Almanac that we know from the poet Hesiod back at the beginning of the Greek traditions—some people thought Hesiod was as old as Homer—he used the stars, the risings and the settings of the Pleiades and Arcturus and other stars, as the guides to not just farming, but even sailing, when it was safe to take your ship out to sea.

All of this was packed in there and most remarkably, it was possible to figure out the zero date, in what year had the thing been set up by working one's way back to the beginnings of these cycles within the little Antikythera device. It was pinpointed to the year 80 B.C.

So here we have a cargo on a ship, filled with treasures from Greece, probably headed, like so many of the other treasures of the Hellenic world, for Rome, in the 1st century B.C., shortly after the sack of Athens in 86 B.C., by the Roman general Sulla, who cut down the olive trees of the academy where Plato used to teach, to make his siege engines, and took columns from Greek tombs to make ballistae and throw those stones over the walls.

Here was this cargo, carrying this treasure, which there was no indication of in any ancient text, which completely surpasses all of our previous ideas about what those ancient Greek scientists were capable of, and anticipates not just computers, but even clock mechanisms, by some 1,700 years, all because of a contrary wind and a group of bored sponge fishermen.

All I can say is, let us all be thankful to the end of our days for that contrary wind that sent them to the bottom and brought up a find that they would have almost left behind, so unprepossessing did it appear. Yet within that corroded mass of bronze remained a secret that implies for us an entire world of Greek bronze engineering and mathematical and astronomical inquiry that otherwise would have remained hidden from us forever.

Lecture Thirty-One
Slaves—A Silent Majority?

Scope:

In the last few lectures, we've discussed engineering, technology, trade, the production of bread and wine, and many other achievements of the ancient world that depended on an element to which we have not yet paid sufficient attention—the institution of slavery. Slaves are, to a great extent, invisible in the archaeological record because they didn't own anything. Our lack of evidence about slaves is problematic, because according to some ancient sources, slaves outnumbered free citizens in many cities. Indeed, that assertion is quite credible when we consider all the slaves who would have worked in the houses and farms, workshops and factories of a city such as Athens. In this lecture, we'll look at a site in the Laurion hills on the peninsula of Attica. In antiquity, hundreds of mineshafts, operated entirely by slave labor, were sunk down into these hills in the search for veins of silver ore.

Outline

I.   We begin with visual evidence of slaves, of which we have little.

    A. As mentioned in an earlier lecture, Athenians had a mania for showing glimpses of everyday life in crafts and artwork. A famous red figure vessel, for instance, shows us the inside of a bronze worker's shop. The craftsman himself sits by the upright column in which the bronze is being smelted. Peeking out from behind the column is the assistant, reaching down to help the master.

      1. Is the assistant the slave, or is this the master's son or an apprentice? Is the master himself a slave, working as an expert craftsman for a master of his own, who then enriches himself with the products of the skilled slave's labor?

      2. We know of many such men in Athens, generals or demagogues, whose fortunes were based on slaves working in the mines or factories. Demosthenes, the famous orator, made his fortune from the labor of slaves who crafted flutes.

B. Similarly, it's difficult to identify evidence of slaves in buildings because, unlike the situation in the American South, slaves were integrated into the domestic architecture of the Greek and Roman world.

  1. We know that sometimes slaves were penned up in rooms that had no doors. Ladders had to be let down from a hole in the roof so that the slaves could climb out and do their daily work.

  2. Such square cubicles were found in the long rows of rooms at the Roman villa at Torre de Palma in Portugal. It's easy for us to think of these rooms as slave quarters, each with its own hearth, all in a row, close to the barns, stables, and granaries, but we don't know that's the case.

C. The problem of finding evidence of slaves is compounded further by the fact that slaves were involved in all parts of society. Again, unlike the situation in the American South, slaves in the ancient world were not basically unskilled and illiterate. Greek or Roman slaves could be craftspeople, scribes, or tutors and often held positions of great trust.

  1. Sicinnus was a slave who tutored the children of Themistocles, an Athenian general in the Persian Wars. Before the battle of Salamis, Themistocles sent Sicinnus to the Persian camp with a false report that the Greeks were planning to flee in the night. In reality, 300 Greek ships were waiting in the narrow straits between Salamis Island and the mainland. The Persians were lured into the strait, and the resulting battle was one of the most important naval conflicts in history.

  2. What became of Sicinnus? So successful was his mission that he was given his freedom and made a citizen of Thespiae. This is one example of the upward mobility possible in the slave system, which again, makes it difficult to recognize slaves from archaeological remains alone.

D. Analyzing the bones and cremated remains of ancient individuals may someday give us better clues about who the slaves were. Stable isotope analysis of the minerals in bones may even be able to tell us the water sources people drank from as children and, thus, their countries of origin.

1. In this way, we might be able to pick out people born in France, Gauls, who were sold as slaves to Greek and Roman wine merchants in exchange for amphorae full of wine.
   2. Analysis of bones can also tell us something about the burdens that slaves were forced to carry or move. Recall the young girl found at Herculaneum, whose massive muscle attachments showed that she had spent her life shifting heavy loads and running up and down stairs in her master's house.

E. One of the most intriguing visual artifacts of slavery we have comes from the Piraeus in Athens. This is a necklace, a band of metal, inscribed with the name of the master of the woman who wore it. This find is an exception, however, to the general rule that material evidence of slaves is lacking.

II. People often note that ancient slavery didn't have a racial basis, as did our brand of American slavery, but this assertion is not entirely true.

A. Texts by Classical Greek writers tell us that most slaves were despised because they came from Asia. They didn't go to gymnasia when they were young, and thus, they were considered soft. As prisoners of war, they became expendable parts of the Athenian economy, of little worth as people because they were barbarians.
   1. Note that the word *barbarian* meant someone who didn't speak Greek, and to the Greeks, there was only one language—Greek.
   2. The semantic arguments we read in the Greek philosophers come from the idea that the gods created one word to be associated with one thing, and that word embodied the essence of the thing. However, this system worked only in Greek.
   3. The term *barbarian* was a way of dismissing people simply because the language they spoke was not Greek.

B. Certainly the fact that one source of slaves was international trade also speaks to a racial element in slavery.
   1. Town trumpeters were well paid and highly respected, and we have some interesting Greek vases that show African trumpeters. It's quite possible that these people

rose within the ranks of the Greeks in their new city-states.

2. We also know that the policemen of Athens were slaves from Russia. They were Scythian archers, bowmen who had been captured during tribal wars in Scythia, sold to Greek slave traders, brought to Athens, and bought by the state.

3. In the case of the Jewish Wars, thousands of captives led to a vast expansion in the world of Roman slavery. Under Nero, the Romans attempted to dig a canal through the Isthmus of Corinth, using perhaps as many as 8,000 slaves from the Jewish Wars. These slaves had been deported from their own country and taken to Corinth to spend their lives digging.

III. Let's go now to the mineshafts in the Laurion hills.

A. The Athenian people themselves, the *demos*, owned the mining district; individual Athenians would pay upfront for leases on the land and keep the profits from the ore their mines produced. This system for mining would not have been possible without the labor of tens of thousands of slaves—men, women, and children, old and young—serving in chains.

B. The silver mines in the Laurion hills were the basis of Athenian greatness. Ironically, if they had not hit a reef of silver ore here in 483 B.C., the Athenians would never have had the wherewithal to build the warships with which they beat the Persians at Salamis. They would never have established their own liberty, fostered democracy, and gone on to become the rulers of a maritime empire—all of which was made possible by the backbreaking labor carried out by thousands of slaves in the silver mines.

C. Each mineshaft was cut as a square, perhaps with a twist as it descended so that it could be braced with wooden frames. Some of the mineshafts reach down 100 yards into the hills. The slaves would have been lowered by ropes down these shafts into complete darkness, but each slave who would be digging also carried a lamp filled with olive oil that would burn for about 9 hours.

D. From the bottom of the shaft, the slaves would move out through galleries into individual tunnels, each man with his pick, crawling into a tunnel that was probably only about 1 meter high. Each slave would probably chip away only about a hand's span into the mountain each day. We believe that children would crawl along the shafts with baskets or sacks to carry away the crushed rock.

E. These miners were destined to die in the mines. They worked in the dark in incredible heat and were deprived of oxygen. They never knew when the next stroke of a pick might release toxic subterranean natural gas that might kill them.

F. Once the crushed ore was brought to the surface, it would be taken to washing areas, great table-like floors, covered with lime mortar, with channels around their edges through which water flowed. Slaves crushed the ore and carried it to the channels, where water washed over it. The heavy ore settled in basins that punctuated the flow along the channels. The ore would then be smelted, using charcoal, at furnaces tended by slaves.

G. At the other end of the Mediterranean, in the Roman world, were the Rio Tinto mines, which yielded lead and other metals. Centuries after serious mining stopped here, the landscape is still stained and polluted.

    1. About 100 years ago, Spanish archaeologists found enormous wheels of wood in the Rio Tinto mines, similar to small Ferris wheels. These were ultimately reconstructed as part of a water-lifting system to allow the mine to be dug below the water table. Excess water would be caught in buckets suspended around the edges of these wooden wheels and carried up to the surface.

    2. Slaves would have been standing inside these wheels all day, walking hour after hour to keep the system moving.

    3. The importance of these mines for Rome cannot be understated. By the year A.D. 79, production at Rio Tinto had reached such heights that lead pollution from the mines blanketed the Earth's atmosphere, reaching the Greenland icecap thousands of miles to the north.

IV. What can we say about the lives of slaves who somehow escaped the animal-like existence of the miners and worked in households?

A. As we've said, in the ancient model of slavery, people moved, at times, out of slavery. Some people became slaves through owing debts. If the debts were paid, they regained their free status. Others were slaves who became so indispensable to their families and so beloved by them that they would be freed on the death of the master. These slaves would ultimately take their places as citizens with full rights.

B. The public baths at Pompeii show us the range of experience for slaves. Below the floors of the baths, in darkness, tending the fires, were slaves whose daily lives were probably not much better than those of the slaves in the mines. Yet at the same time, slaves were also customers of the baths, enjoying the waters alongside their masters or with friends.

C. We also know that some slaves became the owners of businesses and were eventually able to buy their freedom. Among these was a group of silversmiths who were proud of the fact that they worked their way to prosperity and became fully accepted as free citizens.

D. Again in Pompeii, we have found bundles of documents of household accounts that give us a picture of slavery as much more dynamic than we might otherwise expect. Andrew Wallace-Hadrill of The British School at Rome has found documents of one household that included slaves, freed slaves, and offspring of the master and a slave mother.

V. We'll close with an image to counter the happy thought of an upwardly mobile slave population in cities such as Rome and Pompeii.

A. At Laurion, fortified towers guarded the landscape, and we found a similar tower at the Roman farm of Torre de Palma. A recent study by archaeologists from the University of California at Los Angeles, Sarah Morris and John Papadopoulos, has established that such towers existed on farms all over Greece to be used as places of confinement for slaves and to watch for those who tried to make a break for freedom.

B. This side of the Greek and Roman world fits poorly with our high ideas about their philosophy, political science, and cultural achievements, but it's a side that we should never forget.

Suggested Reading:

Thompson, *The Archaeology of Greek and Roman Slavery.*

Westermann, *The Slave Systems of Greek and Roman Antiquity.*

Questions to Consider:

1. How much of the "Classical achievement" depended on a system of slave labor?

2. If the city-states of the Italian Renaissance managed without slaves, why could not Athens and Rome do the same?

Lecture Thirty-One—Transcript
Slaves—A Silent Majority?

Welcome back. We've been discussing ancient engineering, ancient technology, trade and production of bread and wine and many other achievements of the ancient world that depended on an element to which we have not yet paid sufficient attention. That is the institution of slavery. Ancient trade, ancient industry, ancient production of all kinds, depended, to a greater or lesser extent, on the labor of slaves.

These slaves are, to some extent, invisible in the archaeological record. After all, the ancient world was, as we've seen in our section on everyday life, very much—as Madonna would call it—"a material world." You were what you owned, and every aspect of your life as a free person was something you could go shopping for in order to deck out your pastimes and your daily existence with things, things, and things.

Slaves didn't own anything so we can't see them so easily in the archaeological record, except for the occasional finds of shackles, those iron chains with bands around the legs or the arms of an unfortunate slave. Very recently at Pompeii, a skeleton was found outside one of the city gates of a person shackled at the legs. They probably died in their attempt to escape because they couldn't run. That person was certainly a slave.

But in general, the slaves are difficult for us to find, and this is particularly problematic because according to some of our ancient sources, slaves outnumbered free citizens in cities like Athens. Unless we think that doesn't seem very likely, let's remember that in Athens, there were only 30,000–40,000 free citizens—that is adult males of the citizen families. Yet one sector of slaves, the slaves who worked in the silver mines, were so numerous that in the last years of the Peloponnesian War between Athens and Sparta, where Spartans had invaded the territory of Attica, the historian Thucydides tells us that some 20,000 slaves escaped from the mines. We don't know out of what total.

So when we add all of the slaves from the houses and the farms, the workshops and factories of Athens itself, it's quite credible that there were more slave than free in that city which supposedly stood for freedom and democracy. We must always remember that Athenian democracy was much more like American democracy at the time of the Revolution and through the early 19th century, a democracy of free adult males, in which women had some citizen rights, but did not have the vote and could not hold office, and in which there were masses of people enslaved who were doing the work. To what extent slaves actually are responsible for building the Parthenon, working a Roman *latifundium*, sailing a ship at sea, producing the pottery in Athenian pottery workshops, we just don't know.

We have some visual evidence of slaves. For instance, among the objects that represent for us the mania that Athenians had for showing glimpses of everyday life and work, there are pictures of workshops. We can see, for instance, in a famous red figure vessel that shows us the inside of a bronze worker's workshop. The craftsman himself sitting is by the upright column in which the bronze is being smelted. Peeking out from behind the column is the assistant who is reaching down to assist the master.

Is the assistant the slave, or is this the master's son or an apprentice? Is the master himself a slave, working as an expert craftsman for a master of his own who is then taking the produce, the profits from the labor of this skilled slave, enriching themselves? We know there were many such in Athens, men of big figures, generals or demagogues, leaders of the people, and yet their fortunes were based on strings of slaves in the mines, slaves who made beds in factories, who made armor, who made flutes—that was Demosthenes, the famous orator. So even though we have evidence for what looks like menial work in the artistic record, we can't confidently say that's a slave.

Similarly, when we come to the architecture of buildings, we're not dealing with a situation like the American Southern plantation, where slaves had their own row of cabins or quarters. They're very much segregated from the main house of the master and the landowner.

Slaves were integrated into the domestic architecture of the Greek and Roman world in a way that makes it very hard for us to look at a specific room in a specific house and say this is where the slave lived. We know sometimes slaves were penned up in rooms that had no doors. Ladders had to be let down from a hole in the roof so that the slave could crawl out and do their daily work, and then back in they went.

We found such square cubicles in the long ranges of rooms at the Roman villa at Torre de Palma in Portugal that you've heard about before. It's very easy for us to think these are the slaves' quarters, sometimes each with its own little hearth, all in a row, close to the barns and the stables and the granaries. But we don't really know, and we have to deal with the fact that it was a tradition of that local vernacular architecture to sometimes have raised steps leading up to the doorway so you'd keep out snakes and other vermin and stuff blowing in from outside. Are we looking at a room that had no door, or are we simply looking at room where the surviving wall doesn't come up to the level of what would have been the threshold?

These are the problems that we deal with in trying to say where we're looking at slave dwellings, where we are looking at slaves in images in ancient art, and where we're looking at simply free labor of poor people who have a job.

The problem is compounded for us further by the fact that the slaves are involved in all parts of society. We have an idea again from our American experience that slaves were basically unskilled and illiterate. That's not true in the ancient world. You can't confidently say that a skilled craftsperson can't be a slave, or that a scribe who has done extraordinary work in an accounting office or in writing down histories or poems for scrolls of books, that this couldn't have been a slave.

We know on the contrary, slaves had positions of great trust. Slaves were often the tutors of rich families in both the Greek and the Roman world. There was a famous slave at the time of the Persian wars. He worked for the Athenian general, Themistocles, as the tutor to his children. Themistocles sent this slave, Sicinnus, to the camp of the Persians by night to give them a false report that the Greeks, who were holed up with their 300-or-so ships in the narrow straits between Salamis Island the mainland, were going to flee in the night, thus luring the Persian ships into the strait to try to prevent that. This led to the famous confrontation in the Straits of Salamis that Christos Tsountas tried to find the remains of in the 1880s, and which still stand as one of the most important naval conflicts in all of history.

What became of that slave Sicinnus? So successful was his mission that he was given his freedom and made a citizen of another city. We've had the story in brief of Thermopylae and the Spartans and the Thespians at that pass. They were all killed. Thespiae was founded again. This slave became a citizen of the refounded town of Thespiae after the Persian War.

So as I said in an earlier lecture, slavery can be, for the Greek and the Roman world, a source of new citizens. There are people upwardly mobile through the slave system and this, again, makes it harder to recognize them from the archaeological remains alone.

If we could get at the analysis of all of the bones and cremated remains of all these ancient individuals, then someday I think we would not only have better clues about who was a slave and who wasn't, but be able to tell the country of origin of many of these slaves, by tracing back through the analysis, the stable isotope analysis of the minerals in their bones and figuring out the water source they were drinking from when they were children.

In this way, we might be able to pick out those people born in France, those Gauls, who were sold as slaves to Greek and Roman wine merchants in exchange for amphoras full of wine. We know from inscriptions that there were a number of people who were both wine dealers and slave dealers, down in the Greco-Roman world because that was a normal medium of exchange. That's something that bone analysis could reveal.

As it is, we can tell from analysis of the bones of some of the surviving slaves just what crushing levels of weight, of loads, of burdens, they were forced to carry or to move. You may remember from those bodies underneath the arches near the water's edge at Herculaneum, a girl was found whose massive muscle attachments in her body show that she was not the aristocratic young mother of the jeweled baby that she was holding in her arms. She was a slave. She was probably the nursemaid and had spent her life shifting heavy loads and running up and down stairs in her master's house.

One of the most intriguing artifacts that shows us a slave comes from the Piraeus in Athens where a necklace, a band of metal, was found with an inscription on it saying whose property the woman wearing that band was. She had to wear on her neck—like a dog's collar—an advertisement of her slave state and name her master to anybody who would see her.

But this is very much the exception and it's going to be our effort today to try to look at the archaeological evidence for slavery and try to see through it what the conditions for slaves were. Even if we can't pick out an individual from a vase painting, from a tomb, and say slave versus free, I think through archaeology, the big picture can be clear.

One idea that's sometimes talked of about ancient slavery is that it didn't have a racial basis, like the familiar brand of American slavery. That's true and not true. If we read texts by classical Greek writers, we're aware that most of the slaves are despised because they come from Asia. They are soft Asiatics who didn't go to gymnasia when they were young and kept themselves tough. They're prisoners of war who are now expendable parts of the Athenian economy and are assumed to be of little account as people because they are barbarians.

That word *barbarian*, we should spend just a moment with. It meant someone who didn't speak Greek. Nothing would have struck the Greeks of more weird about our system of liberal education than the idea that you needed to learn foreign languages. To the Greeks, there was only one language. There was the real language—Greek.

All of those semantic arguments in the Greek philosophers come from the idea that there was one word that the Gods created to go with one thing and that the word embodied the essence of the thing. But that only worked in Greek. What was everybody else saying? They were saying "bar, bar, bar, bar." Since "Rs" and "Ls" are interchangeable in linguistic systems, that's our modern "blah, blah, blah, blah," projected backward 2,500 years. That was a way of dismissing all of these people simply because of the language they spoke—non-Greek—therefore, slightly subhuman.

There was a racial element in the way the slaves were regarded certainly in the Greek world. The fact that a source of slaves was that international trade which was sending especially wine, but other manufactured commodities of the classical world north into the hinterlands of central Europe—east into Asia, south into Africa—

part of what was being sucked back was a basically archaeologically invisible trade in human flesh, in slavery.

We can certainly recognize the Africans who are often depicted sometimes in positions of great importance. There are some interesting Greek vases that show African trumpeters. Since town trumpeters were very well paid and highly respected, it's quite possible that these people rose within the ranks of the Greeks in their new city-states to be important people.

The policemen of Athens were slaves. Odd for us to think, but by having them owned by the state, you got around any conflicts of interest or possibility of bribes. Where did they all come from? Russia, the same place the grain ships came from. They were Scythian archers, bowmen who had been captured during those tribal wars up in Scythia, modern Russia, sold to Greek slave traders, and then carried down to Athens and bought by the state. They lived in a special building of their own. We don't quite understand their daily life or whether they could ever get ransomed and sent home. But it was true that there was this ethnic element at times to ancient slavery.

In the case of the Jewish wars, thousands of captives led to a great bubble in the world of Roman slavery. There's an attempt on the part of the Romans to dig a canal through the Isthmus of Corinth, where the ancient engineers around the year 600 B.C. had built a stone trackway with grooves in it about a meter and a half apart, to carry the wheels of a little contraption that would carry cargos or even small ships from sea to sea across the Isthmus.

The Romans, under Nero, decided they were going to actually dig a canal. There is a canal there today that's the result of French and Greek engineers working in the 1880s. But Nero started at the western end of the canal. He himself went there. In something that reminds us of the visual symbolisms of the Union-Pacific Railway project, he took a golden pick, he did the first stroke into the sandy soil himself, loaded it up in a basket—in what was the probably the only honest act of work he did in his whole life—took the basket over and dumped it into what was going to be the spoil heap.

Who was going to do the rest of the work? Thousands—some people say about 8,000—slaves, coughed up by the Jewish wars, who had been deported from their own country, taken by their Roman slave masters and anchored there for life, to dig that canal. They might have spent decades there digging it, except that once Nero died, about three years later, the whole project was given up.

But you can still see if you go to the Corinth canal—and I hope you will—that you can get in a boat that will take you through from the west end, over on your right side, the south side, is a miniature Mount Rushmore memorial to Nero. He's in a little plaque carved into the sandstone on the side of the cutting. They didn't get much further than that in their attempt to get through. I believe they thought the thing was sand, as the Isthmus of Mount Athos that King Xerxes had cut through was mostly sand. I think they had no idea the true dimensions of the job that they were getting into, these miles of stones that they were going to cut through.

So there's an ethnic element fed by wars. One of the reasons to keep your periphery destabilized if you're a Greek or Roman power is that this makes it easier to draw slaves into your system. You do need slaves in order for the system to work well.

We've been taking a specific site at each of these last 12 lectures to exemplify some issue of our meditation on these aspects of antiquity. The site that I would like us to focus on in this lecture, as we try to get a glimpse of what it was like to be a slave in the time of Greco-Roman antiquity—is a site almost within sight of Athens itself. It's the nose of the peninsula of Attica, which projects like a great wedge or like the ram of a ship, down into the sea of the southern tip of that landmass of which Athens was the controlling city.

Down near that nose, down near that cape called Sounion, there's a great temple to Poseidon, whose Doric columns still stand. It's a wonderful place to go out and watch the Sun go down over the Saronic Gulf and look at Lord Byron's signature carved on one of the columns. That was famous not only for that temple and for being the first site of Attica for mariners coming from across the sea; it was famous for its silver mines.

The Laurion hills lie to the north, a little bit to the east of that cape. They fill up the lower part of that peninsula. In antiquity, hundreds (350 mineshafts have so far been discovered and there must be many more) were sunk down into those hills to look for the veins of silver ore. This goes all the way back to the Bronze Age. We know people were coming up from Crete during the Bronze Age to exploit these mines. Phoenicians probably came here during the Dark Ages when the Greeks were at low ebb themselves.

These mines were entirely operated during the classical period by people who owned strings of slaves. There was a minimum requirement of the number of shafts you had to sink in order to keep your lease active because the Athenian people themselves, the *demos*, owned the mining district, and individual Athenians would then take out a lease, keep the profits, but pay up front for the lease on the land. So the state got its cut, but it was fostering free enterprise.

All this was unthinkable without tens of thousands of slaves—men, women, and children, old and young—serving in chains, for the most part, in this corner of Attica from which every tree had been stripped in order to provide the charcoal for the smelting of the ore, a bare and blasted landscape that looks sort of like Tolkien's Mordor descriptions from *Lord of the Rings*.

There's a horrible irony for us, that this was the basis of Athenian greatness, that if they had not hit a reef of silver ore here in the year 483 B.C., they would never had had the wherewithal to build the warships, the triremes with which they beat the Persians at Salamis. They would never have established their own liberty, fostered their own democracy by having their own citizens work in this navy, and then went on to become the rulers of a maritime empire, the profits of which paid for the Parthenon. It was all done on the backbreaking labor carried out by those thousands of slaves in these Athenian silver mines.

Let's go to a shaft. It's cut square. It may twist a little as it goes down so that you could brace wooden frames in it as it goes down because it's going to go down a long way. Some of them go down 100 yards into the hills. The slaves would have been lowered by ropes down through these shafts into complete darkness, but each slave who's going to do the digging is carrying a lamp.

Beautiful studies have been carried out by the Greek and French archaeologists who worked on the Laurion site. They analyzed how much olive oil could fit in one of these lamps. Knowing at what the olive oil would burn, they could estimate that the average length of a shift for the miners working under the ground was about nine hours.

From the bottom of the shaft, they would move out through galleries into individual little tunnels, each man with his pick, crawling like a worm back into a tunnel that's probably one meter or less high. He's following that little vein of glittering ore that goes like forked lightning back into the limestone and marble mass of the hills, chipping along, chipping along, pushing the amount of stone that he's just broken up with his pick behind him, working by the wavering light of that little lamp. He's going back probably a hand's span into the mountain's guts each day, and only visited by, we believe, children who would crawl along the shafts with baskets or sacks, push the crushed rock into the container, carry it back to the shaft, and then had it hoisted to the surface.

The lives of these miners were a death sentence. These slaves were going to die in these mines. It was a hopeless life. They were working in the dark. They were working in incredible heat and oxygen deprivation. They were working in an environment where you never knew when your next stroke of a pick would release a little bit of subterranean natural gas that might be toxic and might kill you.

Anybody who thinks that there was something kinder or gentler about ancient slavery than there was about slavery at other periods of history or other parts of the world, needs to go to Laurion and look at those mines.

Once the crushed ore was brought up to the surface, it would be taken to these washing areas, great table-like floors, covered with lime mortar, with grooves around their edges through which water flowed. Slaves had to bring the water for the flow because water was very scarce there in Laurion. Slaves were crushing the ore. This was something that women and old men could do.

It was then put into those little channels, those grooves. The water washed over it. The heavy ore settled in these little basins that punctuated the flow here and there along the channel. This is sort of like the threshing we talked about, only in reverse, going down and with water, instead of up and in the air. But just as the chaff was carried away by the water in the threshing, so the water around those floors where the channels flowed is carrying away the lighter rocky material and leaving the heavy ore behind. This would then be smelted, using charcoal, which was brought by more slaves at furnaces tended by slaves.

This was big business. The little town of Thorikos, out there in that part of Attica, put in a theater for its bustling, prosperous citizen body, and at sometime in the middle of the 5th or 4th century, they had to expand the theater so it would hold 9,000 people. These are not the slaves going to the theater; these are all of those wealthy Athenians who are living in hell, but nonetheless, reaping a profit from it, and from the work of all of those slaves.

Mining is, of course, synonymous with hard labor. If we go to the other end of the Mediterranean and go to the Roman world, out of the Greek world, we can come to the Rio Tinto mines where lead and other metals were taken out of the earth of a period of hundreds of years. The Rio Tinto, "the colored river," it's still colored, centuries after the serious mining stopped. The staining of the landscape, the fouling of the water, the pollution of the soil, and the killing of a lot of plant life has still rendered this a Moon-like landscape.

Down in the mines, the Roman mines of the Rio Tinto, I think it was at least 100 years ago, Spanish archaeologists found enormous wheels of wood, like small Ferris wheels, that they finally reconstructed as being part of a water-lifting process so that the mine could be dug way down below the water table; but all the excess water could be caught in buckets that were suspended around the edges of these great wooden wheels and carried up and up and up, step by step, until it reached the surface and could be sluiced away.

Who was running these great Ferris wheels? Slaves, standing inside. Just as rats in cages have little wheels to exercise themselves in, hour after hour, day after day until they died, those slaves would be walking, walking, walking on that treadmill. It was a brutal—a nonhuman—existence.

There we have one end of slavery. How important was it? We've already described what it did for Athens. Those mines for Rome were so important that we find the mineral, the metal production, the production of ore, reaching such extraordinary heights that by the year 79 A.D., the year that Vesuvius blew up, the lead pollution from the mines down there at the Rio Tinto, has so blanketed the Earth's atmosphere that it is showing up as a spike of lead in the Greenland icecap thousands of miles to the north. This was big business. This was business on a global scale, way back there in those early centuries of our era and even before.

There we have rock-bottom of slavery. But what about the other end? What about the lives of slaves who somehow escaped this animal-like existence of being a beast of burden or a burrower in the earth? Was it any better? Of course it was. There were slaves in almost every rich household throughout the Greek and the Roman world. We can get a picture at a site like Pompeii of the entire range of shades and grades of experience, and even official nomenclature for slaves along that continuum. This was something that was, more or less, lacking in the American model of slavery.

But in that ancient model, there were people who were moving at all times upward out of slavery. Some people became slaves through owing debts. If the debts were paid, they were bouncing back into their freed status. Others were slaves who became so indispensable to their families and so beloved by them that they would be freed on the death of the master, and maybe take the master's name to remind all the world of exactly who it was who bestowed their freedom upon them. They would then ultimately take their places as members of society, citizens with full citizens' rights, though often described on their tombstones as people who had been once slaved and were now free.

Pompeii shows us in its public baths this incredible array of experience for slaves. We know that down below the floors of the baths, in darkness, tending the fires, stoking the furnaces, keeping the whole system going, were slaves whose daily life was probably not much better than that of the slaves in the mines. Yet we know what the same time that from the graffiti, that up top, in the baths in Pompeii, slaves were customers. Slaves were either coming with their masters and enjoying the services of the bath alongside their masters, or coming with friends on their own, writing a little note on the wall to say what a good time they had. This is not our idea of what a slave would normally be doing and yet, it was part of that whole picture of ancient slavery.

Perhaps the most interesting are those slaves who become the owners of businesses and eventually are able to buy their freedom, become independent in the Roman world, wear the toga of a citizen, and represent themselves that way on their tombstones. Among these are certain silversmiths who are very proud of the fact that though they started as slaves, working in someone else's shop, they eventually graduated to a point of prosperity and self-determination, that they could buy their freedom. They could become participating members of society in a fully accepted way as freed men and freed women.

There in Pompeii, we have found, as we've talked about before, bundles of documents of household accounts. Andrew Wallace-Hadrill of the British School at Rome has analyzed some of these and shown that in these household documents, it's clear to us why we're having trouble saying this room belonged to a slave and this room was the dwelling place of a free person. It's because that simple dividing line didn't exist.

In one household, there were the slaves; there were freed slaves; there were slaves—or were they slaves?—who were the offspring of the master and a slave mother; and there was the family itself, all living together, all tied up in each other's concerns, all trying to work out their legal status and their trajectory into the future. This gives us a picture of slavery that is much more dynamic than anyone had suspected before archaeology got into the business of trying to unearth the remains of ancient slavery.

I'd like to leave you with one image to correct that happy note of all of the upwardly-mobile slaves in cities like Rome and Pompeii. We know that at Laurion, there were towers, fortified towers guarding the landscape. There was such a tower at the Roman farm of Torre de Palma where I worked with the University of Louisville. It was in a modern house that used the same aquifer and farmed the same fields as the ancient Roman villa. My colleague, Stephanie Maloney, measured that modern houses and found it had exactly the same dimensions and ground plan as the Roman villa of 2,000 years earlier that it supplanted.

But it had a big tower. We found a room in the heart of our Roman villa that apparently, with its double-thick walls, supported a tall tower. In fact, Torre de Palma, "tower of the palm," it's there in the name. I always thought the tower was for defense until I talked with one of the oldest surviving workers on the farm who could remember back to the days of virtual serfdom who told me, "No. The tower is where the lookout stood to watch for workers who were trying to run away."

An interesting recent study by archaeologists from the University of California at Los Angeles, Sarah Morris and John Papadopoulos, has been able to establish that such towers existed on farms all over Greece. Ancient farms were fitted out with these towers and they believe that the towers served as places of confinement for the slaves and based on what Elias Peixe told me about the function of the tower at Torre de Palma, I can imagine also a guard, standing atop them, looking out over the countryside, watching for those slaves who were trying to make a break for freedom.

It was a side of the world, of those Greeks and Romans, that fits very poorly with our high ideas about their philosophy and their political science and their cultural achievements. But it's a side of their world we should never, ever forget.

Lecture Thirty-Two
Women of Greece and Rome

Scope:

In the last lecture, we looked at a sector of the ancient population whose voices are almost never heard or read in historical texts. This lecture concentrates on another almost voiceless and unrepresented branch of the ancient population, women. As we know, some women rose to prominence, including the poet Sappho and the great queen of Hellenistic Egypt, Cleopatra. For the most part, however, the voices of women are underrepresented or absent altogether from ancient texts. What evidence can we find in archaeology about women's lives and the extent to which this minimalization of women represents the day-to-day reality in the world of Greece and Rome? To answer this question, we'll visit a fort in Brougham, in the far northwest corner of the Roman Empire, on the west end of Hadrian's Wall.

Outline

I. The fort at Brougham was known to exist, but archaeologists who were assigned to the site in connection with a road-building project in 1966–1967 were surprised by what they found there.

   A. The focus of these British archaeologists was a cemetery at the fort, where they found the remains of cremated bodies and grave goods that would have been added to the funeral pyres as the fires were lit.

   B. From the pottery, the archaeologists knew that they were dealing with a cemetery dating to A.D. 3rd century, the period when Roman emperors were trying to stem the tide of barbarian chaos. Rome went through a crisis in the 3rd century, and distant fortification sites, such as Brougham, were affected. Troops were moved there to guard the border.

   C. The remains from the cemetery were separated in boxes according to whether they were found in a tomb or a deposit of cremated material. The lead excavator died in 1980, and this potentially valuable mass of evidence languished in boxes until the year 2000.

1. In that year, Hilary Cool, an archaeologist working for a company called Barbican Research Associates, applied for funding to do what amounted to a dig in those boxes. She wanted to try to "excavate" the material that had been pulled out of the ground in the 1960s.

2. Cool had a multidisciplinary team that included physical anthropologists (specifically, *osteoarchaeologists*) and pottery experts. The excavated material included beautiful examples of red gloss ware, once called Samian ware; bowls, such as the Roman legions used in their mess kits; glass and silver cups; and jewelry.

3. The people had obviously been buried fully clothed because hobnails from boots were found that had been worn when the corpse was put on the funeral pyre. The positions of the boots in some inhumation graves also suggested the possibility that the boots had been placed as separate offerings on the pyre.

4. A zoologist was brought in to study the animal bones, some of which would have resulted from feasting with the dead. Bones of horses were also found, indicating that a cavalry unit had been stationed there and some soldiers had been cremated with their horses.

5. The bones of women, children, and the elderly were also found. These could be distinguished by such features as the gracile nature of the skull bones. Some distinctions could also be made based on the grave material for each person. For instance, the glass drinking cups seemed to be with the male bones and the buckets were with the women's bones. These finds seemed to bear out the traditional cultural divisions of men and women.

6. Surprisingly, though, bone fragments and grave goods were found from what had obviously been high-ranking cavalry officers, and amazingly, they were young women between 20 and 30 years old.

7. Cool thought, perhaps, that these might be the wives of high-ranking officers who were buried with their husbands' badges of rank. In hundreds of other graves, however, there were no other examples of one person buried with the trappings of someone else of a different social rank, gender, or age.

8. Cool finally announced that she had found young females who had penetrated the world of the Roman legions as cavalry officers among the forces on the frontier.

D. Other clues have also been found that women sometimes played men's roles in violent activities, particularly in England. For example, an inscription has been found that clearly describes two female gladiators named Achilleia and Amazona. In another Roman tomb in England, the trappings of a gladiator were found along with the remains of a woman.

E. The population posted at the fort at Brougham seemed to be from the Danube region, perhaps Sarmatians, a troublesome tribe conquered by the Romans sometime around the end of the 2nd century or the beginning of the 3rd. The Sarmatians were cavalry fighters and would have been required to perform service for Rome. It's possible that they carried a tradition of women fighting on horseback from the Danubian provinces.

II. Typically, such authors as Aristotle and Plato have a very low opinion of women, and we generally assume that they are speaking for the society as a whole. But we don't get the same impression in looking at the material remains of the Greek world.

A. Among the burials found in the heart of Athens under the Agora was one of a woman who died in the 9th century B.C. Her tomb was surrounded by others, most of which had elaborate assemblages of grave goods. The most elaborate of all, however, was this woman's, buried at the time of the Greek Dark Ages.

1. This tomb included large pots, jewelry, and a model of a granary that served as her cosmetic box. The granary had five minaret-like domes as its silos, placing it in the property distinction for the highest class of Athenians, the *pentakosiomedimnoi*, "the people whose farms produced 500 bushels of grain."

2. Thus, we see a woman buried, not only with elaborate, costly things to show the wealth of her background, but with a symbol of land ownership and management.

B. If we look even further back in the Greek world, beyond the Classical period in the Dark Ages and into the Bronze Age, it becomes clear that women played an even larger and freer role.

    1. Frescos at Knossos, for example, show men and women together, equally, in a crowd gathered to watch the spectacle of the bulls.

    2. We might also recall the shrine to the mother goddess found by Harriet Boyd at Gournia, representing what may have been a strong matriarchal element in Minoan society, with an emphasis on goddesses as the supreme beings in the pantheon.

C. The prominence of women in religion endured into the Classical Greek period.

    1. Think of the hall at Eleusis, where the ceremonies of the mother goddess were celebrated. The initiates, men and women, seated side by side and completely undifferentiated, were born again as they experienced the mysteries of the goddess and her daughter.

    2. We frequently see that women carried out the rituals of Athenian religion, often apart from men. In many cases, men didn't even know how to enact these rituals, but the community could not survive unless certain rites were conducted by women.

    3. This prominence in religion climaxed at Delphi, where women spoke for the god Apollo as the most influential voice in the Greek world.

III. We sometimes automatically think that the range of role models available to a group of people in society helps shape their consciousness of their place in the world, and it's hard to imagine a stronger set of positive role models than were given to girls growing up in Athens.

A. Athena, the warrior, was never seen without her helmet, her breastplate with a gorgon's head, her shield, her spear, and a great python-like snake, an emblem of her power. At the Parthenon, she is shown with a woman on her hand, Nike, who comes on wings to bring victory in every competition. Also seen with Athena is Artemis, the twin sister of Apollo, and Hera, the reigning queen of the heavens.

B. If we move to the Roman period, we see even greater possibilities opening for women. The supreme example is Cleopatra herself, ruling from a glorious palace; looking out on the Pharos, the lighthouse that was one of the Seven Wonders of the Ancient World; and reigning over her Egyptian kingdom from Alexandria, a city founded by Alexander the Great.

    1. Cleopatra was part of a great tradition of women as rulers and seemed to have no problem holding her own against Caesar, against male claimants of the Ptolemy dynasty to the throne, and against Mark Antony.

    2. Until the end, she represented the most powerful force in the world outside the circle of Roman generals and leaders trying to snatch up the mantle of Julius Caesar. She was an able administrator and military leader and a woman of tremendous education.

C. Inscriptions on the walls of Pompeii further negate the idea that women were marginalized in the Roman world. One is by Eumachia, a woman who funded a public structure in the town and participated in its dedication ceremonies. We also have Julia Felix's advertisement for her property, which she seems to have rented out in her own name.

D. From these glimpses of women in Greek and Roman antiquity, we get a picture that differs from the image of the repressed, silent woman that comes to us from philosophical and historical texts. Our archaeological evidence accords better with the evidence from drama, where many of the tragedies and comedies feature women as heroines and protagonists. What we have found in archaeology calls for a reevaluation of the role and status of women in the Classical world.

Suggested Reading:

Lewis, *The Athenian Woman: An Iconographic Handbook.*

Pomeroy, *Goddesses, Whores, Wives, and Slaves: Women in Classical Antiquity.*

Questions to Consider:

1. To what extent can any culture's material remains reveal the relationships between the sexes, or the relative status of men and women?

2. Both Greeks and Romans were adept at delivering what we might call "propaganda" messages in art and other images. How might this affect our view of ancient women?

Lecture Thirty-Two—Transcript
Women of Greece and Rome

Welcome back. Last time, we spent half an hour looking at the lives of a great sector of ancient population whose voices are almost never heard or read in the historical texts. We are going to spend this session with another almost voiceless and unrepresented branch of ancient population. Last time it was slaves; this time it's women.

There were some very prominent women who were writers, and the Greeks valued the poetry of Sappho from the island as Lesbos as highly as those of any other lyric poet. We're also going to be spending a little time today going down to Alexandria and Egypt so that we can be close to he archaeological remains of the palace of the Great Queen and the famous leader of Hellenistic Egypt, Cleopatra. But in spite of the fact that some women did rise to positions of tremendous power and authority, for the most part, the voices of women are underrepresented or absent altogether from our ancient texts.

What does archaeology have to do, or have to say, in presenting us with evidence for women's lives and seeing to what extent this minimalization of women that we find in the historical record represents day-to-day reality in the world of Greece and Rome?

To kick off our examination of this important topic, we are going to the far northwest corner of the Roman Empire, to the west end of Hadrian's wall, way up there in northern England, that wall—whose maker, Hadrian, we will be spending an entire lecture with next time—and to a little fort south of the west end of the wall, where a garrison was established in order to guard that perimeter of the Roman Empire.

It's at a place called Brougham, a name derived from the ancient Roman Brovacum, which was the name of the fort. In the 1960s, the British highway department, in its wisdom, decided that they needed to reroute a road. It being 1966–1967—in an era before most of the western European and American countries put in laws about doing archaeological surveys first to see what public road-building projects or other works were going to be disturbed—that road went through so quickly that no archaeological plan could be worked out for a systematic survey and recovery of what lay there at the fort.

Everybody knew the fort was there. From planes flying over, you could see the marks in the soil of the square of the old Roman rampart and ditch, and there was a medieval castle sitting on one corner of it. It was known that there must have been a cemetery, a little town for the soldiers and their families, and then all of the military buildings of the fort. Nonetheless, the archaeologists who were assigned to the project were taken by surprise by the start of road building and earth moving in 1967. They rushed to the site and carried out, just in front of and alongside the bulldozers, a rescue dig that concentrated on the cemetery.

There were the remains of cremated bodies and lots of grave goods that would have been on top of those funeral pyres as the fires were lit and the bodies of the deceased and all those belongings that had been placed on there by their loving families were carried up in flames.

The pottery showed them that they were dealing with a cemetery dating to the 3rd century A.D., in those periods of the 200s when emperors like Septimius Severus were trying to stem the tide of barbarian chaos. Rome went through a crisis in the 3rd century and distant fortification sites like Brougham were affected by that crisis. There were movements of troops. New folks were sent up there to try to guard that border. In fact, Septimius Severus sent his own sons up there, hoping that a stint of military service on the northwest frontier would straighten out those juvenile delinquents (which I'm sorry to say didn't work).

At any rate, here was a cemetery, one of the largest ever found attached to a fort in Britain, of human bones and animals bones, all of the grave goods. They were separated box by box, according to whether they were found in a tomb or in what looked like a more hasty deposit of cremated material, and knowing that it was incomplete because some of the tombs had been destroyed by the bulldozers.

The excavator died in 1980 before there was time to go through all the material. So this potentially incredibly valuable mass of evidence languished in those boxes until the year 2000. In that year, an archaeologist named Hilary Cool, who worked for not a university, not a museum, but a company of archaeological associates called Barbican Research Associates, applied to English Heritage for funding to do what amounted to a dig in those boxes. She wanted to try to excavate the material that had been pulled out of the ground in the 1960s, and see what information could be derived. In some ways, it was probably a good thing that it was going to be looked at in the 21st century because back in the 1960s, many of the analytical techniques for saying the age of death of a person's remains, or what sex, and things to analyze the animal bones and the remains of plants were all lacking.

So Hilary Cool and her team were funded and they began systematically to work their way through those boxes. They had a multidisciplinary team that included physical anthropologists, and pottery experts. There were beautiful examples of that red gloss ware that used to be called Samian ware; bowls, such as the Roman legions often used in their mess kits that had become part of the communities; table service; glass cups; silver cups; jewelry. These people had obviously been buried fully clothed because they were there hobnails from boots that had been worn when the corpse was put on the funeral pyre. There was a very rich mass of material.

There was a zoologist there to study the animal bones. Some of the animal bones seemed to derive from feasting with the dead. A funeral meal would have been placed on the pyre to go up in smoke with the dead person, so you got joints of meat. But something that had never been documented before in England—the bones of horses were there. This had been a cavalry unit and some of the people, some of the soldiers, the cavalrymen, had been buried with their horses and those bones were part of the cremated remains.

There were also the bones of women, children, and old people—apparent non-combatants. They could be distinguished, of course, if there was enough left to the cremated bone, by things like the gracile nature of the skull bones—more gracile, a woman; more robust, a man—clues such as that. There was also some distinction between what was in the assemblages of grave material for each person. For instance, the glass drinking cups all seemed to be with the male bones and the buckets all seemed to be with the women's bones.

So it seemed to bear out, in a very simple and non-problematic way, this traditional idea that men were men, women were women, and culturally speaking, never the twain would cross into each other's territory.

But that was before they examined the bone fragments from a couple of elite graves in which the horse had been cremated. This was obviously a cavalry officer. Among the finds there were parts of sword scabbard fittings that have been burnt on the pyre with the body. Placed in the grave were expensive and unusual vessels such as a wine cup with a drinking motto—the 3rd century equivalent of "cheers." One had been accompanied by a roast set on a platter. These are very important people. And they were women. They were young women between 20 and 30 years old. Nobody was ready for this. The physical anthropologist was absolutely sure that the bone fragments she was looking at had to come from the skeletons of women.

Hilary Cool knew that she was immediately going to be under fire from all of her colleagues saying, "Oh, you're a bunch of women, you're looking at these things, and you're interpreting them from a very feminist point of view." So she asked herself every possible question. Was it possible these were the wives of high-ranking cavalry officers who were buried with their husbands' badges of rank? The husbands, perhaps killed on distant campaign; the wife dying maybe in childbirth during his absence or after the report of his death, buried with the honors that would have been given to him.

But they had hundreds of graves and they had no other example of somebody buried with the attributes, the trappings that should have gone with a person of a different social rank or gender, sex, or age. They didn't have children buried with their parents' objects as a mark of respect.

So finally, she just decided to bite the bullet and publicly let the world know that a couple of members of the Roman forces up there on the frontier, riding those horses, keeping the barbarians at bay, were young women.

Everybody, of course, was very excited or appalled by this announcement. It was not what was expected. The last area where you would have thought you might have had women penetrating the Roman world was the world of the legions and the military. In fact, there were times when the legionaries themselves were expected to maintain a hands-off attitude toward women, not get married until they got out.

But there had been some other clues that women were sometimes playing men's roles in violent activities, and England showed up again and again in these. There had been an inscription found in which a couple of gladiators were clearly women. Somebody figured out that the female form of the word—and one we don't need to worry about now—was gladiatrix. But these gladiators had names, Achilleia and Amazona, which don't sound to me like they're given names at birth by their loving parents, but rather the kind of stage names that female performers would take. Achilleia, named after Achilles, the great hero of the Trojan War; and Amazona named for those legendary horsemen, those women who, according to Greek myth, were minus a breast and therefore "a-mazon," minus a breast, without a breast. So they could be better with their shooting, their archery. Their missing breast would allow their hand to come right back past their body, as man's would, if they shot their bows. Since they weren't very interested in the domestic life or motherhood, this wouldn't be a problem for those Amazons. So here's Amazona as a gladiator.

To everyone's amazement, a few years ago, a tomb was found in England of a Roman burial and in that burial were all of the trappings you would expect if you were gladiator. But the body, the remains of the body, was that of a woman.

So there was a precedent, there were clues already out there that what was found by Hilary Cool and her team at Brougham or amongst those things from Brougham was a possibility. But this was the first time that it had been nailed down in such a spectacular, overt fashion.

They got into a little more work on who was up there at that frontier. Because, of course, to say something is Roman by the 3rd century A.D., you can be talking about people from the Danube, from the Sahara, from the Euphrates, from the Atlantic coast of Iberia. The Romans themselves had become a tiny minority within their own empire.

There was a name of a town, Stratonice, and these people posted there were from Stratonice. Unfortunately, there are too many places of that name dotted around the empire. But there were some other clues that the people were from the east, the Danube provinces, names that are common from Illyria, mentions of places in that province of Dacia that Trajan had conquered.

So they seemed to be from the Danube, and it was known that at the beginning of the 3rd century, or the end of the 2nd century, the Romans had conquered a very troublesome tribe on their borders in that northeast corner of the empire called the Sarmatians. They were cavalry fighters. They were from that same area that the Amazons were supposed to be from. Part of their duty, part of their service as people who had surrendered to Caesar, was that they would do cavalry service for the Romans in whatever part of the empire they might be posted.

So one obvious line of thought would be that those people in those graves way up there by Hadrian's wall in northern England, in fact, were born all the way at the other end of the empire in the Danubian provinces. They would have carried their tradition of women fighting on horseback (if they indeed had such a tradition, which is not absolutely clear) with them when they went up there to England.

As I've said before when we were talking about the isotope analysis on bones that will allow us to say where a person grew up, this is another round of tests that could now be brought to bear on some of these cremated remains. We can see where those people originated, judging by what minerals formed their bones from the water they were drinking when they were children.

But there is a problem here, as Hilary Cool has pointed out. Cremation is not the form of burial in the part of the Roman Empire. Cremation is a typically Roman form of burial. And if there's one thing that people are conservative about, it's the form of burial that they use for their dead.

So we have to confess that many elements of this remarkable discovery are mysteries, but nonetheless, I think it forms a proper place for us to look at this whole question of the role of women in the Greek and Roman world.

Typically, we look at authors like Aristotle and Plato, who have a very low opinion of women, and assume that they are speaking not just for all men in that society, but for that society as a whole. I have to say as an archaeologist, looking at the material remains of the

Greek world and even of classical Athens—where Plato and Aristotle ran philosophical schools—this is not the impression we get.

If we go back to that agora where John Camp showed us around a few sessions ago, you may remember that I had mentioned that it was a new civic center created at the end of the 6th century B.C. on top of what had been cemeteries and private homes in earlier centuries, things that had been swept away.

Among the burials in that cemetery in the heart of Athens was one of a woman who died in the 9th century B.C. She was surrounded by other tombs. All those tombs had, more or less, elaborate assemblages of grave goods. But the most elaborate one of all was hers, at a time when we imagined the Greeks there in the Dark Ages, defended by their aristocratic warrior chiefs and living perhaps in a very uncertain and unstable kind of world, where the warriors truly might be called upon at any moment to defend those little communities. Here in that world, a woman is being given pride of place with the most elaborate burial.

She had big pots; she had jewelry; she had all kinds of elaborate and beautifully decorated things in her tomb. The most amazing thing of all was a little model of a granary. It was, in fact, her cosmetic box. If you lifted the lid off where the silos were, there were places inside where she could have put her different paints and face creams and so on.

But the thing itself, this granary, beautifully painted in geometric designs, had five domes, minaret-like domes that were the silos. There was a property distinction for the highest class of Athenians that was called *pentakosiomedimnoi*, "the people whose farms produced 500 bushels of grain." That's the *penta* and there is the five.

One interpretation of her little cosmetic box with its five domes is she's one of those 500-bushel people and each dome is 100 bushels there in that little granary.

But we see a woman here not only buried with elaborate, costly things to show the wealth of her background, but with a symbol of land ownership, of management, something that you just wouldn't expect to see on a woman's dressing table on the average farm.

If we look even further back in the Greek world, back beyond the classical period in the Dark Ages and into the Bronze Age world, we're in an age where it's very clear to us the women played a larger and freer role than in the classical period. You can see frescos of dances with bulls at the great palace of Knossos. We see the crowd seated there, animatedly talking to each other as they're getting ready to watch the spectacle of those bulls charging around and tossing young men and women in the air as they vault over the backs of the bulls.

Men and women together, equally, are in the crowd. The women are simply shown by their white faces—whether that's makeup or because they stay in out of the sun more than the men—but they're there as complete equals in the crowd. We remember Harriet Boyd finding the shrine of the Mother Goddess there at Gournia, representing what we think may have been a strong matriarchal element in Minoan society, with an emphasis on goddesses as the supreme beings in the Pantheon. Then there were those priestesses with their arms held out, snakes crawling up their arms as emblems of their power over nature.

It was very much a religion centered around women. If we look at classical Greek religion, we can see that that endured. Yes, the women are not typically visible on the streets or in the markets; yes, women do not attend the assembly; women are not in Greek armies. But the religion was very much in the hands of those women.

Think of our hall at Eleusis, where the ceremonies of the great Mother Goddess are celebrated. The initiates come in, they are born again as they go through the mysteries of the great goddess and her daughter. They have revealed to them the mystery of the growing, sprouting grain coming out of the dead seed. That was in the hands of women. As we look around that assembly of up to 3,000 people crowded into that dark cave-like hall, we will see men and women are seated side by side, completely undifferentiated, equally able to come in and be born again in their own right as new men and women who have seen this revelation and are now part of that big band of initiates into the mysteries.

As we look at the rituals of Athenian religion, time and time again, we see that there are women who are carrying out the rituals, often apart from men. Men often don't even know what is going on at these rituals. They only know that the community cannot survive unless the women are able to carry out those rights.

This climaxes at Delphi with that woman sitting on the tripod over the cleft in the crypt of the temple, speaking for the god Apollo. She is the most influential voice in the entire Greek world. It's a voice of the religious side of experience and it's the voice of a woman.

We sometimes automatically think that the range of role models available to a set of people in society help shape their own consciousness of their place in the world. We're very big on the idea that you need to have positive role models. It's hard to imagine a stronger set of positive role models than were given to girls growing up in Athens.

Athena, the warrior, never seen without her helmet and her breastplate with the gorgon's head on it, and her shield and her spear and her great python-like snake that's an emblem of her power. On her hand on the temple at the Parthenon is Nike, another woman, the winged victory who's come down, as she must, in every competition, whether it's athletic or musical or a battle, to bring victory to the winning side. There's another woman with a bow and arrow and a short tunic of a hunter—Artemis, the twin sister of Apollo. There's Hera, a reigning queen up there in heaven.

The Fates, justice, all these are role models for girls; all these show them possibilities of being feminine, being a woman, and yet if you read the literary sources about the lives of women in Athens in the classical period, the 5th and the 4th century, you would never dream that this range of possibilities was in front of those young girls as they grew up, was shaping their consciousness of themselves and of what it meant to be a woman.

If we move to the Roman period, we are really struck, I think, by the opening up of possibilities for women, in a very practical and everyday way. Cleopatra herself, ruling from that glorious palace, looking out on the Pharos, the lighthouse that's one of the wonders of the world, reigning over her Egyptian kingdom from Alexandria, a city founded by Alexander the Great, where other Cleopatras have reigned before her. She's from the last dynasty of pharaohs. They are Macedonian rather than Egyptian. They all speak Greek, except for herself, who speaks Greek and also took the trouble to learn Egyptian, the language of her subjects.

She's part of a great tradition where women ruled. She seems to have no problem in holding her own against Caesar; against male claimants of the Ptolemy dynasty to the stone; against Mark Anthony. She finally stubbed her toe against Octavius, Caesar, and Augustus. That was the end. Anthony dying, she committed suicide with the asp.

But up to that point, she had been the most powerful force outside the little circle of Roman generals and leaders who were trying to snatch up the mantle that had been dropped by Julius Cesar when he was killed. She is the single greatest force. Her navy is extraordinarily well equipped. She knows how to manage it. We saw that one signature of hers, that line that that wrote, "Let it be done," on a papyrus, where her own hand scratched across the sheet of papyrus. She was an administrator; she was a military leader; she was a person of tremendous education, interested in everything; a family woman interested in the upbringing of her children. What a role model she was for all of these girls of the Greek world and the Roman world who had her as part of their lives.

Finally, if we get to the women of Pompeii, I think we can see that whatever idea we had that women are seen and not heard, are really a silent majority in the Roman world, is completely false. I just want to read you a few inscriptions (some of them just painted on walls) that have been unearthed in Pompeii since the digging started there in 1748. Some of these came up very early and have contributed all along through the development of classical archaeology to an awareness that there is more to the condition of women in the classical world than the literary text would have us believe.

There's one about a woman, "Naevoleia Tyche, freedwoman of Lucius" So this is a woman who started life as a slave and is now free and, as we will see, is carrying out some important tasks here, for herself and for "Caius Munatius Faustus, member of the Augustan College and District Magistrate, to whom the city council, with the assent of the people granted an honorific chair on account of his services." So here's this freed woman of Lucius, linking herself to this very important magistrate in a common action. "This monument Naevoleia Tyche made for her own freedmen and freedwomen and for those of Caius Munatius Faustus, during her own lifetime."

There are two households, apparently. A woman now in charge of her own life as a freedwoman; on behalf of freedmen and freedwomen who were her slaves, who she freed, is making a dedication; and also on behalf of this magistrate to whom she seems to be pairing herself almost as an equal. This is an extraordinary thing to find in what would have seemed to be a place where women had no role.

> Eumachia, daughter of Lucius, holder of a public priestly office, in her own name and in that of her son, Marcus Numistrius Fronto, built a portico with a crypt, a covered corridor, to concord and to piety, at her own expense, and she also dedicated it.

She was not only the funder of the thing, but she came publicly to the ceremonies of dedication and officiated there at this religious moment where this portico and this porch were dedicated to the gods of concord and the gods of piety. This would have probably been, then, a public amenity available to anyone to come in to use, to get down in the crypt on cold days, or to be in the shade of the portico on sunny ones.

Finally, we need to go back to our dear old friend, Julia Felix, whose house was excavated way back in the 1750s by Karl Weber, who was so intrigued by this grand property. On the outside of the house, there was painted, for all to see, an advertisement by this extraordinary businesswoman, Julia Felix. "In the property, [the *Praedia*], of Julia Felix, daughter of Spurius, there are for rent a bath, shops, sheds, upper rooms, from the 15th of the month of August next, for five years, running until the 15th of August five years from now."

There are other descriptions about the beauty of this property, that it's got a bath worthy of Venus, that it has an outdoor dining room, that the shops below are attached to apartments above where one can sleep. So she is a canny person. She apparently inherited this house from her father, Spurius. She is not running it through a manager; she is advertising it in her own name.

She's very smart. Remember there was an earthquake in Pompeii, 17 years before the big blast of Vesuvius in 79 that wiped out poor Julia Felix and buried her house. The public baths were not working so canny businesswoman that she is, she knows that if she offers baths for rent to the general public here, that bath-seeking population, bereft of their normal entertainment in the public bath, will provide a great market for her offer.

From these little glimpses of women throughout the Roman world, the Greek world, the inheritance they had from the Bronze Age, we get a picture that, as I said, differs—in some respects radically—from that image of the repressed, silent woman that comes to us from the philosophical texts and comes to us by implication from great histories like Thucydides. In these, there are literally only one or two women among the hundreds of people who appear (and one of whom is just a mysterious woman who hands a man an axe during a little battle in the town called Patea), not even named. You would get the impression women just didn't matter.

Our archaeological evidence accords better with the evidence from drama, where so many of the tragedies in the comedies feature women as heroines and as protagonists.

I'm not trying to say that there was some sort of equality. I am saying that in the realm of religious experience, women certainly played a vital role and may have played a dominant role for both Greeks and Romans. But above all, I would say that the archaeological evidence is sufficiently at variance with what's in our historical texts that it calls for a complete reevaluation of the role and the status of women in the classical world.

Lecture Thirty-Three
Hadrian—Mark of the Individual

Scope:

In the last few lectures, we have looked at Greeks and Romans in the multitudes—women, slaves, people on the streets, engineers—thus, it seems appropriate to devote one session to a single person. There is a great conflict in the way we approach ancient history between those who are oriented toward the study of individuals—rulers, generals, and so on—and those who see the past as a succession of great movements and shifts involving entire populations. To what extent does the individual have an impact? Admittedly, looking at the ancient world through the lens of one person, in this case, a Roman emperor, is loading the dice toward seeing the power of the individual to change history. But when we turn our attention to the Emperor Hadrian, we see someone who truly did change the world of the Romans and Classical antiquity in a way that would have been difficult to predict before his time. The site where we will begin this lecture on Hadrian is Troy.

Outline

I.   You may recall that the Romans linked their own existence to the refugees from Troy, specifically the Trojan prince Aeneas who fled across the Mediterranean and established a town in Italy that led to the rise of Rome.

    A. When the Romans took what is today Turkey into their empire, Troy was one of the cities they targeted for the establishment of a new civic center, calling the city there Ilium.

    B. Recently, the Roman levels at Troy have been dug by archaeologists from the University of Cincinnati, led by Brian Rose. In 1993, this team was working in the odeon and discovered that it had been refurbished by and dedicated to the Emperor Hadrian; they also found a larger-than-life statue, in marble, of the emperor.

        1. The statue is wearing a very simple *cuirass*, bronze body armor, with just one decoration on the chest. He looks like a true field commander, and Hadrian was, indeed, one of the soldier-emperors.

2. The statue shows Hadrian with the smooth-shaven face and bowl-style haircut of a proper male Roman, but this image of a soldier is somewhat deceptive. Hadrian, in spite of being a successful general, was the emperor responsible for setting limits to the Roman Empire and stopping the relentless process of expansion.

3. Even the statue's beardless cheeks send a cultural message. Hadrian was the first emperor to wear a beard, which was not a neutral matter of choice in Roman culture. In wearing a beard, he presented himself as a Greek and revealed two conflicting strands of imperial thought: The love of things Greek and the desire to champion Greek culture stood in opposition to his position as the leader of the warrior culture that had conquered the world, as well as his own desire to set defensible limits to the empire.

4. These desires sum up some of the conflicts in the character of Hadrian himself, who is certainly the most complex and difficult to understand of all the Roman emperors.

C. In this lecture, we'll try to understand Hadrian through his works, tangible artifacts that have been left behind from his reign which archaeologists have discovered across the Mediterranean world and up to the northern frontiers of England. These artifacts range from a single coin to an entire defensive wall running for many miles across the land.

II. Hadrian was born in Italica, in the south of Spain, in A.D. 76. When his father died, Trajan took charge of the boy, and because Trajan was childless himself, Hadrian became his heir and married Trajan's great niece.

A. By A.D. 117, when Trajan died, Hadrian had campaigned across the empire and had come to know it on a personal level from having fought on its frontiers. As emperor, he and his wife, Sabina, traveled around the provinces, visiting some of the thousands of cities, establishing new towns, and erecting or refurbishing buildings.

B. Up to his time, the provinces were regarded as captives, an array of nations and regions that the Romans had conquered and that were now tied by conquest to Rome. In contrast, Hadrian saw the provinces as a family of peoples linked to Rome by ties of community, common purpose, religion, and culture.

C. Hadrian struck coins and created images that would send this message to the Roman people. He erected fabulous buildings throughout the empire and funded public works projects. He had his artists create iconic statues of the provinces, personified as women and linked to Rome, the ultimate mother figure, in this great family of peoples.

D. Among Hadrian's most popular moves was the reduction of taxes. In fact, we get a glimpse of his largess to cities throughout the empire in the matter of taxes from a rare discovery. In Aphrodisias, the city of Aphrodite in Turkey, letters from Hadrian to the town have been found inscribed into stone for all the citizens to read. One letter in particular releases Aphrodisias from paying a tax on iron.

III. Hadrian was aware of problems all along the northern frontier—the frontier where the German tribes had massacred the Roman legions in the Teutoburg Forest in A.D. 9.

A. The emperor toured the northern frontier and created a massive defensive line, stretching from Eastern Europe to the Rhine, with walls, fences, cleared zones, forts, and camps.

B. He then crossed over to England and toured that province. One of his methods for gaining inside information was to remove his insignia of rank, wrap himself in an old cloak, and sit with the soldiers at night to hear what the rank-and-file were talking about.

    1. We have one report written on a wooden tablet from Vindolanda that sums up the kind of information Hadrian might have gathered in this way: The soldiers complained that the Britons, whom they called Brittunculi, "wretched little Britons," didn't stand still to fight and were able to throw their javelins from running horses.

2. In response, Hadrian decreed that a wall should be built from sea to sea across the northern narrow neck of Britain. The wall would have watchtowers along it, gates, and forts. This immense fortification was, on the one hand, a proclamation of Roman power and wealth, but on the other hand, an admission of partial defeat.

3. Hadrian had given up on the dream of Alexander the Great and early emperors that Rome would continue to expand until it truly ruled the world.

4. The line drawn across Britain that we know as Hadrian's Wall—that line of fortifications all through central Europe that gave the army a feeling of security—represented a turning point in Rome's history and in Rome's idea of itself.

C. In this situation, it was all the more important to emphasize the positive—Rome's previous triumphs and the happy family of provinces. For this reason, Hadrian erected triumphal arches, completed a gigantic temple to Zeus begun by the Peisistratids, and funded other projects.

D. The province of Judea gave Hadrian great trouble during his reign. Jews there rebelled against pressure to embrace Roman culture, particularly pagan gods. Hadrian ultimately went to Judea himself to repress the revolt and built a triumphal arch in Jerusalem, proclaiming his victory over the Jews. His exile of the Jews from their own country resulted in the diaspora of the Jewish people.

IV. Hadrian was also responsible for extraordinary projects in Rome. In fact, whenever he traveled, he was accompanied by engineers and architects to carry out his wishes for a new aqueduct, arena, or some other feature for a remote city.

A. Hadrian erected a temple of Venus and Rome and a great bridge across the Tiber River, leading to a gigantic cylindrical building that would ultimately serve as his tomb.

B. He decided also to rebuild a structure that had been built by one of his predecessors, Augustus, a *pantheon*, that is, a temple for all the gods.

1. Hadrian's name is not on the Pantheon; instead, he preserved the inscription from the original building erected by Augustus, which attributes the construction of

this great temple to Marcus Agrippa. This inscription deceived people for centuries about the true date of the Pantheon.

2. Archaeologists finally determined the real date by studying the structure of this engineering marvel. The Pantheon is a circular building with a great dome, a masterpiece of Roman concrete engineering. It sits, as archaeologists discovered, on a vast donut of brick and concrete sunk into the ground. The cylinder rises to the base of the dome; then the dome soars out—a perfect hemisphere.

3. From the top of the dome, which has a 30-foot-wide *oculus*, or "open eye," to the floor in the center of the circle below is exactly 142 feet. Half of that is the hemisphere that is the dome itself. The other half would be a perfect invisible hemisphere with the south pole, as it were, on the floor and the north pole being up in the oculus. The structure is a perfect mathematical solid, a cylinder and half a sphere.

4. Within the building, we can see one final testament to Hadrian's genius. The lower parts of the cylinder and the dome use heavy stone for the aggregate in the concrete of which they are made. As the dome rises over the floor, the Roman engineers switched to pumice for the aggregate. Thus, the structure actually gets lighter as it rises and was, therefore, more capable of holding itself up, which it has done for 2,000 years.

V. We see much of the public side of Hadrian, but what do we know about the private man?

A. We know that Hadrian loved hunting because he loved to show himself at the hunt. Circular reliefs often show Hadrian with one foot planted on a lion. One of his horses was named Borysthenes, and when the horse died, Hadrian had a monument erected for it that included a poem reminiscing about his wonderful equine companion.

B. At some point on his journeys, Hadrian met a young man from a Greek community called Bithynia, near the southwest end of the Black Sea. This young man's name was Antinoös, and he became part of Hadrian's court as he traveled around the empire.

1. Antinoös was one of the most handsome young men of the age. He died when he was about 20, but during the few years that he was with Hadrian, we know he was also a companion of the hunt.

2. A recent archaeological study uncovered a jar in Egypt containing a papyrus that records an epic poem describing a lion hunt that Hadrian and Antinoös went on together.

3. We don't know if Hadrian's relationship with Antinoös was another example of the emperor's expressing his love of all things Greek, or if Antinoös took the place of a son for Hadrian. We do know how strongly Hadrian felt about Antinoös because when the boy died on a state visit to Egypt, Hadrian made him a god.

4. A city was built on the banks of the Nile, Antinoopolis, in memory of the young man. His worship was taken up with enthusiasm by people throughout the Roman Empire who were looking for a religious savior figure.

5. At Delphi, French archaeologists discovered a marble statue of Antinoös, dedicated by the people of Delphi to Hadrian as a mark of honor, because this emperor had done so much for Delphi, as he had done for Athens and other Greek cities.

C. When Hadrian became old and ill, he retired to a villa called Tiburtina (Tivoli) that he had created outside Rome. Here, acre after acre was filled with a sort of theme park of buildings in imitation of different places around the empire: Erechtheion, the porch with the maidens as caryatids, holding up the roof; the Acropolis at Athens; or the Canopus, inspired by the Nile River and his visits to Egypt.

D. Hadrian died on the Bay of Naples, leaving behind a poem about his life that is as enigmatic as everything else we know about him. In the poem, he calls himself, "*animula, vagula, blandula,*" "little spirit, little wanderer, little charmer." For the emperor of the world to view his own soul as a drifting wanderer leaves us with a final question mark.

1. If we look at the work of the man, spread across the Roman Empire, we can see that he tried to remake that

empire, set limits to it, and glorify its Hellenic elements—both in his public and private lives.

2. Just as the emperor's great wall was both an emblem of glory and an admission of defeat, so were his attempts to Hellenize the empire, to hold back time and change. We see a record of failure with Hadrian, an inability to keep at bay the shadows that would soon fall over the Roman Empire, even in the midst of incredible glory.

Suggested Reading:

Birley, *Hadrian: The Restless Emperor.*

MacDonald and Pinto, *Hadrian's Villa and Its Legacy.*

Questions to Consider:

1. According to one Roman biographer, Hadrian died "hated by all." Does his record suggest the reason?

2. Would the material record of our modern world suggest the presence of any individual Hadrians since the time of the Renaissance?

Lecture Thirty-Three—Transcript
Hadrian—Mark of the Individual

Welcome back. We have been looking at Greeks and Romans in their multitudes—women, slaves, people on the streets, engineers—so it seems fair to have one session devoted to just one person. There's a great conflict in the way we approach ancient history between those who are oriented toward the study of individuals—rulers, generals, lovers, dramatic conflicts between people—and those who would prefer to see the past as a succession of great movements and shifts involving entire populations.

I think this is really well summed up in Tolstoy's *War & Peace* when he gets after those who want to have the cult of the individual dominate their view of human history when he says that Napoleon, for all his grandeur and power, was no more really in charge of the invasion of Russia by French troops than a child who imagines he is driving his father's carriage just because he's holding onto the strap.

There's one of our essential problems in history. To what extent does the individual have an impact? I was lucky enough to be an undergraduate at a time when the great anthropologist Margaret Mead was still lecturing. She came to our university. I can remember sitting in the auditorium and hearing her tell all of us students, "Never doubt the power of the individual to change history because it is the only thing that ever has."

There is Tolstoy turned on his head with a vengeance—and from an anthropologist too, someone who was accustomed to looking at humans from the cultural point of view of large populations and their behavior rather than the historical view of person by person.

Admittedly, looking at the ancient world through the lens of one person, and choosing a Roman emperor to do that, is loading the dice towards seeing the power of the individual to change history. But I feel that we are looking, when we gaze on that emperor Hadrian, at someone who, thanks to certain unique parts of their past, elements of their character, truly did change the world of the Romans and the classical antiquity in a way that would have been hard to predict until Hadrian himself came along.

We've been starting each of our lectures in this last third of the course with a specific site or find, so let's go to Troy to meet Hadrian. Troy has faded from our consciousness over the last few lectures. You remember it was the site where Heinrich Schliemann took all the credit for rediscovering the actual tell, the actual mound that enclosed King Priam's Troy, the site of the *Iliad*. You may remember we discussed how the Romans came to put a great value on that hill of Troy because they linked their own existence to the refugees from Troy, specifically that Trojan prince Aeneas who fled across the Mediterranean and ultimately established a town in Italy that led to the rise of Rome.

The Romans did not forget this. When they took what is today modern Turkey into their empire, Troy was one of the cities they targeted for the establishment of new civic places. So a little city was created on top of that tell at Troy, adding yet another layer to the layer cake of cities entombed in that artificial hill, and the Romans called it Ilium, which was there version of Homer's Ilion, which gives us the name *Iliad* for the epic.

Recently, the Roman levels at Troy have been dug by the University of Cincinnati, the same great American archaeologically-minded university that was responsible for some of the digging at Nestor's palace at Pylos. The chief archaeologist has been Brian Rose. In 1993, they were in the part of Roman Troy, Ilium, that included the odeon, the little covered theater or music hall which had its steps perfectly preserved. One of the great memories of my life is being privileged to actually stand in that theater on that stage and give a lecture at one point.

As they dug down through it, they came to an extraordinary thing. Just a reminder that in 1993, after more than a century of digging at Troy, it was still possible to make monumental finds. It turned out that that odeon had been perhaps paid for, certainly refurbished, at any rate, dedicated by, or to, this emperor Hadrian, who is of great interest to us today because they found a larger-than-life statue, in marble, of Hadrian.

He's wearing his *cuirass*, his bronze body armor, but very simple. If you look at the body armor worn by Augustus in that famous Prima Porta statue, it's covered with symbols and emblems of Rome's history and greatness. Hadrian looks like a real field commander.

He's just got one little divine head right here on the chest, and then the straps that held it on, and you can see a bit of his toga coming out underneath. It's like he might actually be ready to go out and command an army. He was one of the soldier emperors. He campaigned as a young man, with his predecessor Trajan, in Parthia (modern Persia), in Germany, all along the northern frontier.

So he's showing himself as a soldier and he's showing himself as a proper Roman. He's got the nice haircut, as if somebody just stuck a bowl over his head and trimmed around the edges. He's got this smooth, shaved cheeks and chin of a proper Roman adult male. Here he is, presiding over all the shows and entertainment that would have been given on that stage in this new Romanized city, sitting on top of the hill at Troy.

But this is a very deceptive image. Hadrian, in spite of being a great soldier and a very successful general, is the emperor responsible for setting limits to the Roman Empire and stopping the relentless process of Roman expansion. He's the one who said, "Enough."

As for the beardless cheeks, it might be hard to imagine that these are sending a cultural message. But when you find coins of Hadrian from the time of his reign, he's always bearded—the first emperor to wear a beard. This was not a neutral matter of choice in Roman culture. He was presenting himself not as a Roman, but as a Greek. These two strands of his imperial life—the love of things Greek, the desire to champion Greek culture and the Roman world; and also this conflict between Rome, the mistress of legions, the great warrior culture that had conquered a world, and the desire to set limits to that empire that could be defended—these sum up some of the conflicts within the character of Hadrian himself, certainly the most conflicted, the most complex and difficult to understand of all the Roman emperors.

So what I'd like to do today is try to understand him through his works, through the tangible artifacts that have been left behind from his reign, which archaeologists have discovered all over the Mediterranean world, way up to the northern frontiers of England. These artifacts range from a single coin, whose design tells us something important about Hadrian, to an entire defensive wall running for many miles across a neck of land, and cutting off the

Romans and their civilized world to the south, and the barbarians to the north on the outside.

This is our work for the day then, is an attempt to use archaeological materials to illumine the life and the character of this most enigmatic of emperors.

Hadrian was not born in Rome. He was born in a city called Italica, in the south of Spain, Hispania, a city which lies very near Seville, and is well worth a visit. It's sort of a Spanish Pompeii. If you go there and see all those beautiful mosaics and remains of fantastic buildings, you're looking at a city that was not only the birthplace Hadrian, but of his predecessor Trajan also. These are Spanish emperors from good Roman families who emigrated to Hispania and who set down roots there. When Hadrian's own father died, Trajan took over the charge of this boy and brought him up. Ultimately, since Trajan was childless himself, Hadrian became his heir and he married Trajan's great niece, thus cementing his ties to his benefactor, Trajan.

He was born in 76 A.D. By 117 A.D., now a mature adult, he has campaigned all over the empire and traveled around and seen provinces in a way that even those earlier peripatetic emperors rarely did. So he knew the empire better than most. He knew it on a personal level from having fought at its frontiers and traveled through its different provinces.

Trajan died in 117 A.D. and Hadrian was recognized as emperor. Never was there an emperor before who spent so little time in Rome. He himself, often in company with Sabina, his wife, traveled around the provinces, going to some of the thousands of cities that existed within the Roman Empire, trying to create new buildings, establish new towns, and refurbish old ones. His own hometown of Italica was immensely enriched with new buildings because he wanted it to shine as a true gem of Roman urban life way out there in the west.

He began to strike coins and to create images that would send certain messages to the Roman people. Up to the time of Hadrian, the provinces were definitely regarded as captives, a whole array of nations and regions of the earth that the Romans had conquered and captured and which were now held by ties of conquest to Rome. Hadrian wanted to change that. He wanted the provinces to be seen as a family, a family of peoples linked to Rome by ties of family feeling, love, common purpose, worship of the same gods, partaking of the same culture.

He built all sorts of fabulous buildings all over the empire for the people of these provinces. He was a very lavish giver to the provinces. Many of the public works in the provinces go back to Hadrian. He put up arenas, even though he doesn't seem to have liked gladiatorial combats much himself, but he knew the people liked them.

He created, or had his artists create, these iconic statues of the provinces, personified as women who are linked to Roma, the ultimate mother figure, in this grand family of peoples. So there's a shifting from an imperial and oppressive image of conqueror and captives, to a family feeling of those united in one grand bond of amity and concord.

Among his most popular moves was the elimination of a lot of taxes. He, as I said, used coins for propaganda. There's one coin whose design has Hadrian with his Greek beard on one side; on the other side, people bringing in buckets of tax documents and burning them. We get a little glimpse of his largess to cities and to people throughout the empire in this matter of taxes from a rare archaeological discovery. This site, we've briefly mentioned before when we talked about the tombs of some of the charioteers that were adorned with long strings of their trophies, their little wreaths of victory.

This was Aphrodisias, the city of Aphrodite in Turkey in the Maeander River valley. Recently, in Aphrodisias, there have been studies made of these inscriptions in which the town—delighted to have received several letters from Hadrian himself—had them inscribed on stone for everyone to read. One of them has to do with the remission of the tax on iron. It begins this way:

> The emperor Hadrian [and then a whole lot of titles, which I will omit], Greeks, the magistrates, the council and the people of Aphrodisias, your freedom, your autonomy, and your other privileges given to you by the senate of Rome and the emperors who have preceded me, I confirmed earlier. [Notice he is certainly emphasizing here a sort of honorable

relationship between Rome and this city, almost as if they were equals, rather than a thing that has been acquired by Rome through conquest.]

But having been petitioned by an embassy from you, about the use of iron and the tax on nails [imagine the ruler of the world having it take in during the course of his day Aphrodisias' requests to consider the tax on nails], although the matter is controversial, since this is not the first time that the tax collectors have undertaken to collect it from you too, nevertheless, knowing that the city is, in other respects worthy of honor, I release it from payment of the tax. I have written to Claudius Agrippinus, my procurator, to instruct the contractor for the tax on iron in Asia to keep away from your city.

Just a little aside here about the instructions to the tax collector. You may remember from gospel readings that tax collectors like Matthew were loathed and despised by everyone. They were hated people. This was because of the way that ancient Greeks and Romans collected taxes. We pay our taxes in arrears, after the year is over. It's calculated how much we owe, and we pay it to the government. Greeks and Romans had privatized taxation. There was an auction. Rich people came down and bid for the right to collect the tax on nails, the tax on cargos entering a harbor, the tax on prostitutes and brothels—whatever the tax might be. They all came up, one after the other, for auction. You bid up to a point where you thought you could still make a profit when you're collecting.

After you bid, you then have to pay the state the tax—you, the rich person. So the state collects its tax for the coming year immediately and you then have 12 months to use any means, fair or foul, at your disposal to wring out of those people who bought the nails or those prostitutes or those ship owners more than you paid to the government. Apparently no tax collector ever went hungry so they were very good at extorting more than they had paid to the state for the tax.

Hadrian is trying to address this. He's trying to relieve some of the cities from these onerous burdens of taxation.

Hadrian was aware that all along the northern frontier—that frontier that caused the conflict with the German tribes that led to the massacre in the Teutoburger Forest, as it's called, in the year 9 A.D.—there were many troops stationed, trying to keep the German tribes out of the empire. He was aware that this was a problem area. We know, in fact, this is the frontier that gave way first as barbarian tribes in the 4th century entered the Roman Empire.

He did a tour of that frontier. The result was that he created a massive defensive line, stretching all the way from Eastern Europe to the Rhine, with walls, fences, cleared zones, forts and camps up and down that line. Then crossing over into England, he toured that province too. The Romans had never succeeded in conquering Scotland in the far north of England. They'd had some campaigns up there, generals like Agricola. They won some battles, but they couldn't win the war and so they'd retreated.

There were forts up there and one of those forts we've already visited, Vindolanda, that fort where all those people wrote all those letters and documents on those little tablets of wood. These were miraculously preserved in the wet soil of the fort, down to our own time, the ones where the legionary commanders' wives are sending birthday greetings to each other.

There was a little report that has come down to our own time in one of those documents written on the wooden tablet. This report tells us the kind of thing that Hadrian heard when he went to assess Britain, by doing something that Shakespeare shows Henry V doing before the battle of Agincourt. Hadrian would take off all of his insignia of rank, bundle himself up in an old cloak, and go around to the soldiers' watch fires at night, just to see what the rank-and-file were complaining about.

In this little document, you can see that they're complaining about the way that Britons fight. They call them Brittunculi, which means "wretched little Britons," a word we only know from these recently recovered letters. They are very difficult for the legionnaires to deal with because they don't stand still and they can shoot their javelins from a running horse. So it's very hard to control these people. Morale was very low on that northern frontier.

What did Hadrian do? He decreed a wall, a wall to be built from sea to sea, across the northern narrow neck of Britain, a wall that would have great watchtowers along it, gates, and lines of forts. This was an immense fortification that was, on the one hand, a proclamation of Roman power and wealth, that they could create this thing; but on the other hand, an admission of something like defeat, an admission that it is not going to be Rome's destiny to rule the world. This had been around as an idea since the stories were told about Alexander the Great, the young man who set out to conquer the world and died weeping because in an infinity of worlds, he still hadn't managed to conquer even one.

Hadrian gave up on that dream. That dream seemed to have motivated most of the early emperors and the generals of the republic before them, people like Julius Caesar, that Rome would just keep on expanding until it truly ruled that world.

That line drawn across Britain that we know as Hadrian's Wall—that line of fortifications all through central Europe that gave the army a feeling of security—is a real turning point in Rome's history and in Rome's idea of itself.

It was all the more important, then, to emphasize the positive, all of their previous triumphs, all the happy family of the provinces. So we find triumphal arches put up. He didn't have any triumphs of his own to celebrate as emperor in that way. But he created a triumphal arch in Athens, a city he dearly love, where there's a Great Arch of Hadrian, proclaiming that on one side is the ancient city of Theseus, that the Athenians had been living in since the Bronze Age (it doesn't actually say the Bronze Age on the arch). On the other side, it says this is the city of Hadrian, the new city, the city paid for with Roman gold (also not on the arch), but an expansion of Athens, an investment of imperial money in Athens so this university town could shine again.

He finished one of those projects that the tyrants way back in the 6th century B.C., the Peisistratids family, had left unfinished: a gigantic temple to Zeus. It was to Hadrian's credit that that temple was finally completed. In all these ways, he is trying to bolster up his image as someone who is a strong and victorious sort of person.

One province gave great trouble during his reign. Part of the effect of his Hellenization was a great impatience for the many cults that were engaging the faith of people throughout the Roman Empire, including Christianity and Judaism. He wanted all these people to get in line, get with the program, be more Roman, be more Greek. This was putting pressure on Jews, after they had already been beaten once by his predecessors, Vespasian and Titus, in the great Jewish revolt. But the Jews of Hadrian's own time rebelled again.

To this disloyal province, he was ruthlessly harsh in sending generals—and then going himself—to repress that revolt. So there's a great Hadrianic triumphal arch not only in the Athens, but in Judea as well, in Jerusalem, proclaiming his victory over these Jews. It showed his determination to recreate Jerusalem as a Roman city and, dating from that time, the true Diaspora of the Jewish people. Because Hadrian decided that the only way these people could be controlled was to break them as a people and send then out as exiles from their own country, thus creating one of those wounds in human history that never seemed to heal. It's from Hadrian and his desire to have everyone embrace one culture—a culture with a Greek face on it—that that Diaspora of the Jews originates. Because, of course, the Greek gods, the Roman gods that are at the core of Hellenic and Roman civilization, were exactly the point at which the Jews had to draw the line and refuse to worship in a healthy Roman/Greek kind of way all of those pagan deities.

Hadrian, in addition to this grand public life, out through the provinces, did some extraordinary things in Rome. In fact, whenever he traveled, he had engineers and architects with him so he could instantly proclaim that a new aqueduct should be made or an arena put up or a new feature of a remote city. But in Rome itself, he made some of the truly extraordinary monuments. A Temple of Venus, in Rome, was put up. A great bridge was put up across the Tiber River, leading to a gigantic cylindrical building that was ultimately going to be his tomb, Hadrian's tomb, on the far side of the Tiber from the little City of the Seven Hills.

He decided also to rebuild a structure that had been put up by his predecessor, Augustus, a pantheon, a temple for all the gods (that's what the word means). If you go to Rome today, you don't see Hadrian's name on this temple. He was famous for not signing his works. Given the average instinct of Roman aristocrats in the republic and of Roman emperors during the Imperium—who put their names on everything—this really marks Hadrian out. He didn't have any desire to take credit for his works.

In the case of the Pantheon, he preserved the inscription that stood over the porch from the original building that Augustus had put up, that attributes the construction of this great temple to Marcus Agrippa, who had been three times consul. He made this. That inscription deceived people for centuries as to the date of the Pantheon. It was believed to date to the early empire in the time of Augustus, when its true date is really more than a century later.

How was it finally figured out? This engineering marvel was studied by archaeologists. It's a circular building behind that old rectangular porch. It's got a great dome, the greatest in the ancient world. It's a masterpiece of Roman concrete engineering. It's sitting, as archaeologists discovered, on a vast donut of brick and concrete that's been sunk into the ground. The cylinder rises to the base of the dome and then the dome soars out—a perfect hemisphere.

If you go from the top of the dome, which has a 30-foot-wide oculus, or "open eye" at the top to let in the sunshine, if you drop from there down to the floor in the center of the circle below, you've gone exactly 142 feet. Half of that is the hemisphere that is the dome itself. The other half would be a perfect invisible hemisphere with the south pole, as it were, right on the floor; the north pole up in the oculus. It's exactly planned, a perfect mathematical solid, cylinder and half a sphere.

By the way, it was the brick stamps that showed it was made during his reign. The contractor for the bricks had put a stamp of Hadrianic date onto all the bricks in the building so when they found those, the archaeologist knew this is not Augustus' pantheon.

Within the building, we can see Hadrian's genius, one final marvel. The dome is concrete. The lower parts of the cylinder and the lower parts of the dome have very heavy stone for the aggregate in the concrete travertine and so on. As it gets out over the floor with that soaring final reach of seemingly miraculous suspended concrete, archaeologists have bored into the fabric of concrete. They switched over to pumice for the aggregate. The pumice is so light, it will float.

So this very light volcanic rock was taking the place of the heavy aggregate lower down. So the structure actually gets lighter as it rises and was therefore more capable of holding itself up, which it has done for 2,000 years.

The Pantheon was a great work; his own tomb was a great work; the bridge; the temple to Venus in Rome. All this is the public side of Hadrian.

What about the private man? We know he loved hunting because he loved to show himself at the hunt. These little circular reliefs that show Hadrian often show him with a foot on a lion as if he were a modern hunter on the Serengeti Plain, surrounded by his friends. He loved to go out hunting on horseback. He had a horse called Borysthenes. When Borysthenes died, he had a monument erected for Borysthenes, with a little poem of his own, written on the monument as he missed this wonderful companion of his hunting days and of his military campaigns.

At some point on his journeys, he met a young man from the Greek world from a Greek community, a place called Bithynia, up near the southwest end of the Black Sea. This young man's name was Antinoös. He became part of Hadrian's court, part of his suite, as he traveled around the empire.

Antinoös was one of the most handsome young men of the age; we've got a lot of statues of him. He died when he was about 20, but during the few years that he was with Hadrian, we know he was the companion of the hunt. We see him on some of those circular reliefs, one of which is on a triumphal arch in Rome.

A recent archaeological discovery is a jar in Egypt with papyrus in the jar and the papyrus records an epic poem describing the lion hunt that Hadrian the emperor and his young favorite, Antinoös, went on together, in a sort of epic Achilles and Patroclus kind of way; Alexander and Hephaistion.

This young man stayed with him for a few years, traveled around the eastern Mediterranean with him, was in company with him and with Sabina, Hadrian's wife. Is this just another example of Hadrian, who was now in his 50s, expressing his Greekness? Zeus, after all, did have his Ganymede, his handsome young man, to be the cupbearer of the gods. The homosexual relationship between an adult male and an attractive teenager was part of Greek tradition. Is Hadrian just expressing that? Was he lonely because he didn't have a son, and this boy was taking the place of the son?

We don't have much from Hadrian himself, although Marguerite Yourcenar's novel, *Memoirs of Hadrian*, would make you think he left reams of diaries. She, in fact, had to piece together all sorts of information to come up with that autobiographical novel.

We don't really know what was in his mind; but we do know how strongly he felt about Antinoös. Because Antinoös died in the Nile River during one of the state visits to Egypt and Hadrian's reaction was extraordinary. There is now a city that archaeologists have been able to excavate, on the banks of the Nile called Antinoopolis that was built in memory of Antinoös.

Antinoös was made a god. We find him in Egypt with the headdress of the pharaohs. We find him throughout the empire. In fact, if you do a count of Antinoös statues throughout the empire, there are double the number that there are for Hadrian himself. He was taken up by enthusiasm with people who, in that 2nd century of the modern era, throughout the Roman Empire, were looking for new religious figures—savior kind of figures.

At Delphi itself, we had the French archaeologists discovering a marble, a beautiful statue of Antinoös, dedicated by the people of Delphi to Hadrian as a mark of honor because this emperor had done so much for Delphi as he had done for Athens and all these other Greek sites, in pouring so much wealth into their city.

When Hadrian became old and sick, he retired to a fabulous villa that he'd created outside Rome, a place called Tiburtina, which we call Tivoli. Here, acre after acre was filled with a theme park of buildings that were in imitation of the Erechtheion, the ports with the maidens as caryatids, holding up the roof; from the Acropolis at Athens; or Canopus, a thing inspired by the Nile River and his visits to Egypt. So in this vast park and palace, he recreated beautiful things from all over the empire.

He didn't die there. He died down on the Bay of Naples, looking out over the blue waters. He left behind, at the very end of his life, a little poem about his life that is as enigmatic as everything else. It begins:

> *Animula, vagula, blandula,* [little spirit, little wanderer, little charmer] you who are the guest and the companion of the body, you are now going away to a place that is pale and harsh and cold. And when you are there, you won't make those little jokes that you're accustomed to.

From the emperor of the world, who seemed to have achieved everything and worked on an epic scale throughout his life, to view his own soul as a little drifting wanderer, down to the underworld, whose greatest concern is that it won't be possible to make little jokes there anymore, this is a final question mark over his nature, over his reign, over his personality, that has continued to cause scholars and people who try to understand Hadrian to scratch their heads through the centuries.

But if we look at the work of the man, spread all over the Roman Empire, we can see the work of a man who tried to remake that empire, who tried to set limits to it, who tried to glorify one particular element of it—the Greek element, the Hellenic element—both in his own person and his own private life, and ramming it down other throats of members of the empire throughout its expanse.

Ultimately, there's a sadness about Hadrian because, just as the great wall is both an emblem of glory and an admission of defeat, so with his attempts to Hellenize the empire, so with all of his other attempts to hold back time and change. We can see a record of failure with Hadrian, an inability to keep at bay the shadows that are soon going to fall over the Roman Empire, even in the midst of all of that incredible glory.

Lecture Thirty-Four
Crucible of New Faiths

Scope:

One of the themes we touched on in our last lecture was religion, specifically new religions emerging in the Roman world. Hadrian, the emperor we looked at last time, was himself the target of devotions by cities and launched a new religion by establishing the cult of his dead favorite, the young man Antinoös. This was in line with the essentially polytheistic basis of Greco-Roman civilization; people worshiped many gods and had no difficulty accepting new ones. Throughout the ancient world, there was a blending of gods from different cultures. But in A.D. 1st and 2nd centuries—the time when the emperors, starting with Augustus, were trying to distract the attention of the population with shows and entertainments—a contrary force was operating in the empire. This force took the form of a craving for religious experience over the "virtual reality" of the sports world. Although their everyday lives may have become more comfortable, the people were politically oppressed under Roman rule, and many desired something more, perhaps something like the mysteries of Eleusis, a feeling of direct contact with divinity. To look at the archaeological record of that desire, represented by the creation of new cults, we'll go to the eastern extremities of the Roman world, to a site called Dura-Europos.

Outline

I.   In the spring of 1920, a troop from India, part of a multinational peacekeeping force assembled after World War I, discovered a fresco at a bivouac on the Euphrates River. The spot was itself a natural-seeming fortification, a high place with earth and mounds around it that looked like ramparts.

    A. This fresco showed auxiliary troops of the Roman Empire—almost 2,000 years before—lined up behind their Roman commanders. These were men who had obviously served from this area of Syria under Roman command to secure this spot on the Euphrates for Roman control.

    B. Off to the west was Palmyra, a caravan city whose queen, Zenobia, was troublesome to the Romans. Palmyra was part of a caravan route into the heart of Asia, which brought precious metals, gems, spices, silk, and other treasures out of Asia and into the Roman world. This newly discovered spot would seem to have been part of the network of caravan cities on the eastern fringe of the Roman Empire, but no one had known of a Roman presence at this point on the Euphrates.

C. Later that year, James Breasted, a young American archaeologist, working at the Oriental Institute at the University of Chicago, was invited to come to the site to do some digging. His initial exploration touched off years of excavation and quickly uncovered an inscription showing a goddess of the town whose name was Tyche, the "good fortune" of Dura.

D. This discovery led the archaeologists to a name for this site: Dura-Europos. Europos had been the Greek name when it was founded in about 300 B.C. by the successors of Alexander the Great, and Dura was the name that the Romans had given to it, meaning "fortress." The site is still being worked today, because it offers evidence about Roman military life on the frontier and an unmatched array of religious centers for different faiths.

II. The Romans took over Dura in about the year A.D. 160, holding it for just under a century before it was recaptured by the Parthians, the ancestors of the modern Persians and Iranians.

A. The military aspects of the site were spectacular. Thanks to the siegeworks and the walls of the town, such artifacts as the frescos that were found in some of the religious centers were sealed in and preserved under the fallen ramparts.

B. Archaeologists found graffiti, dated to the year that we would call A.D. 238, that read, "The Parthians have fallen upon us." Obviously, there had been an attack from the east; evidence of an assault by a Parthian army was also found outside the Roman garrison.

C. Towers were found in the fortification wall, under which the Parthians had dug a tunnel, a mine, held up with a wooden framework. Their plan, apparently, was to set fire to the wood, which would collapse the mine and bring down the tower. The Romans must have gotten wind of this plan, because they dug a countermine, but the Parthians also destroyed that. An underground battle took place, leaving the bodies of Roman soldiers still inside the countermine, to be discovered by archaeologists 1,800 years later.

III. In the heart of Dura-Europos was a Greek agora, just like the one in Athens, a central civic and religious space. There were temples to the Classical gods of the Greco-Roman pantheon, along with a Jewish synagogue and one of the oldest places of Christian worship ever identified.

    A. The people of Palmyra had come to Dura and created a temple to their gods, such as Bel or Baal, who were part of the ancient Near Eastern tradition. There was also a temple to the god Mithras, from the Persian tradition. The cult of Mithras was particularly popular with the legionnaires. Mithras represents the kind of cult that could have become dominant in the centuries to come but didn't.

        1. In the cult of Mithras, men would go down below ground level into an artificial cave, set up as a rectangular chapel, with rows of seats. In rituals of initiation that involved slitting a bull's throat and spilling the blood on the initiate, they paid tribute to their god.

        2. Mithras was a young man, wearing a stocking cap that was a mark of Phrygians and Asiatics. In some representations, he kneels with one knee on the back of a bull, an emblem of brute nature; Mithras pulls the bull's head back and cuts its throat.

        3. Through the act of killing the bull, Mithras represented the triumph of light and good over darkness and evil. This image of a divine hero, fighting on behalf of humanity and overcoming the powers of darkness, was an appealing one. It came into Christianity in the guise of the *Manichaean heresy*, the idea that the world was a battlefield between forces of light and darkness. God would triumph, but it was a battle that hung in the balance and involved heroism in the winning.

4. In spite of its popularity, Mithraism finally fell out of favor, perhaps because the religion was limited to adult males, particularly soldiers.

B. Just up the street from the temple of Mithras was a Christian center. The Christians had just been expelled from synagogues across the empire by Jews, who no longer saw any compatibility between the Jewish traditions and the new Christian ones.

1. Christianity became an underground religion, its adherents, mostly women and slaves, meeting in secret. This religion would grow in a way that neither Mithraism nor Judaism could.

2. At Dura, the Christian shrine was a house converted to religious use. The Christians did some remodeling of the interior structure, and on the walls, they added scenes from the Old Testament and from the life of Christ and his ministry.

C. We must always be careful, from an archaeological standpoint, in judging a faith by its symbols, but it's possible to make certain assertions about early Christianity from the kind of place that enshrined its worship. Archaeologists are interested in the places of worship, the artifacts used in ceremonies, the symbols, the paintings and statues, and finally, any traces of rituals that were performed.

1. Just the fact that they worshiped in a house tells us something about early Christians. There is a sense of informality and family; women and slaves were part of the natural picture because the worship took place in a family dwelling.

2. There was no sign in this church of hierarchies with powerful church figures on top and a subservient congregation accepting their words and their rulings below. All were equal.

3. In this early Christian period, although not specifically represented at Dura, we know that worship had a feature called the *agape*, the "love feast." This tradition descended from family meals of the ancient pagan world, in which people imagined that they were feasting with their dead loved ones.

4. The symbols of the early church—fish, anchors, ships, lighthouses—emphasize the feeling of life as a voyage. All these watery images, of course, also call up the idea of God separating the waters from the rest of the Earth, as well as the baptism in water, which is important symbolically in Christianity.

5. The fish fits in with the watery images and, in itself, is a secret anagram. The letters of *fish*, *ichthys* in Greek, are the opening letters of the Greek phrase "Jesus Christ, God's son, the savior." Just by showing a fish, early Christians could evade the attention of the Roman authorities but proclaim themselves to others who were also part of that secret cult.

IV. As we know, Christianity experienced an extraordinary flowering at the turn of the 3rd century.

A. Toward the end of the 3rd century and the beginning of the 4th, the Roman Empire was under attack and besieged from within by dissension among its leaders. One of the leaders who was trying to establish himself at that time was Constantine.

B. Camped at the Milvian Bridge and knowing that he would soon face the armies of another contender, Constantine told his army that he had had a dream, in which he had seen the symbols of Christianity—his mother's religion—on their banners and shields. He had heard in his mind a voice saying, "*In hoc signo vinces*," "In this sign, you will conquer." The soldiers put on the Christian symbols, went into battle the next day, and were victorious; Constantine became emperor.

C. Ultimately, Constantine would have an impact as great as that of Hadrian on the fabric of the Roman Empire. He created a new capital in the east in the ancient Greek city of Byzantium, which he called Constantinopolis, "Constantine's city." In so doing, he divided the empire in two and ensured that the eastern side, with its Greek center, would survive long after the western side, now divorced from the exclusive attention of the emperors.

D. Constantine had also embraced Christianity—not Mithraism, not the religion of Isis, not any of the other possible cults—

but Christianity. His sons, including Constantius II, who was a fervent Christian, began the process in which the pagan temples would be closed.

E. The whole empire recognized the arrival of Christianity as the state cult. The religion that had been condemned, the religion that had been persecuted, now was brought into the light of day, honored, and fused with imperial authority.

    1. An extraordinary archaeological find from the Palatine Hill shows us how despised Christianity had been. In a guard's house there, dating from sometime in A.D. 1st or 2nd century, is a graffito showing the image of a cross. Crucified on the cross is a being with the body of a man and the head of an ass. A man is off to one side with his hands raised in the position of adoration. Underneath, a cynical Roman soldier has written, "Alexis worships his god."

    2. It's amazing that this religion, which had been outlawed and scorned for centuries, was now brought into the limelight as the official religion of emperors.

F. With its new status, Christianity needed a new home. There had always been a tradition in the Greek and Roman world that temples lay at the heart of communities, that the state religion was an essential part of experience. Thus, Christianity would have to move out of small houses for worship, and the family feeling would be lost.

    1. The new building form chosen, the basilica, traditionally used for large buildings that could accommodate crowds of people, left its mark on the nature of the religion itself.

    2. Within the space of the basilica, hierarchies were naturally created, with a sense of power and judgment that was miles away from Dura-Europos and the warm family feeling embodied by Christianity when it was still a small cult struggling for recognition on the frontiers of the Roman Empire.

Suggested Reading:

Mancinelli, *The Catacombs of Rome and the Origins of Christianity.*

Ulansey, *The Origins of the Mithraic Mysteries: Cosmology and Salvation in the Ancient World.*

Questions to Consider:

1. To what extent can the physical trappings of a religion truly convey its beliefs?

2. Did the Greco-Roman culture in which Christianity developed play a greater role in shaping the new religion than its Judaic roots?

Lecture Thirty-Four—Transcript
Crucible of New Faiths

Welcome back. One of the themes that emerged in our last session together, as we looked at the evidence for the reign of the emperor Hadrian—the most archaeologically visible of all Roman emperors—was that of religion, specifically new religions emerging in the Roman world.

Hadrian himself, as emperor, was target for the devotions of cities and people involved in the imperial cult and the Roman emperors. He finished that great temple of Zeus at Athens. He refurbished the shrine of the Delphic Oracle in central Greece. He built a new temple to Venus and to Rome, in the city of Rome itself. All these grand things were part of mainstream religion. At the same time, by establishing the cult of his dead favorite, the young man, Antinoös, who drowned in the Nile long before his time, he helped to launch a new religion into the Roman world.

The Greco-Roman basis of civilization was essentially polytheistic— many gods and no great difficulty about accepting new ones. It's very amusing to read about the evangelizing religious crusader, Paul, coming to Athens as he's spreading the word of Christianity, and finding it so impossible to make any headway with the Athenians because they put up no resistance. They just were quite ready to accept one new god and add that deity to their pantheon.

So by launching the religion of Antinoös, Hadrian was doing something that was very much not just of his time, but of the whole fabric of Greco-Roman civilization. Dig in most of the great cosmopolitan centers of the Greek world or the Roman world, and you will find alternative cults. At the Piraeus, the harbor city of classical Athens, space was set aside so that the Phoenician traders could worship their own Phoenician gods and goddesses, right there in classical Athenian territory. Over in Rome, up on the Palatine Hill, Cybele the Mother of Gods from Asia Minor, with her exotic cult involving eunuchs and ecstatic dancers, she had a little temple right there.

There was always a blending, a merging. If we go to Pompeii, we will find Isis, the Egyptian goddess, the consort of Osiris, with little shrines and water features dotted all through the city, sacred to her.

But in the 1st century and 2nd century A.D., the time of the Roman Empire—at the time that the emperors, starting with Augustus, are trying to more or less distract the attention of these vast populations with shows and entertainments—there was a contrary force operating within the empire. These were people who did not want to go to the shows, who did not want that thing I've called the "virtual reality" of the sports world, to be the first thing in their minds.

They were people who valued the sort of religious experience that we saw when we visited, during our talk about bread and wheat. That was the shrine of Eleusis, sacred to the Mother Goddess and the young maiden Kore, and to the grain, the sacred grain, that by dying and springing up again from the ground, gave life to humanity.

That was a mystery religion. It took place in a dark spot. It gave you a sense of personal contact with the gods, which we have to always remember was not the main feature of classical Greek and Roman religion, where the god's image is living inside a small chamber with colonnades all around it, in that thing we call a temple. There was a priest or a priestess to be the intermediary between you, who bring the sacrifice up to that open-air altar, and the god inside.

Eleusis was a real unusual thing in that Greco-Roman world and it was that kind of experience that more and more people came to crave, a feeling of direct contact with divinity, about doing something for their own soul, about looking behind this life and into the next one. There was a surge of desire on the part of so many people. These people were now politically oppressed under Roman rule, however beautiful their lives may be, however easy their existence now that the Romans have run aqueducts to their cities and provided public fountains and good roads to the next town and security from marauding bands of robbers. All those things had happened and yet the people of the empire want something more.

To look at the record, the archaeological record of that desire, taking the form of creating new cults, I'd like us to go today to the very eastern extremities of the Roman world. The Greeks got all the way to the Hindu Kush and to the Indus River—thanks to Alexander the Great—and planted cities all along the way. But for the Romans, the remoter areas of the Near East were areas that they never succeeded in adding to their empire.

It was a great surprise in the spring of 1920, a part of the multinational peacekeeping force, featuring British armies and French armies, was trying to cut up the southern portions of the old Ottoman Empire after World War I was over. They wanted to create that array of states, which are still, in many cases, on the map of the Near East and Middle East today. They caused a group of troops from India, under a British command, to go up the Euphrates River and bivouac for the night at a spot where there was already a natural-seeming fortification, a high place with earth and mounds around it that looked like ramparts.

They continually had to deal with the Arab Freedom Fighters, who were not keen, having finally gotten rid of Ottoman rule, to simply introduce the rule of European powers over their affairs. They wanted to be free. So groups like these troops of Indians (from India) were continually at risk out there in the countryside, so they were looking for strong places to entrench themselves.

As they dug down into the soil of that massive rampart-like place, one of the soldiers hit a fresco, an ancient wall painting. They cleared it away and what did it show? It showed auxiliary troops of the Roman Empire—almost 2,000 year before—lined up behind their Roman commanders, people who had obviously served from this area of Syria under Roman command to secure this spot on the Euphrates for Roman control.

Way off to the west was Palmyra, a famous caravan city whose queen, Zenobia, gave the Romans all sorts of trouble. Palmyra was part of a caravan route into the heart of Asia, which brought precious metals, precious gems, spices, silk, and other treasures out of Asia and into the Roman world. This newly-discovered spot would seem to have been part of that network, of which the famous city Petra down in Jordan is also part, the caravan cities on the eastern fringe of the Roman Empire. But nobody had known that there was a Roman presence at this spot on the Euphrates.

Word was carried out that these soldiers had found something remarkable. A young American archaeologist, working at the Oriental Institute at the University of Chicago, a man named James Breasted, was invited to come later that year, 1920, and do some digging, some exploration. That touched off years of excavation at this site. Pretty soon, an inscription showed up showing a goddess of the town whose name was Tyche "the good fortune of" Dura.

Once this was discovered the archaeologists knew what name to put on this mound. It was Dura-Europos. Europos had been the Greek name when it was founded in about 300 B.C. by the successors of Alexander the Great, who were establishing Greek cities all over the area of Asia that Alexander had conquered during his lifetime. And Dura was the name that the Romans had given to it, meaning fortress.

They knew it was Dura-Europos. As the years went by, such celebrities as Michael Rostovtzeff of Yale University—the man who introduced the idea of economic history to the study of the Roman Empire—he became involved in the dig. It's still being worked on today because the site is so extraordinary and so rich for its blending of different cultures, and for representing both incredible evidence about Roman military life on the frontier and an unmatched array of religious centers for different faiths.

The Romans took over Dura in about the year 160 A.D., so we're a bit after the death of Hadrian, who we spent our time with last time. They only held Dura for just under a century before it was recaptured by those folks off to the east who are beginning to work away at Roman control in Asia: the Parthians, who lie behind the modern Persians and Iranians.

The military side was, in itself, spectacular. Thanks to the siegeworks and the walls of the town, certain things like the frescos that were found in some of the religious centers were sealed in under the fallen ramparts. So they were preserved the same way that, archaeologically speaking, way up there in the site of the Teutoburg battle, near the River Rhine in Germany, the fall of a rampart had sealed in a beautiful silver cavalry mask and the bones of a donkey and so on. In the terms of creating archaeological sites, military activity can be very favorable for the preservation of parts of a site.

What they found was graffiti, dated to the year that we would call 238 A.D., saying "The Parthians have fallen upon us." So obviously there was an attack from the east. Then the archaeologists found the evidence of a great assault by a Parthian army outside, targeting the

Roman garrison inside, all those legionnaires and all those Syrian auxiliaries.

They found there were great towers in the wall and they found that the Parthians had dug in under the towers with a great tunnel, a mine, which they had held up with a wooden framework and their plan was then to set fire to the wood. As it burned into the mine, the wood would burn out, the mine would collapse, and the tower should fall. This was the plan.

The Romans got wind of what they were doing, apparently, because they dug a countermine. But the Parthians saw to it that the Romans in that countermine were destroyed. There was an underground battle, and when the archaeologists opened up the countermine, the bodies of the Roman soldiers were still inside, 1,800 years later.

Ultimately, the Parthians succeeded in burning their wooden structure inside their mine, but the wall simply dropped without falling over. Nonetheless, they did create a big siege ramp. Ultimately that wall, which was mainly mud brick, did topple over, falling into the town and burying a Jewish synagogue and one of the oldest places of Christian worship ever identified.

Let's go right into the middle of the town and look at it as it grows. In the heart of it is a Greek agora, just like the one in Athens, a central civic and religious space. There are temples to the classical gods of the Greco-Roman pantheon—Artemis, Zeus. Then we get the Roman additions, with some Roman gods added; and a pretorium that is a place for the soldiers; and these new places of worship for some of the cults that are bubbling up from below in the Roman world in our 1st and 2nd century.

So the people of Palmyra, which is that caravan city off to the west, they've come here. They're at what's called the Palmyra Gate. And they've created a temple to their gods, gods like Bel, which were part of the ancient Near Eastern tradition. We've already mentioned the Jewish synagogue, this Christian house church which we'll come back to in a moment.

There was also a temple to the god Mithras. Mithras somehow comes out of the Persian tradition. He seems to have gotten staying power as a religious figure in the Roman Empire, somewhere in Asia

Minor, perhaps in the city of Tarsus. From there, he and his cult spread like wildfire throughout the empire. This is a particularly popular cult with legionnaires, soldiers in the Roman army.

Mithras shows us the kind of cult that was out there that, as things held in the balance, could have become the dominant cult of centuries to come—but didn't. In the cult of Mithras, these men (because it was very much a man's cult and particular a soldier's cult) would go down below ground level into an artificial cave, set up as a rectangular chapel, with rows of seats along the side.

In rituals of initiation that involved the slitting of a bull's throat and the spilling of the blood all over the initiate, and in other rituals that we can only guess at, they paid tribute to their god. Their god was a young man named Mithras, wearing that little stocking cap that is a mark of Phrygians and Asiatics. He is kneeling with one knee on the back of a bull, pulling the bull's head back, and then cutting the bull's throat. We can always remember how the bull was an emblem of brute nature, all the way back to those frescos that Arthur Evans found in the palace of Knossos.

We know very specifically that Mithras, through that act of killing the bull, was representing the triumph of light and good over darkness and evil. Even though this was something that the original Christians kept insisting was not part of their religion—after all, if their god was all-powerful, there was never a time when he was threatened by darkness.

Nonetheless, the appeal of this image, of the divine person as hero, fighting on behalf of humanity and overcoming these powers of darkness, was a very appealing one. It came into Christianity in the guise of what was called by the early Christians the Manichaean heresy. This was the idea that the world was a battlefield between forces of light—God—forces of darkness—the devil, if you will— and that God would triumph; but it was a battle that hung in the balance and involved heroism in the winning. This seems to have come straight out of the Mithraic tradition.

What happened to Mithraism? It finally went under, in spite of the fact that we find hundreds of these Mithraeans all over the empire. In Rome, there are Mithraeans. Up in Britain, there are Mithraeans that are specially associated with the legionary camps. But I think the people who designed the Mithraic religion made a fundamental mistake. They limited their demographic: adult males and especially soldiers. That's a very powerful group of people, but a small one.

Just up the street, we have our little Christian center. They've just been expelled from the synagogues all over the empire by Jews. The Jews felt there was no longer any compatibility between their Jewish way of life, seeking a traditional path, and these new Christians, who wanted to interpret things differently. So Christians had moved out. Christians are an underground religion. They've been persecuted. The famous example was in 64 A.D. when, after the great fire in Rome, Nero blamed the Christians specifically and began the persecutions and the throwing of the Christians to lions and other wild beasts in the amphitheaters of the empire. Different pogroms, different persecutions had occurred again and again throughout the following years.

So Christianity was an underground religion, meeting in secret, sharing as a secret its cult, and involving women and slaves—huge portions of women, 50 percent; slaves, perhaps, outnumbering free. Here is a religion that is going to grow in a way that Mithraism cannot and in a way that Judaism really cannot. Christianity has the seeds of its success already sewn there in its earliest years, in spite of the martyrs—and perhaps in some way, because of the martyrs, they were being created by those imperial persecutions.

At Dura, the Christian shrine was a house. In fact, it was built as a house and just converted to Christian use. The Jewish synagogue is elaborately adorned with wonderful wall paintings that show scenes from the Bible of Noah, Moses, the exile, the Exodus, Solomon establishing the temple, Ezekiel and his visions—all these scenes around the walls.

So the Christians, in their little house, transformed it from an ordinary dwelling into a place of Christian worship. This was done not so much by reorganizing its interior, although they did knock out one wall so they had a big house for worship. Remember, they are a communal, corporate kind of worship now. It's important to get everybody together as you did in that hall at Eleusis to get a critical mass of believers in one place.

They did that, and they added to the main room of the house a little baptismal font so that baptisms could take place there, but otherwise, it still looked like a house in ground plan. On the walls, they added Adam and Eve and other scenes from the Jewish tradition, the Old Testament, as they were coming to call it, and then scenes from the life of Christ and his ministry. These include scenes of healing the paralytic; talking to the woman at the well; conversing with Peter; and finally, a vision of paradise. All of these images are around the walls to remind people of the content of their religion.

Judging a faith from its symbols is a very tricky thing archaeologically. I used to assign my undergraduates the task of going to a place of worship somewhere in Louisville and trying to reconstruct the belief system based on what they could see. It's a reminder of how careful we have to be in assuming that the obvious explanation is the true one.

The most memorable one for me was the student who came back from a visit to a Roman Catholic church and said, "It's obviously a place of mother worship, where Mother Goddess presides there. The largest figure was a blue old lady with a white veil who outranked and certainly outstood any of the male figures. The male figures were sacrificial victims nailed to crosses or babes in arms. There must have been a big animal cult element to it because there were fish, doves, lambs, and lions."

You could justify all of these conclusions from what that student saw; but it's certainly not an accurate reflection of what the average Roman Catholic, polled about their faith, would say is the content of belief or the ranking of those figures in importance. In fact, the most important element—God—is usually just not represented at all.

So we have to be careful in looking at these images from these early Christian sites. But I think you can say certain things about early Christianity from the kind of place that enshrined the worship, the act of cult. Archaeologists, after all, when we try to reconstruct an ancient religion, we're not so much worried about details of theology or belief. For us, the content that we're looking at is the places of worship; the artifacts that were used in the ceremonies; the symbols; the paintings; the statues; the artwork which was used to carry a religious message; and finally, any traces of the rituals that were performed.

Just the fact that they are worshipping in a house tells us something about those early Christians. There is a sense of informality; there is a sense of family; there is a setting in which women and slaves are part of the natural picture because it is a family dwelling. There was no sign in this little church—one of the earliest ever found—in Dura of great hierarchies and separations with powerful church figures in one place and a subservient congregation accepting their words and their rulings, segregated off in another place. All were together.

In that early Christian period, not specifically represented at Dura, we know there was a feature called the *agape*, the "love feast," which had descended from the family meals of the ancient pagan world in which you imagine that you were feasting with your dead loved ones—a renewal of the grief, but also the family feeling that you felt at a cemetery after the burial. So special tables were created, which all, in a sort of feeling of equality, were drawn up for their meal together at this *agape*.

The symbols of the early church—fish, anchors, ships, lighthouses— emphasize the feeling of life as a voyage, life as a quest, life as a movement. All of those watery images, of course, are calling up the idea of God separating the waters from the rest of the Earth (in the book of Genesis), and also the baptism in water, which is so important symbolically in Christianity since it's part of the gospel story about Jesus himself with John in the River Jordan.

The fish, not only going along with all of those other watery metaphors of ship and anchor and lighthouse, also, in itself, is a little secret anagram. The letters of fish, *ichthys* in Greek—Iota, Chi, Theta, Upsilon, and Sigma—are the opening letters of the Greek phrase "Jesus Christ, God's son, the savoir." Just by showing a fish, you could evade the attention of the Roman authorities, but proclaim yourself to anyone who was also part of that secret cult—a Christian.

Later on, we will see these things that we find at Dura, changed. When Christianity was small, underground, or enclosed within this world of houses, with their central little courtyard and their array of humble rooms opening off of it, that setting has to have had its own effect on the attitude that people had toward their religion and their faith.

But an extraordinary thing happened to Christianity. Toward the end of the 3rd century, the beginning of the 4th century, the Roman Empire was under attack and it was besieged from within by dissension among its leaders. One of the leaders who was trying to establish himself at that time of the turn from the 3rd century or the 4th century, the 200s to 300s, was a great leader named Constantine.

When he was camped at a place called the Milvian Bridge, knowing that he would face the next day the armies of another contender to the position of emperor, he told his army he had had a dream, that he had seen in this dream the symbols of Christianity—his mother's religion, not his—on their banners and on their shields. We don't know whether this was the cross or whether it was a Chi-Ro symbol (the "Chi" and the "Ro" being the first two letters of the Greek word Christos, "the anointed one"). But at any rate, he somehow heard in his mind a voice saying, *in hoc signo vinces*, "in this sign, you will conquer." So the soldiers dutifully put the Christian sign—whatever it was or whichever it was—on their shields, their banners, went into battle the next day, were victorious, and Constantine became emperor.

Ultimately, he was to have effects as great as those of Hadrian on the fabric of the Roman Empire. He created a new capital off in the east where there was an ancient Greek city called Byzantium, guarding the Bosphorus, that little narrow neck of water that led water from the Black Sea down into the Sea of Marmara, through the Hellespont, and then out into the Aegean and the Mediterranean.

There at Byzantium, he created what he modestly called Constantinopolis, "Constantine's city," which has been worn down first to Constantinople and then Istanbul. Thus, he divided the empire in two and ultimately—as we will, of course, see—ensured that the eastern side, with its Greek center, would survive long after the western side, which was now divorced from the exclusive attention of the emperors and its glorious radiant position as the seat of the emperors, that it would ultimately pass into the shadows.

But he had embraced Christianity—not Mithraism, not the religion of Isis, not any of those other possible cults, but Christianity. We have to imagine that his mother, who was a very strong-willed person, had something to do with this acceptance by her son of what had been, for centuries now, a prescribed and forbidden cult.

So Constantine and—although he didn't convert himself until he was near his deathbed—his sons, including his son Constantius II, who was a fervent Christian—saw to it that the empire was set on a path where the pagan temples would ultimately be closed (as happened in the year 391 under Theodosius. It was under Constantius II that that basilica-shaped church that we visited at Torre de Palma (in the remote Roman province of Lusitania, way out on the western edge of the empire), that it was built sometime in the 350s.

The whole empire recognized the arrival of Christianity as the state cult. The religion that had been condemned, the religion that had been persecuted, now was drawn up into the light of the day, honored, and actually fused with imperial authority. In an extraordinary move, having brought it up out of the ground, underground, it was necessary to find some sort of home for it.

It had been a despised thing. Just to show you how despised, we've got an extraordinary archaeological find from that Palatine Hill where we spent so much time, where the hut of Romulus was, the temple of Cybele, the house of Augustus. There was also a little guard's house there and dating from some time in the 1st century or 2nd century A.D. is a graffito on the wall where one guard has scratched an image of a cross. Crucified on the cross is a being with the body of a man and the head of an ass (a donkey). A little man is off to one side with his hands raised in the position of adoration. Underneath, the cynical Roman soldier has written "Alexis worships his god."

So it wasn't just the laws against Christianity, it wasn't just the brutal repression—it was this air of mockery, of scorn, that had been heaped on this religion through the centuries. And now here it was, out of the shadows and into the limelight as the official religion of the emperors.

It couldn't go on being in the churches. There had always been a tradition in the Greek and Roman world that temples lay at the heart of communities, that the state religion was an essential part of experience. It was part of civic pride—national pride, imperial pride—to look at the temples of the gods. Christianity needed a new home. No more in a house, no more family feeling, no more of that easy acceptance of women and slaves and all ranks together. And no more love feast. It was banned in the 5th century.

Instead, the new building form chosen set its mark on the nature of the religion itself. Roman architects knew how to build a certain range of buildings. The one that was chosen was the basilica, something that had served for halls of justice, as well as for those bathhouses, such as the one we saw at Bath in England where the great bath was enshrined in a basilica. It was a way of creating a big building that lots of people could come into.

But it was a way, also, of creating a physical space that would leave its mark on this resurgent religion, coming up into the light of day, now fixed to the imperial family, now presided over by not just the emperor himself, but bishops who were like princes. It was a way of creating a space in which it was very natural to create hierarchies, feelings of power, of law, of judgment that are miles away from Dura-Europos, that little house, and that warm family feeling that Christianity was still a small cult struggling for recognition there on the frontiers of the Roman Empire.

Lecture Thirty-Five
The End of the World—A Coroner's Report

Scope:

Our theme in this lecture is the end of Classical antiquity and the fall of the western Roman Empire, an event we can't date with precision. We have some convenient years to start with, such as 376, the year in which the Goths crossed the Danube into the Roman Empire, or 476, the date of the last western Roman emperor, Romulus Augustulus. We might point to the year 391, in which Theodosius closed all the pagan temples and banned pagan worship, including the consultation of the Delphic Oracle and the Olympic Games conducted in honor of Zeus. In 409, Rome itself was sacked, leading in 410, to the recall of the legions from such provinces as Britain. All these dates are popular choices for pinpointing the end of Classical antiquity, but history shows us that the fall of the western empire was a process, not an event. In this lecture, we'll look at the material evidence for important changes between the Classical world and the time that came after it, revisiting the site of Torre de Palma, the villa in the ancient Roman province of Lusitania.

Outline

I. The writer who perhaps gives us the best view of the end of the Classical world is Edward Gibbon (1737–1794) in his gigantic work, *The History of the Decline and Fall of the Roman Empire.*

    A. Gibbon's work starts when the Roman Empire appears to be at its height and ends in the 15th century, with the final seizure of Constantinople by the Turks.

        1. Gibbon gives us a beautiful image to illustrate his view of those centuries; he compares the gradual fall of the Roman Empire to a fabric that crumbled due to its own weight.

        2. That image also sums up what archaeology has to show us about the end of Classical antiquity. It was not immediate; the empire was like a fabric of woven threads going in different directions, interlocking, each thread depending on the other, and it crumbled, rather than being torn.

3. Gibbon carefully chronicles all the barbarian invasions that brought hordes of Germans, Goths, and other outsiders into the former territories of the Roman Empire to claim the provinces as new barbarian kingdoms. Gibbon is aware that these invasions were the final blow to the empire, but the real cause was something from within.

B. The idea that the Roman Empire fell is modern. Ancient writers were not aware that events were happening in their lifetimes that brought on the end of their way of life.

1. The idea of a fall took hold in the Renaissance, in Florence, with thinkers who were involved in the revival of Greek and Roman learning. They perceived a vast space across the centuries that separated them from the Greeks and Romans and the present, a period they called the Middle Ages. There must have been a decline into darkness, then, from which the Renaissance thinkers could emerge.

2. Some of the famous names of the Italian Renaissance were involved in this debate. Petrarch, inventor of the sonnet and a scholar and collector of antiquities and coins, promoted the idea that the Roman Empire fell apart from within. Machiavelli, who studied ancient Greek and Roman warfare and politics, put the blame on the barbarians. Without them, he believed that the empire could have survived.

C. Some modern scholars hark back to the medieval view that the empire never fell—it just gradually transformed itself. Indeed, this theory has become popular among historians today. These scholars see a period of *transition*, not a decline or fall, between A.D. 2nd century, after Hadrian, when events start to turn against the Romans, and the year 800, when Charlemagne was crowned in Rome and revived, in a political sense, the Holy Roman Empire.

D. From an archaeological point of view, I believe that the evidence shows a death, although many historians might disagree. One of the questions we must ask in looking at the end of the Roman Empire is: What evidence do we emphasize—indications of continuity or indications of loss of cultural traditions and changes? My impression from the evidence is that a great civilization did go under, but some of its interlocking parts spun off separately and survived.

II. As you remember, the villa at Torre de Palma was a fantastic complex with a manor house, bathhouses, and gardens, all decorated with mosaics and frescos. The villa shows us the amenities of a rich Roman house, whether in Rome itself, or Pompeii, or the Portuguese countryside.

   A. Surrounding the villa was a working farm with a gigantic olive press, stables for racehorses, quarters for slaves, granaries, and wine presses. The farm was obviously an economic powerhouse, not only supporting the local people, but producing cash crops and livestock in such abundance that they became an important element in the imperial economic system.

      1. As a site, Torre de Palma survived almost to the time of the Arab invasion shortly after 700, when the Moors came across from North Africa, eliminated the remains of Visigothic royal power, and made most of Iberia part of the Islamic world. After that period, we have only a few of sherds of Islamic pottery from Torre de Palma; we know then it was not an active farm.

      2. Roman traditions and tools survived at Torre de Palma, however, right into the late 20th century, which would seem to be good evidence for continuity of the civilization.

   B. If we go a little bit north from the villa and come to the basilica, we find the tombs of those who were running the farm in the centuries after Roman power was broken.

      1. In these tombs, we find bits and pieces of the Roman villa itself, torn out and carried to the churchyard. Huge rectangular slabs of concrete that served as the gutters around the impluvium were later used as the walls or capstones of tombs. Column capitals were pulled from the house and lintels from doors; roof tiles were used to line the tombs, which tells us that the roof no longer existed.

      2. These architectural pieces became meaningless in their new role as part of a tomb. At the base level of

agricultural tradition, we find continuity, but the great emblem of Roman civilization, the villa itself, was dismantled.

C. In walking around the villa, we notice places where the mosaics have been roughly patched or even paved over by people who no longer have the money or, perhaps, the technical skill to repair them.

D. The lovely colonnades around the atrium, once open to the air, are now filled in with solid walls for security.

E. We get a mixed feeling from the tearing apart and gradual transformation of the villa. We see the demise of a great system, of which the villa was a flower, and the system itself, now dead, leaving behind only the base level of continuity and a new cultural tradition, based on the basilica, rising to the top.

III. What was happening at the same time elsewhere in the empire?

A. The Roman Empire was, among other things, a great economic engine. It was the center of a global trading system that had its western end in the Canary Islands and reached all the way east to China. From north to south, the network ran from Sweden and the Baltic to equatorial Africa, and all the lands in between were part of this vast system.

B. From archaeological evidence, we know that this system went under. What had been commonplace—markets in every town of the Greco-Roman world, where goods from faraway places were available to all—disappeared. As the centuries progress, we find a subsistence economy based on short-range trade and around far fewer major centers.

C. The great cities themselves went under. In the year A.D. 609, the pope petitioned the emperor in Constantinople for permission to turn the Pantheon into a church. Rome was, at that time, a village of a few thousand people, where it had once been a city of 1 million. All its gigantic monuments were now empty or in shambles.

D. Remember that we are looking at A.D. 3rd, 4th, and 5th centuries of the western empire. The eastern empire was still thriving, to some extent, thanks to that older, more entrenched Greek tradition and the presence of the emperor in Constantinople. But the western empire was in decline. Rome's fate is emblematic of many cities, most of which were abandoned.

1. Most of the cities in the western empire were no longer safe. Regional security was in the hands of a few strong military leaders, and villas in the countryside became the headquarters for these people, the nuclei of new towns. The cities were targets for wandering hordes because they were filled with goods that could be sold, but they were dangerous for settled life.

2. The great trading systems and the system of cities—the *polis* of the Greeks, the *urbs* of the Romans—were bedrocks of Classical civilization. The idea of a human being, a citizen in the Greek and Roman world, was tied to a city. If the cities were no longer habitable, Classical civilization could no longer exist.

3. We can see a flight of people, particularly the wealthy, from the cities in the final centuries of the Roman Empire in the west. These people moved their households to the country and created islands of civilization outside the city.

E. We see the same trend in Greece. In the 2nd century, when Hadrian was traveling through Greece, he was invited to the Roman-style villa of a famous Athenian, Herodes Atticus.

1. This man had donated a gigantic theater on the south side of the Acropolis to his fellow citizens, in keeping with the tradition of his predecessors in Attica. His own home, however, was not in Athens; he had built himself a palace, far to the south in a seaside town called Nafplio.

2. Archaeologists are now bringing this villa to light. Among the other visitors, besides Hadrian, were philosophers, entertainers, and public figures. All the influential people from the city had retreated to the countryside.

F. Thus, even this fall of the cities seems to be something that we can associate with Gibbon's crumbling fabric; forces from within were pulling the economic and social support for city life out from under those who must remain in the city to make their living.

IV. The environment also played a role as the backdrop to this picture of decay and decline.

A. The Mediterranean environment was steadily degrading. Pollen studies show that once the first farmers came into the Mediterranean, 7,000–8,000 years ago, a process of deforestation began; at the same time, good soil was loosened from the slopes. As mentioned in an earlier lecture, Plato himself was aware of these changes.

B. Scientists on the research vessel *Aegeao* have used subbottom profilers to see how thick the sediment is on the floors of the seas around Athens and the Greek coast to the north. In some places, they have found what appears to be up to 45 feet of mud. These are sediments that came sweeping off the mountains in historic times, completely covering the sea floor. The mountains themselves are bare down to the water's edge.

C. This deforestation, in turn, had an impact on rainfall, the temperature, the number of crops that could be raised, and the extent of farms; the very basis for wealth in that world eroded away.

D. Even cities suffered from environmental problems. In Ephesus, the river that comes out of the interior of Asia Minor was silted up at its mouth from the erosion of the mountains and hills along its upper course.
  1. In the days of the Ionian Greeks, Ephesus was one of the greatest cities in the Greek world, and it remained so into the Roman period.
  2. In time, however, Ephesus was left high and dry, miles from the coast, as the river filled up its delta; marshy swamps teeming with mosquitoes made the city dangerous to inhabit. Ephesus was left behind, gradually becoming a ghost town.

E. Through these processes, populations, cities, and economic systems were lost. All these factors together are threads in Gibbon's fabric, which archaeologists can see, one by one, were broken. Which thread was the one that ultimately caused the fabric to crumble beyond repair is an issue we continue to debate.

Suggested Reading:

Brown, *The World of Late Antiquity, AD 150–750.*

Ward-Perkins, *The Fall of Rome and the End of Civilization.*

Questions to Consider:

1. Based on the physical record of the Classical world, was the collapse of the western Roman Empire and Classical civilization inevitable?

2. From a historian's viewpoint, Gibbon saw the decline and fall as the crumbling of a fabric. What other metaphors might the archaeological record suggest?

Lecture Thirty-Five—Transcript
The End of the World—A Coroner's Report

Welcome back. Let's start today with a little poetry, some lines by Wordsworth:

> And what if she should see those glories fade, / Those titles vanish and that strength decay? / Yet shall some tribute of respect be paid / When her long life has reached its final day. / Men are we, and must mourn when even the Shade / Of that which once was great is passed away.

Our theme today is the end of classical antiquity and the fall of the Western Roman Empire. Those lines of Wordsworth—apt though they may be for the situation in the Mediterranean in the 3rd, 4th, 5th, 6th centuries of our era—were actually written about the extinction of the Venetian republic in Wordsworth's own time. During this time, a very small force of French soldiers and mariners sailed into the harbor at Venice and put an end to 1,000 years—and more—of Venetian independence and Venetian republican government.

That was the event that moved Wordsworth and that was a date you could mark on the calendar. Before that date, there had been a Venice, with an unbroken tradition stretching back into the past, a free and noble city. Go read the whole sonnet. It's a very beautiful evocation of that lost world.

And after that date, it was gone. But this is our problem for the Roman Empire. We can't find a date. There are some convenient years to hang one's hat on, if one is looking for a date for the fall of the Roman Empire. The year 376, the Goths crossed the Danube into the Roman Empire, pushed in desperation by the attacks of the Huns on their territory. One hundred years after that—476—we see the last Western Roman emperor, bearing the appropriate name, Romulus Augustulus. His first name calls forth memories of, Romulus, the founder of Rome; and that diminutive for Augustus, Augustulus, 'little Augustus," symbolizes how far the Imperium has fallen from the days of the first emperor.

Then there is the year 391. How about that for the fall of pagan antiquity? Theodosius closes all of the pagan temples, bans all pagan worship, including the consultation of the Delphic oracle or the contests of the Olympic Games for Zeus at Olympic.

Or the year 410 A.D., when Rome itself is sacked, leading one year later to the recall of the legions from provinces like Britain, and leaving them to their fate as the Roman emperors, or the claimants to that position, need the legions closer to home.

All of these are popular choices for naming a point where we can see that great classical antiquity finally ending. We're addicted to that—we want to find nice, correct answers for test questions where there's one date and one only.

I'm afraid that history is not going to oblige us. We're going to have to face the fact that it was a process and not an event. I think the person who gives us the best view of this is that famous chronicler of the last centuries of the classical world, Edward Gibbon, in his gigantic work—more honored than read—The [History of the] Decline and Fall of the Roman Empire, whose multiple volumes grace many bookcases. The very title, with its talk of a fall, has fooled many people into thinking that Gibbon was a proponent of the event theory, that there would be a day you could say it fell.

Gibbon was not so simplistic. I always have tremendous respect for anybody who pulls back from the trenches to try to get the big picture, which is what he did. He starts when the Roman Empire appears to be at its height. The centuries go by. He won't finish until the 15th century, and the final seizure of Byzantium, Constantinople, by the Turks. After all, the Byzantine Empire is an etymological invention of our modern historians. Those Byzantines called themselves Romans. After all, Constantine had shifted the headquarters of the Roman Empire to that new city of Constantinople. The tradition kept right on going and Edward Gibbon chronicles it, right to the end.

Gibbon gives us a beautiful image—a depressing thing, but a beautiful image—to understand the way he saw those centuries. He said, "The fall of Rome was like the crumbling of a fabric, which gives way due to its own weight."

I think that you could look for a lifetime and never find any single image that more clearly sums up what archaeology has to show you about this end of classical antiquity. It was not immediate; it was something to do with a system, as a fabric of woven threads going in different directions, interlocking, each thread depending on the other. Yet it crumbled, rather than being torn. It gave way thread by thread so there's no point at which you can say it's past darning or mending or reweaving. But we all know there does come a point where you can't salvage what's left.

Finally, it gave way of its own weight. Gibbon, chronicles so carefully all those barbarian invasions, which brought horde after horde of Germans, Goths, other people from outside the empire, into the former territories of the Roman Empire, claiming province after province to be new barbarian kingdoms. He shows us all that in detail. He's aware that that is the sort of axe which finally cuts off the head—but the real cause, he sees as something from within.

The idea that the Roman Empire fell is modern. We can't find ancient writers—not that there are very many of them after the 4th century—who seem aware that something happening in their lifetime could be called a fall of the Roman Empire. After all, the emperor's still living out there in Byzantium. There are various kings of Ostrogoths and others who seem to have taken the emperor's place in the west.

You have to get all the way to the Renaissance, in Florence, to find people who are involved in the revival of Greek and Roman learning that we called the Renaissance, "the rebirth." They look back across the centuries that separate them from the Greeks and Romans whose literature they are enjoying so much and finding so much inspiration in, and whose art they are trying to imitate. They perceive that there's a vast space, that they are going to call the Middle Ages, between them and what they like to think of as their prototypes, back there in the Greco-Roman world. That has to have ended then. There has to have been a fall, a decline into darkness, from which they then will emerge as the heroic figures who bring light, learning, classical values back to Europe.

Some of the famous names of the Italian renaissance were involved in this debate. Petrarch—inventor of the sonnet and a scholar as well as a collector of antiquities and coins—promoted the idea that the Roman Empire got sick and fell apart from within. This was Gibbons' take on it also. Machiavelli, who studied ancient Greek and

Roman warfare and politics, he put the blame on those barbarians. Without them, he feels that the empire could have kept right on going.

So we have warring camps among scholars. Is it event-based or is it processed-based? Is it due to internal weakness and failure of the system or is it more to be laid at the door of those barbarian hordes who just got so numerous and so warlike and aggressive that they were able to overcome what was left of the great Roman army military machine?

Then are those modern scholars who really want to hark back to the medieval view, as we would see it now chronologically, that it never fell—it just gradually transformed itself. After all, isn't the pope, in Rome, creating a sort of spiritual capital for Christendom, just the transmogrification of the Roman emperors, into a more spiritual plane?

This has become a very popular theory among historians today, that we should just take that chunk of time from about the 2nd century A.D. where things start to go wrong—and with the successors of Hadrian, Marcus Aurelius, poor fellow up on the Danube, trying to protect those provinces from marauding Germans—go all the way up to Charlemagne in 800, who was crowned in Rome and revives, in a political sense, holy Roman Empire.

There's a nice millennium. Let's say that's a period of transition; let's call it late antiquity; and let's not get into this decline, fall, civilization, Dark Age kind of debate.

What I'd like to do for our time today is look at the material evidence for big important changes between the classical world and what came after it. From an archaeological point of view, we're looking at what you find in the soil, what you find left behind. We go all the way back to our first time together when we talked about a crime scene where you were calling different teams of scholars. The historians would take down everyone's own personal account of what they'd seen or experienced; but the archaeologists would be down on their knees, picking up the evidence for the crime.

If we think about that situation where the historical record and the archaeological one can be at odds, I'd like to look at what the physical evidence has to tell us. First of all, to make the point that, from purely the physical evidence itself, the archaeologists would be gathering and then giving to the coroner for the coroner's report on this. There was a death. I believe that the archaeological evidence shows something died. This is something that many historians would not be ready to admit. Let's say right away, it's going to be a matter of ongoing debate. A lot of it is just the old "glass half empty and half full" (a metaphor I am not really fond of). Which are you going to emphasize—the evidence for continuity, or the evidence for loss of cultural traditions and changes?

I want to give you today my own impression of the archaeological evidence, for the fact that a great civilization did go under and that that civilization, being a system, is made up of interlocking parts, some of which may spin off separately and survive, while the system itself goes under.

For our type-site today, I'd like to go back to a site we've already visited, that huge Roman farm, that villa at Torre de Palma in Portugal, the ancient Roman province of Lusitania. When we visited there, way back in Lecture Twenty-Four, we saw a place where probably a Roman military man, Marcus Caelius Celsus, had created, out in the middle of the Lusitanian countryside, a fantastic complex with a manor house at its heart, bathhouses, gardens, ultimately and generations to come, mosaics, and frescos. These were all the amenities of a rich Roman house, whether it was in Rome itself or Pompeii or out here in the Portuguese countryside.

Surrounding it was a working farm with a gigantic olive press, stables for racehorses, quarters for slaves, granaries, wine presses—a fabulous establishment, gigantic in scale. Obviously an economic powerhouse, not only supporting the local people with their own produce, their own handcrafts, but producing cash crops and livestock in such abundance that they are actually an important element of the whole imperial economic system.

Torre de Palma, as a site, keeps on going strong right up to close to the time of the Arab invasion, when the Moors come across from North Africa, knock off what's left of Visigothic royal power, and make most of Iberia part of the Islamic world. That happened shortly after the year 700. We only have a couple of sherds of Islamic pottery of Torre de Palma so we know it wasn't an active farm in that period.

But up until that time, there's evidence for building, there's evidence for a lot of activity. And as I told you before, it's fascinating to see the Roman agricultural tradition, its tools, its annual schedule, its daily routines. After all, the words for that rest hour in the middle of the day—in Portuguese, *sesta*; in Spanish, *siesta*—they're from the same Latin word sixth, the sixth hour. If you count from dawn, that was the hour when everybody could take their break and go off and sleep in the shade.

So the Roman name has been preserved, along with the Roman tradition and along with all of those specialized Roman iron tools that formed such spectacular archaeological finds at Torre de Palma and survive, in living use, right down to the late 20th century. Here would seem to be good evidence for continuity.

But when I go a little bit north from the villa and come to the basilica—which, as we saw, was probably laid out by Roman architects in the middle of the 4th century A.D., and had fine Roman cement worked into its walls and lovely white marble veneer on its floors—there I see the tombs of the people who were running the farm in the centuries after Roman power was broken. Our last coin from Torre de Palma dates from the time of that emperor Honorius, who was emperor in 410, when they had to let Britain go.

So we extend for centuries after that, but what do we see in those tombs? We see bits and pieces of the Roman villa itself, torn out and carried over to the churchyard. Huge rectangular slabs of concrete that were the gutters around the little impluvium that was like an atrium in the heart of the old Roman house, now just used to be the walls or capstones of tombs. There are column capitals pulled from the house; lintels from doors, which means the door isn't there anymore.

All of these things brought over, reused. We can still see the cuttings and facings that the Roman masons put them for their original place, now useless, meaningless, in their new role as just part of a tomb for a Visigothic landowner or a person descended from the Romans, who's still there working the land and doing the agricultural work. After all, that's the majority. Modern Portuguese is a dialect of ancient Latin. In fact, if you're careful, you can write a page of modern Portuguese and know that Cicero could have read it.

So linguistically there's continuity; in the base level of agricultural tradition, there's continuity. But the great emblem of Roman civilization, the villa itself, is being dismantled. Here, we find those roof tiles pulled down and used to line the tombs. The roof is gone now in the villa. The rain is getting in. Those adobe walls that sat on top of the stone footers, they're beginning to slump and bury the site under the weight of its own walls.

If we walk around the villa, we can now notice places where the mosaics have been roughly patched or even paved right over by a people who no longer have the money, or perhaps even the technical skill, to repair them.

The lovely colonnades around the atrium, open to the air, open to the sunshine and the blue sky, those spaces between the columns are now filled up with solid walls because now just security and warmth are the issues for the people who are surviving in this place.

So we get that mixed feeling here and yet I do believe, from the tearing apart and gradual transformation of the villa, we are seeing the demise of a great system, of which the villa was a flower, but the system itself, now dead, can only leave the base level behind of existence, and a new cultural tradition, based very much on the church, rising on top of it. That is, after all, a very conventional view. I'm not claiming any original notion here.

Let's pull back and let's look empire-wide and see what's happening. The Roman Empire was, among other things, a great economic engine. It was the center of a global trading system that had its western end in the Canary Islands, where we find Roman trade artifacts and where we know geographers like Ptolemy set their longitude that was zero line for their world maps. We can then follow that trading system all the way east to China, whose silk production was very important to Romans. In fact, Tiberius had to make certain legislation about paying gold for silk because so much Roman gold was being sucked eastward along the silk routes.

All the lands in-between are part of this vast dynamo—the Roman economy. If we want to go north to south, we can take it from

Sweden and the Baltic, with its amber supplies in the north, all the way down to equatorial Africa with its gold and its ivory.

That system is broken. That system goes under. What has been a commonplace—to find markets in every town of the Greco-Roman world, where these goods from faraway places are commonly available to all—that disappears. As the centuries progress, we find a subsistence economy based on very short-range trade, based around far fewer centers.

The great cities themselves go under. In the year 609 A.D., the pope in Rome petitioned the emperor in Constantinople for permission to turn the Pantheon into a church—St. Mary of the Martyrs. Rome was, at that time, a village, a few thousand people. It had been a city of 1 million. All of these gigantic monuments were now empty or in shambles. Thank goodness he asked for permission to transform the Pantheon or it would have ultimately gone as well. He was told by the emperor, get rid of all that pagan trash first, so it was stripped of its pagan remains.

But what a transformation for Rome, the seat of power, the very heart of that classical civilization in its final centuries, to be reduced to a place where sheep are grazing in what had been the forum.

Remember always, we are talking here at this stage, as we look at the 3rd, 4th, 5th centuries A.D., of the western empire. The eastern empire is still going pretty strong, thanks to that older, more entrenched Greek tradition, thanks to the presence to the emperor in Constantinople, among other things. But the western empire is going under. Rome's fate is emblematic of all of those cities, most of which are abandoned.

Most of the cities of the western empire are now empty because they're not safe anymore. Regional security is now in the hands of a few strong military leaders, chiefs, and warlords. You've got to attach yourself to them. In a small and humble kind of day, villas out in the countryside become the headquarters of these people, the nuclei for new towns. The cities, these great targets for wandering hordes—since they're still filled with a jumble of salable stuff—they are not safe enough for settled life.

The great trading systems, the system of cities itself—the *polis* of the Greeks, the *urbs* of the Romans—was one of the pieces of bedrock under classical civilization. The idea of a human being, a citizen in the Greek and Roman world, is tied to a city. Take away the cities, how can we have classical civilization anymore? In my view, we cannot.

We can see a flight of people from the cities (I'm just reiterating what we saw earlier when we were at Torre de Palma), a flight of the rich, the senator's class, from the cities in the final centuries of the Roman Empire in the west. This happened as—for whatever reason—rich people stopped being the donators of monuments and amenities to public life in the cities. They take their wealth, their households and move out to their country estates and create little islands of civilization, palaces, in the countryside. That's the period when the most beautiful mosaics are put in, the most beautiful frescos, and the loveliest columns.

Let's visit, for a moment, Greece. Already back in the 2nd century, Hadrian was going through Greece, living, traveling in that land that he loved so much. During that time, he was invited to the villa, the Roman-style villa, of a famous Athenian, Herodes Atticus. Go to Athens today, go to the south side of the Acropolis, and there's a gigantic theater, all set for modern performances. I was lucky enough to hear Jose Carreras and Sumi Jo singing there in the summer of 2005, under the lights. As the crowd filled up, I was thinking of how we look just like all those thousands of ancient Athenians who would have enjoyed being there, thanks to Herodes Atticus and his largess.

With one hand, Atticus was doing something his predecessors would have done in Attica. He claimed descent from Miltiades and Cimon, those great heroes of the Greek 5th century B.C. He was giving a grand public work to his fellow citizens, an entertainment center. But where was his own home? Was he in one of those modest little houses right there in Athens the way his ancestors would have been? No. He had built himself a palace, far to the south, south of that beautiful seaside town of Nafplio. Greek archaeologists are bringing it to light now. It's got a gigantic central courtyard, very much like the one in the Villa of the Papyri that J. Paul Getty duplicated at Malibu in California.

There we know from the records, Hadrian visited this Greek multimillionaire, along with his wife Sabina, and his favorite, Antinoös, and all the rest of the court. We know that they probably went hunting from there.

Who did they find? All the philosophers were there, the entertainers, the public figures. They're all now in that enclosed little box of that countryside retreat, pulled out of the city, and now bringing the amenities of life to a select wealthy clientele, leaving the cities to go to hell. That is what happened.

So even this fall of the cities seems to be something that we can associate with Gibbon's crumbling fabric, that forces from within are pulling the economic and social support for city life out from under those who must still stay in the city in order to make their living.

The environment too is playing a role, as a background to this picture of decay and decline. The Mediterranean environment has been steadily degrading. Pollen studies show us that once the first farmers came into the Mediterranean, 7,000–8,000 years ago, a process started of steady deforestation. But even though it started way back in the Neolithic, it's a remarkable thing that the Romans and Greeks could still find masts for their ships, timbers for their temples, from their own hills and from their own forests, of a size and a majestic quality that just don't exist today in the Mediterranean. Little by little, it was deforested. As it was deforested, the good soil was loosened from the slopes.

Plato himself was aware of this. I believe I mentioned this when we talked about his vision of Atlantis. Atlantis dated to a time when Athens still had rich soil and forests on its hills. When the forests were cut down (which had happened in the time of grandfathers of Plato's generation), the soil was loosed, it flowed down to the sea, and the result was a wasted skeleton of what had once been a healthy landscape. The deforestation was pointed to by Plato—a contemporary of apart of this process—as the culprit.

In that research vessel, Aegeao (that I've been privileged to be on), using subbottom profilers, to see how thick the sediment is on the floors of the seas around Athens and the Greek coast to the north, there are places where we find what appears to be up to 45 feet of mud. These are sediments that have come sweeping down off the mountains in historic times, completely covering whatever might lie there on other seafloor. The mountains themselves are bare, right down to the water's edge.

This has impact on the rainfall, the temperature, the number of crops you can raise, the extent of farms—the very basis for wealth in that world was eroded away. Even great cities suffered in a very direct way from this.

Go to Ephesus and you will see that river that comes down out of the interior of Asia Minor, having silted up at its mouth from all of the erosion of the mountains and the hills at its upper course. Ephesus, in the days of the Ionian Greeks, was one of the greatest cities in the Greek world, and still in the time of the Romans—probably second only to Rome as a great city—was left high and dry, miles from the coast now as the river fills up its delta, as marshy swamps filled with mosquitoes make the place a danger to live in. Ephesus was left behind, gradually strangling, finally going under, and becoming a ghost town.

In this way, through all these processes, as we lose population, cities, economic systems—the environment itself, failing to provide the rich resources that a huge population needs—all of these things together are threads in Gibbons' fabric, that archaeologists can see, one by one, are being broken. Which thread is the one that ultimately causes the fabric to crumble beyond repair is something we could continue to debate.

I hope that as more effort is made—especially in the environmental area—to understand, moment-by-moment, year-by-year, the transitions within that ancient world, we will have a clearer idea of exactly what happened.

But of one thing I have no doubt. When we see those Roman buildings of the imperial age torn apart for what is called archaeologically the *spolia*, "the spoils" of those buildings that will now be put into the tombs, the buildings of the Ostrogoths and the Visigoths, we have indeed witnessed the end of something that, as Wordsworth said, "once was great."

Lecture Thirty-Six
A Bridge across the Torrent

Scope:

We've come a long way in this course since we first followed Roque Alcubierre down the well shaft at the site of Herculaneum in 1738. We witnessed the birth of Classical archaeology when he came back to the surface and wrote down what he had seen, keeping a day-by-day record of the exploration of this buried site. Since then, we have traveled through North Africa, Asia, Europe, and from end to end of the Mediterranean, looking at Greek and Roman sites, as well as culturally hybrid sites where the Greeks and Romans came in contact with peoples on their frontiers. We've tried to see exactly what it is that archaeology can reveal to us about these great ancient civilizations. In each of our final 12 lectures, we have visited a site that was somehow emblematic of one of our themes. In this lecture, we'll look at the legacy of the Classical civilizations we have explored at a site that is today called Alcántara, Arabic for "the bridge."

Outline

I.   Alcántara is in the far west of Spain, the site of a bridge spanning the gorge of the river that the Romans called Tagus (modern Portuguese, Tejo; Spanish, Tajo), one of the great rivers of Iberia that rises in the highlands of Spain and flows westward to the Atlantic Ocean at Lisbon.

   A. The bridge at Alcántara is one of the Romans' most extraordinary engineering and architectural achievements. It was the highest bridge in the Roman Empire, standing 175 feet tall, with six grand arches carrying a 25-foot-wide roadway for 600 feet from bank to bank.

   B. The architect and engineer who was in charge of erecting the bridge included in his work a temple—a shrine with a pair of columns framing a doorway—so that in crossing the bridge from the north, the temple was directly ahead.

   C. On that temple was a list of all the municipalities in Lusitania that, in the year 106, the time of the Emperor Trajan, had contributed money to build the bridge. Then, there was the name of the architect, Lacer, and a statement by him: "*Pontem perpetui mansuram in saecula mundi,*" "I have built this bridge to last forever, through the ages of the world."

D. The bridge at Alcántara symbolizes for me an important element of Classical civilization that makes it still worth studying today: the desire to create something of value that would last. Whether it was a philosophical argument or a poem or a building or a work of engineering, these things were built to last.

II. Many different approaches can be taken to the study of the ancient world.

A. We started these lectures with Johann Joachim Winckelmann, the man who called art history into existence when he studied Greek and Roman statues. Winckelmann believed that we should study antiquity because the Greeks and Romans had created a perfect standard of art, something that we should try to emulate. He also believed that this perfection in art was shared by the entire culture in which the ancient Greeks lived.

B. As mentioned in an earlier lecture, Winckelmann ignored the evidence of color on ancient marble statues. He imagined that they were all pure and white. I think that one of the great achievements of archaeology has been to put the color back in, to show us the polychrome richness of effect that the ancients loved to achieve in their art and that we can find in their lives.

C. That richness, that complexity that we see in the art, is emblematic of what has been lost through the ages in our view of ancient civilization. The modern popular perspective on Greco-Roman antiquity is still dominated by Winckelmann's idealizing view of Greece and Rome and the belief that we should study these civilizations as models.

D. To some extent, this view was enhanced during our own American Revolution with Roman ideas of republicanism and Greek ideas of democracy. The founding fathers of the United States looked back to Classical antiquity as a source of inspiration and validation for their ideas about how a country should be run.

E. I believe that all these assumptions and claims about the ancient world not only go too far, but they miss the point. By idealizing, one fails to see the humanity and the complexity of this civilization and fails to learn all that these people had to offer.

F. A contrary tendency among some scholars and historians is to emphasize the negative: the injustices, the horrors, the unrelenting warfare, and slavery.

   1. In this context, Winckelmann had some sound advice for archaeologists: "Don't be like schoolboys who simply look at their master to criticize and point out all the faults. Until you have fully understood the good that a person has achieved, you are not ready to look at the bad."

   2. I think this approach is wise; we should assess the achievements of the Greeks and Romans, then consider aspects of those civilizations that were not so successful.

III. I hope this course has introduced the idea that the Greeks and Romans resemble us in uncanny ways. Their legacy has come to us through direct descent, convergent evolution, and deliberate imitation.

A. Many of our institutions are direct descendents of the ancient world, having survived through the intervening centuries. One example is the agricultural system, derived from Roman villas in the form of modern ranches and haciendas.

B. Some features of our world that are similar to those in antiquity have come about through convergent evolution. For example, some of our forms of government came to be like the Greek world and the Roman world, simply because we're the same kind of people with the same kind of economies and the same kind of urban life.

C. Finally, the framers of the American Constitution deliberately imitated the example of the Greeks and Romans in establishing our government. Palladian forms of houses and buildings that hark back to Classical models became our standard for architecture. Many of our ideas about painting and sculpture can be traced back to the Greeks and Romans. All of this makes them a living presence in our world.

D. The point of any study is to achieve what was written on the outside of the temple of the Delphic Oracle: "Know thyself." We should all strive to know ourselves and our world, but doing so while we are in the midst of that world can be difficult. We must look to worlds that most resemble ours to see where other civilizations went wrong and take steps to avoid the same mistakes.

1. One element of the past that I hear challenged again and again from my students is warfare. Wasn't the Roman Empire basically a product of its legions? Isn't the Parthenon the end result of the Athenians' naval conquests?

2. Those assertions are true, but are we then forced to say that the whole Classical achievement would have been impossible without warfare? I don't think the evidence supports that conclusion.

3. Most of the sites in Greece today do not date from the 5th century, the time of the Peloponnesian War between Athens and Sparta. Only after those wars were over did the economy blossom. From the 4th century on, we get the major building projects that still adorn Greek city sites today.

4. In Rome, we learn that before there were legions, before there were wars, before the first conquest of a neighboring city, the Romans had already resculpted their Seven Hills and laid the foundations for their city. Their work wasn't the fruit of militarism but a product of a confident citizen body directed by charismatic leaders.

IV. Above all, I think we should learn from the Greeks and Romans the value of the individual engaging in the life of the community.

A. In an earlier lecture, I quoted Pericles on this subject: "We have no respect for the person who keeps aloof from public affairs, who tries to lead a private life. That person is not valued in Athens. We expect people to be participants in the life of their city." This statement applied to all citizens in democratic Athens and republican Rome. The wealthy made offerings of great public works; the middle class and the poor participated in festivals, warfare, and the commerce of the city.

B. Pompeii in A.D. 79 was deeply into the period of the Roman Empire. The imperial government was an absolute autocracy, but each city still managed its own affairs. And what we do find on the walls of Pompeii? Election slogans, showing us an image of people engaged with their world.

V. The remains of the Greeks and the Romans and their civilization are slipping through our fingers.

A. Cites that are excavated are often subject to more destruction than they would have been if they had been left underground. Further, there is scarcely enough money in any governmental treasury, anywhere in the realm of the old Greek and Roman civilization, to deal adequately with all that has been pulled up from the ground by archaeologists.

B. In Pompeii and Herculaneum, pigeon droppings have marred many of the statues, reliefs, and frescos, and falcons have been brought in to keep the pigeons at bay. The weather, too, has destroyed frescos and other artifacts. Under the water, shipwrecks have been looted by treasure hunters and sites damaged by the effects of uncontrolled trawling.

C. Does this destruction matter? If we consider an artifact such as the Antikythera device, I think we can see the answer. We have hundreds of thousands of artifacts from the Greco-Roman world, but nothing else like this device. It is the sole representative, surviving into our modern world, of a completely lost tradition for making complex astronomical calculations. Without this chance find, every modern scholar would deny that the ancients were capable of that kind of science.

D. We have important things to learn from the Greeks and Romans about the durability of civilization. Who would have believed, walking the streets of Rome in the time of Hadrian, that this civilization would soon be finished? By 409, the gates of Rome would be battered down and there would be a German army in the streets. Yet in the time of Hadrian, the world seemed completely secure, and those "barbarians" seemed so distant.

E. The system itself reminds us again and again that it's its own worst enemy. It's like the cloth that is so heavy that the fabric crumbles of its own weight. As strand by strand goes, we can see how the Greco-Roman world eventually went under, but we also know that the ancients weren't aware of the decline at the time. There was no call to action.

F. For those of us who have come after, every day is a time for action. We must always struggle to perceive the dangers in our society, to choose the right path to correct the errors we have made, and to ensure that the world we live in will continue—and will improve.

VI. The buildings and artifacts we have seen in this course have outlived the legions and their military victories. These are works of human craft, artistic genius, engineering skill, and imagination.

A. Looking at the bridge at Alcántara recalls some beautiful lines from the *Iliad*. Late in the book, King Nestor is coaching his son, Peisistratus, on how to win a chariot race. Peisistratus does not have the fastest horses nor is he the most powerful contender in the race. But Nestor tells his son that he can win anyway, because achieving victory comes through wisdom and art:

> It is not strength, but art, obtains the prize,
> And to be strong is less than to be wise.
> 'Tis more by art than force of numerous strokes
> The dexterous woodman shapes the stubborn oaks;
> By art, the pilot, through the boiling deep
> And howling tempest steers the fearless ship;
> And 'tis the artist wins the glorious course;
> Not those who trust in chariots and in horse.

B. The achievements of the ancients in power, might, and military victory have vanished. What is left behind, as we roam through the regions of the Classical world, are the achievements of its artists, craftspeople, engineers, thinkers, and designers. It's a legacy that not only illuminates and beautifies our own world but, just as Winckelmann said, should be a beacon for us, even if it's not perfect. Then, we should try to surpass it. Perfect or not, let us try also to create things in our world about which we can say, with pride, "This will last forever."

Suggested Reading:

Dyson, *Ancient Marbles to American Shores: Classical Archaeology in the United States.*

Taplin, *Greek Fire: The Influence of Ancient Greece on the Modern World.*

Questions to Consider:

1. The process of exploring, excavating, and preserving Classical remains is costly. Is the expense justified?

2. What should be the highest priorities for Classical archaeologists in the future?

Lecture Thirty-Six—Transcript
A Bridge across the Torrent

Welcome back. For the last of our 36 sessions together, we've come a long ways since we first followed Roque Alcubierre down that rabbit hole—or, rather, well shaft—at the site of Herculaneum on that October day in 1738. We witnessed the birth of classical archaeology when he came back up and wrote down what he had seen, and started a day-by-day record of the exploration of this buried site.

Since then, we have traveled through North Africa, Asia, Europe, from end to end of the Mediterranean, Greek sites, Roman sites, and sites that are those hybrid cultural places where the Greeks and Romans came in contact with peoples on their frontiers. We've tried to see exactly what it is that archaeology can reveal to us about these great ancient civilizations.

In each of our final 12 lectures, we've been visiting a site which somehow is emblematic of the subject. Today's subject is the legacy of those classical civilizations. So please come with me to the far west of Spain, and the gorge of the river that the Romans called Tagus (the modern Portuguese, Tejo; and the Spanish Tajo), one of the great rivers of Iberia that rises in the highlands of Spain and flows westward until it flows into the Atlantic Ocean at Lisbon.

In that gorge, which was on the edge of the territory of the Roman province of Lusitania, the Romans had to span a great gulf between two cliffs in order to get traffic across the Tagus River. So they built one of their most extraordinary, epic engineering and architectural achievements. This was the highest bridge in the Roman Empire, standing 175 feet tall, six grand arches carrying a 25-foot-wide roadway for 600 feet from bank to bank at a place that is today called Alcántara, Arabic for "the bridge."

I've never been there except in the late afternoon because I would come from the sites where we were working in Portugal during the mornings. After the field day was over, we'd get in the car and drive over to sit on that steep bank, in amongst the briars and dry stocks and burrs, watching the river sliding through the gorge below, looking over at the Sun shining on the western face of that beautiful bridge at Alcántara. Then looking beyond it to a modern engineering marvel, humming in the background, a great hydroelectric dam, which in the 20th century, spanned the same gorge.

I don't know how long that dam, the creation of our own world, is going to be there. But I know what the Romans thought about their bridge. The architect and the engineer who was in charge of putting up the bridge included in his work a little temple—a shrine with a pair of columns framing a doorway—so that if you came across the bridge from the north, it was straight ahead of you, just before the road took a sharp turn as it reached the far bank.

On that little temple was the list first of all the municipalities in Lusitania that, in the year 106, the time of the emperor Trajan, had contributed the money to build the bridge—solid granite blocks, no cement or concrete. Then there was the name of the architect, Lacer, and a statement by him: *Pontem perpetui mansuram in saecula mundi*, "I have built this bridge to last forever, through the ages of the world."

As I look behind me then at the handiwork of Lacer and of all those Romans who worked with him and think about their confidence that, yes, somebody would still be standing there in 2,000 years, able to admire that bridge and, in fact, still able to drive across it, and I look upstream at that concrete dam and I'm wondering not just about that dam, but about everything else that we create in our society. On which work of our own engineering would we have the courage to put the words, "This will last forever"?

The bridge at Alcántara symbolizes for me an important element of classical civilization that makes it still worth studying today. That was a desire to create something of value that would last. Whether it was a philosophical argument or a grand poem or a building or a work of engineering like that bridge, the things were built to last.

There are many different approaches to take to the ancient world. We started off with Johann Joachim Winckelmann, the man who called art history into existence when he studied those Greek and Roman statues and used them for models of what he thought a perfect set of art would be. He believed that we should study antiquity because the Greeks, especially, and the Romans, somewhat in their shadow, had created a perfect standard of art, something that the best we could ever do was try to emulate. He also believed that the perfection of the art, as he saw it, was shared by the entire culture and world in which those ancient Greeks lived.

I think it's emblematic of Winckelmann, as I said when we were talking about him a number of sessions ago, that he ignored all evidence of color on ancient marble statues. He imaged they were all pure and white—even though there were some pigments to be seen, if you look closely, on the very ones that he was looking at there in the pope's collection and in things that had come up out of the ground at Pompeii and Herculaneum. But he ignored them. Classical antiquity should be something pure, something bleached, something refined, something unstained by ordinary human experience.

I think it's been the great achievement of archaeology to put the color back in, to make us realize the columns of ancient temples were often painted red, that all of those statues that we admire in white marble were originally tinted with flesh tones. The hair was colored; the lips and the nipples and the eyes picked out in appropriate shades; and even bronzes, like the Riace Warriors, show us that polychrome richness of effect that the ancients loved to achieve.

That richness, that complexity that we see in the art is, to me, emblematic of what has been lost through the ages in our view of ancient civilization itself. The modern popular view of Greco-Roman antiquity is still dominated by this "Winckelmannesque" idealizing view of the glory that was Greece and the grandeur that was Rome, and the belief that we should study them because they are somehow models.

To some extent, this was even enhanced during our own American revolution with Roman ideas of republicanism and Greek ideas of democracy (although in the 18th century, the democracy was associated more with religious freedom and idealism). Nonetheless, we are aware that the founding fathers of the United States were looking back at classical antiquity as a source of inspiration, as a source of validation, for their ideas about how a country should be run.

It's been very famously noted by one philosopher that all of modern philosophy is just a set of footnotes to Plato. I'll stay out of that one.

I feel that all of these assumptions and claims not only go too far—more than that, they miss the point. By idealizing, one fails to see the humanity; one fails to see the complexity of the record; one ignores all the troubling elements; and one puts oneself in a position where it's very hard to actually learn what those people had to offer.

I'd like to read you a very short passage from an address that was made on the Acropolis in the year 1838 when the Greek wars of independence were over and the Greek Archaeological Society was having its very first meeting up there on the Acropolis, as the archaeological representatives of the new nation of Greece. One of their company, Rizos-Nerulos, stood up and addressed his companions, "Gentlemen, these stones, thanks to Phidias, Praxiteles, Agorakritos, and Myron [all very famous sculptures] are more precious than diamonds or agates. It is to these stones that we owe our political renaissance."

Here is putting a burden of meaning and idealism on the past, to a truly epic degree, to say that a modern nation is resting on the skeleton of what is endured from those ancient times.

Obviously, the ruins of Greece have played an important role in the Greek renaissance in modern times, just as the ruins of Rome were an inspiration to the modern nation of Italy, as it formed itself in the 1860s during those wars of unification and liberation.

But still, we miss the point, to a large degree, if we just look at the past for a bland feeling of inspiration. We need to take the good with the bad because only then can we really understand all that they have to tell us—not just about themselves, but about ourselves too.

There has been a contrary tendency among some scholars and some historians to emphasize the negative, the injustices, the horrors, the unrelenting warfare, the slavery. They were stuck with slavery, they felt. Aristotle made the famous statement, "Until we have looms that can weave of themselves and lyres that can pluck themselves, we shall have slaves."

He was picturing, perhaps, a mechanical age that would do all those tasks for you, a mechanical age he certainly did not live long enough to see. It was a mechanical age that the Romans turned aside from when they ultimately gave up on that steady advance of technical knowledge and engineering expertise that might have led to the industrial revolution and machine-driven age that allows us to get rid of slaves.

But before we pat ourselves on the back for being a slave-free society, let's consider how many decades went by after the industrial revolution before the tide finally turned against slavery, in our own society.

Does this justify it in the ancient world? Absolutely not. But it's part of the archaeological approach to try to see both the good and the bad.

In this context, Winckelmann said a beautiful thing. Remember, he was very hard on Alcubierre and those other early excavators of Pompeii. But in another context, he said something that I think is always worth remembering as you look at the record of a person or an entire people, "Don't be like schoolboys [he was a former teacher himself] who simply look at their master to criticize and point out all the faults. Until you have fully understood the good that a person has achieved, you are not ready to look at the bad."

I think we should that approach, that we would like to assess the achievement and then consider the bad—and there is bad. We are taking the right approach to any period of history. After all, I hope you've been able to get the feeling that the Greeks and the Romans resemble us in uncanny ways. That's partly because we grow directly out of the world of Greece and Rome. Many of our institutions survived through the intervening centuries; the agricultural system that they developed; the modern ranches and haciendas that are direct descendents of Roman villas. All of this is a direct link.

Then there are the things that we evolve through convergent evolution. Some of our forms of government came to be like the Greek world and the Roman world, simply because we're the same kind of people with the same kind of economies and the same kind of urban life and many of the same issues that we deal with and try to overcome.

So direct descent, convergent evolution, and finally, a deliberate imitation. Those framers of the American Constitution were all familiar with Greek and Roman writing about politics, what makes a good citizen, what makes a just state or a just city. It had been on the minds of Greeks; it had been on the minds of Romans. We were following their examples. Some of their ideas were deliberately revived in our own modern world, just as Palladian forms of houses and buildings that hark back to classical models became our standard for architecture. Many ideas about painting and sculpture go straight back to the Greeks and Romans. All of this makes them a living presence in our world.

I would say that the point of any study is to achieve what the Delphic oracle had written on the outside of her temple. When you finally make your way up to that trail on the side of Mount Parnassus and came around the final corner, that was the grand altar for sacrifices on your left, but straight ahead of you was the temple façade. There, written either on plaques or hanging like a slogan, were the words, "Know thyself."

We should all strive to know ourselves, strive to know our own world—but it's very difficult to do. It's as if our world is a mountain that we are scaling. Our noses are right up against the rock. We can see the little bit of the mountainside to the left and right of us and a little bit behind and a little bit ahead, but we can't see the mountain. We can only see other mountains in the same range.

I would submit to you that the one that most resembles ours, the one that can give us the best inkling to what our particular modern mountain looks like, and where we are headed, is that edifice, that enormous geological structure—to continue the mountain metaphor—of the ancient Greek and Roman world. We see it in politics; in the world view; in the idea of what an individual is within society. We see it in silly ways, like the quest for leisure and comfort, which in some ways, went out of the world with the end of the Roman Empire and its mass production of luxury, easily-available items, which allowed everyone to have this lifestyles of abundance, security, and ease. They resemble us and we resemble them.

For all these reasons, we need to think about the past. We need to study their ways, try to understand where we would feel they went wrong—as they certainly did in slavery—and try not to take the same steps or make the same mistakes.

One element of the past—one which I certainly hear challenged again and again from my students—is the warfare. Isn't the Roman Empire basically a product of those legions? Isn't the Parthenon standing there because the Athenians went so much in for conquest that they created a navy that no one could withstand, and brought 150 Greek cities and islands into an empire whose product was that Parthenon?

For many Athenians at the time, those stones had blood on them because they represented the unjust taking of wealth from those who had no interest in supporting Athens and creating beautiful temples out of that tribute.

That's all true. But do we really have to say that the whole classical achievement would have been impossible without the warfare? I think there is contrary evidence. If you walk around the sites of Greece today, look at a wall, look at a ruin, look at a temple, look at any sort of remarkable public work and ask for its date. It's not likely to be from the 5th century, the time of all those wars, the famous Peloponnesian War between Athens and Sparta. It was once those wars were over that the economies blossomed. It's from the 4th century and the centuries after that that we get the major building projects that still adorn all of those Greek city sites today.

If we go to Rome and follow our grand investigator of subterranean Rome, Ammerman, as he puts his cores down, we learn from him the lesson that before there were legions, before there were wars, before there was the first conquest of a neighboring city by the Romans, they had already resculpted their seven hills, their little valley by the Tiber. They had done the backbreaking labor of raising the level of what was to become the forum by two meters of artificial fill throughout its extent, adding on to one of those seven hills, the Capitoline, with an enormous artificial plateau on which they placed a gigantic temple to Capitoline Zeus.

This wasn't the fruit of militarism or conquest or legions. This was the confidence of a citizen body led by charismatic leaders, those Etruscan kings, who were able to transform that site into a great city.

I believe that in this way, we can see that there are alternatives to the view of militarism, the view that slavery alone can account for all of those achievements. These were people who were reaching out for other means of achieving their ends.

Above all, what I think we have to learn from the Greeks and Romans is the value of the individual engaging in the life of their community. I mentioned in an earlier presentation the words of Pericles, as recorded for us or invented for us in one of the speeches in Thucydides' history. But since Thucydides himself was a contemporary of Pericles and an Athenian, we can hope here that he's representing the ideas of his fellow citizens.

Pericles said, "We have no respect for the person who keeps aloof from public affairs, who tries to lead a private life. That person is not valued in Athens. We expect people to be participants in the life of their city."

That was true in democratic Athens; it was true in republican Rome. If you were rich, you made great offerings of public works (the Appian Way, aqueducts, theatres); and if you were of middle or poor class, you participated in the festivals, in the warfare, in the commerce of one's city on a regular basis. It's this that, to me, shines through.

Pompeii has recorded for us all the graffiti on all the walls from which plaster would have otherwise crumbled away, leaving us nothing behind. So we know what day-to-day people were talking about. In Pompeii, 79 A.D., we're far into the Roman Empire. It's an absolute autocracy on top; but each city is still managing its own affairs.

What we do find all over the walls of Pompeii? Election slogans. Vote for this person; vote for that person; he is of estimable character; the Guild of Fuller supports so-and-so for council, for magistrate. Even women—who can't vote—are writing up the candidates they prefer so that everyone will know who they support.

It's an image here of a world that was engaged. It's not until we get to that later period we talked about last time, when the rich start to pull out—building those little enclaves in the countryside, retreating into those pleasure gardens and enclosed manor houses—that that public element falls away.

At that point, I feel the classical age really has ended. It doesn't matter if the houses are beautiful and the mosaics are repeating the motifs of ancient myths. The essential element of the classical spirit is gone—the spirit that I feel would be most worth preserving in our own world.

It's a matter of urgency, I feel, that people think about this, that everybody realize that we have here a precious resource, the remains of the Greeks and the Romans and their civilization, because it is slipping through our fingers. It is being destroyed. Sometimes sites, when they're excavated, are subjected to more destruction than they would have if they had been left underground. In fact, that's almost axiomatic. There's scarcely enough money in any governmental treasury, anywhere in the realm of the old Greek and Roman civilization to adequately deal with all that has been pulled up from the ground by archaeologists.

Let's go back to Pompeii and Herculaneum where, in Herculaneum, we will suddenly find shadows passing over our heads. These are falcons that have been brought in with falconers in an attempt to deal with the pigeons. You may remember that Fiorelli, in the 1860s, instituted a policy of leaving the frescos and the other objects in place. That's fine, but not all the buildings are roofed. The pigeons are actually—through their droppings, which now mar and cover the statues, the frescos, the reliefs—contributing to the degradation of this site. The falcons, I'm happy to say, have been pretty effective at keeping the pigeons at bay.

In Pompeii, we find Wilhelmina Jashemski, the very noted archaeologists and scholar of ancient gardens, whose work we saw when we talked about the scientific approach to studying ancient sites. She records how, a few years ago, she went to Pompeii, fought her way through a thicket of scrub within one of the old courtyards (because there's not enough money for anything except the main touristic areas clear of weeds), because she knew that somewhere on a far wall, there was a fresco showing a garden scene. It was her last day of fieldwork. She was with her husband. They had their cameras. By the time they got through the undergrowth, the light was too dim to take the picture. But they saw the fresco and they thought, we'll come back first thing in our next season and get the picture.

When they came back, there was no fresco on the wall. There was just a crumbled pile of plaster at the bottom of the wall where it had finally given way, the assaults of the winter rains, and was completely destroyed.

Pompeii is a striking case, but it's hard to find any archaeological site anywhere in the Mediterranean area that isn't suffering from the same kind of decay.

Under the water, shipwrecks are continually being attacked by looters; by treasure hunters; or just by the effect of uncontrolled trawling, which is wiping out a lot of the biota of the Mediterranean, but at the same time, destroying forever these underwater sites.

Does this really matter? Obviously it's my life so I think it does. But if we consider something like the Antikythera device (that 1st-century B.C. bronze computer that came off the Antikythera wreck), it's unique. We have hundreds of thousands of artifacts—perhaps millions of artifacts—from the Greco-Roman world. Nothing would have prepared us for that device. It can't be a one-off object. It is the sole representative, surviving into our modern world, of a completely lost tradition, otherwise unknown, of creating those clockwork-like mechanisms out of all those bronze gears, putting them in those wooden cases, using them to do incredibly complicated astronomical calculations. One chance find by a sponge diver. Without that, every modern scholar would deny that the ancients were capable of that kind of science.

We have important things to learn from the Greeks and Romans about the durability of civilization. Who would have believed, walking around the streets of Rome in the time of Hadrian, that this civilization, within a couple of hundreds years in that city, would be finished? But by 409, the gates of Rome would be battered down and there would be a German army in the streets. No one would have believed it. The world seemed completely secure; the underpinnings, economic and military and social, seemed so strong, so many, so secure. Those barbarians, as they liked to call them, seemed so distant, so shadowed.

But the system itself reminds us again and again that it's its own worst enemy because it's top-heavy. It's like that cloth that is so immensely heavy that the fabric itself can crumble at its own weight.

As strand by strand goes, we can see how the Greco-Roman world eventually went under. But we also know that they weren't aware of it themselves at the time. That means that there was no one to tell them, "Now is the time for action."

But for those who come after, every day is the time for action. We must always struggle to perceive what the dangers are, to follow these different possibilities down to their conclusions. We must try to choose the right path to correct the errors we're making now, the injustices, the wrong choices, and to ensure that the world we live in will continue—and will get better.

When I sit and look at the bridge at Alcántara, I reflect on the fact that all those legions, all those military victories, they've not survived. What has survived is a work of human craft, of human artistic genius, engineering skill, and imagination.

I think, when I look at that bridge, of some beautiful lines that carry us all the way back to the world of Homer and the *Iliad*, when old King Nestor, late in the *Iliad*, is coaching his son, Peisistratus, on how to win a chariot race. Peisistratus does not have the fast horses. He's not the powerful one in the race. But Nestor tells his son, you can win anyway. Because it's really about wisdom. It's about intelligence. It's about art. To give you the passage in the beautiful words of Alexander Pope, this is what Nestor said:

> It is not strength, but art, obtains the prize,
> And to be strong is less than to be wise.
> 'Tis more by art than force of numerous strokes
> The dexterous woodman shapes the stubborn oaks;
> By, art the pilot, through the boiling deep
> And howling tempest, steers the fearless ship;
> And 'tis the artist wins the glorious course;
> Not those who trust in chariots and in horse.

Their achievements of power, of might, of military victory, these have vanished. What is left behind, as we roam through those regions of the old classical world, are the achievements of their artists, of their craftsmen and craftswomen, of their engineers, of their great thinkers and designers. It's a legacy which not only illuminates and beautifies our own world, but just as Winckelmann said, should be a beacon for us, even if it's not perfect. Then we should try to surpass it. But perfect or not, let us try also to create things in our world to which we could say, with pride, "This will last forever."

We've come to the end of our voyage together through classical antiquity. Thank you for making it with me. I learn more and more every time I consider these ancient sites and these remarkable achievements of the past.

I'd like to leave you with the motto of those young diving archaeologists from Greece and Denmark who are currently working in the harbor of the Piraeus, one of the most polluted bodies of water on Earth, as they pull on their dry suits and get ready to pull their masks down on their faces. They will look at you and say three words which I think we should all keep in mind as we think about the past and the future.

They say, "Peace, love, archaeology."

Timeline I
Important Periods of Greek and Roman History

Note: Important sites mentioned in the lectures are listed under each period. Dates for periods are approximate.

10,500–7000 B.C. .... **Mesolithic or Middle Stone Age**. Obsidian deposits in Franchthi Cave, Greece, show that Mesolithic mariners had seagoing vessels capable of crossing the Aegean to the volcanic island of Melos.

7000–3600 B.C. .... **Neolithic or New Stone Age**. Farming communities spread across Greece, creating distinctive painted pottery and establishing such villages as Dimini and Sesklo.

3600–2100 B.C. .... **Early Bronze Age in the Aegean**. (Late Neolithic in Italy and the western Mediterranean.) Important settlements at Troy and Knossos.

2100–1600 B.C. .... **Middle Bronze Age (Aegean)**. Eruption of Santorini volcano circa 1620 B.C. destroys Akrotiri on the island of Thera, a major center of Cycladic civilization.

1600–1100 B.C. .... **Late Bronze Age**. Mycenaean contacts with Italy and Sicily. Proliferation of Minoan sites on Crete, most of which share the fate of Gournia and are abandoned or destroyed in about 1450 B.C. Greek-speaking Mycenaeans rule from such palaces as Mycenae on the Greek mainland and Knossos on Crete, using the Linear B script for their accounts. Shipwreck at Uluburun off southern Turkey, circa 1320 B.C. Legendary time of the Trojan War, variously dated to 1250 B.C. or 1184 B.C. Ultimate destruction of palaces at the end of the Bronze Age.

1100–800 B.C. .... **Iron Age or Dark Age**. Site of Rome settlement about 1000 B.C.; Ionian Greek cities in Asia Minor settled about the same time. Lefkandi, Euboea, is the center for "Homeric" chieftains and Near Eastern trade at about 950 B.C.

800–500 B.C. .... **Age of Colonization; Age of the Polis**. Greeks and Italians adopt alphabet from the Phoenicians. Greek colonies established near the Bay of Naples and in southern Italy and Sicily. Homer composes the *Iliad* and *Odyssey*. Rise of ritual activity at Delphi and Olympia—first Olympic Games held in 776 B.C. (traditional date). Rome founded in 753 B.C. (traditional date). Etruscans dominate Rome; local tyrants rule in many Greek city-states. Eastern and western Greek colonial cities surpass the cultural achievements of Corinth, Athens, Sparta, and others in the heartland. Archaic period of art, circa 580–480 B.C.

500–330 B.C. .... **Classical Age**. Romans expel the last king circa 500 B.C. Greeks involved in wars with Persians in the east and Carthaginians in the west. Athenians begin to develop the Agora northwest of the Acropolis as a grand civic center. After the Persian Wars, Athens rules as a maritime empire thanks to its fleet of triremes. After 450 B.C., Athenians build the Parthenon and other temples on the Acropolis. "Golden Age" of Athens. Phidias creates monumental statues of Athena at Athens and Zeus at Olympia. Romans begin to expand their territory, taking over Veii circa 396 B.C. The archaic temple at Delphi is destroyed circa 372 B.C. and is replaced by a 4th-century temple. In 334 B.C., Alexander the Great embarks on his conquest of the Persian Empire, founding Alexandria in Egypt in 331 B.C.

330–28 B.C. ....**Hellenistic Age; Roman Republic**. Successors of Alexander the Great created Hellenized kingdoms in the eastern Mediterranean and Near East. Ptolemaic dynasty in Egypt inaugurates the lighthouse at Alexandria in 283 B.C. Romans conquer Samnian territory (including Pompeii and Herculaneum) by 290 B.C., establish maritime colonies at Cosa and Paestum in 273 B.C., and are embroiled in the Punic Wars with Carthage from 264–146 B.C. Alexandria and Rhodes become literary and scientific centers, as shown by the famous bronze Antikythera device. Romans conquer Athens in 86 B.C. In 30 B.C., the Roman general Octavian captures Egypt. The last queen, Cleopatra, commits suicide, and Octavian's military and administrative successes bring an end to both the Hellenistic Age and the Roman Republic.

27 B.C.– A.D. 96. ....**Roman Empire: Julio-Claudian and Flavian Dynasties**. The former Octavian, now Caesar Augustus, rules as emperor—a status that will eventually grow into a divine cult. From 20 to 9 B.C., Roman engineers help construct a harbor city called Caesarea Maritima for Augustus's friend and client Herod of Judea. Augustus's legions suffer a great loss in Germany at the Teutoburg Forest in A.D. 9. The emperor Claudius launches a successful Roman invasion of Britain in A.D. 43. Eruption of Mt. Vesuvius in A.D. 79. buries Pompeii and Herculaneum. The great amphitheatre known as the Colosseum is inaugurated in A.D. 80, having been built with spoils

brought back to Rome from Judea after the Jewish Revolt.

A.D. 96–235.................**Roman Empire: Trajanic, Antonine, and Severan Dynasties**. During the reign of Hadrian (117–138), limits, such as Hadrian's Wall, are constructed to mark the imperial frontier; a high-water mark of Hellenization is reached in Roman culture; and the cult of Antinous is introduced. Emperors continue to sponsor extraordinary engineering works in concrete up through Caracalla (211–217) and his baths, the largest in Rome.

A.D. 235–284.................**Crisis of the Third Century**. Economic collapse, weakening of centralized power, and widespread "barbarian" invasions threaten the existence of the Roman Empire. In 267, the Heruli from the Black Sea launch a maritime invasion of Greece, sacking and burning the Agora at Athens.

A.D. 284–476.................**Late Roman Empire**. Economic edicts and coinage reforms of Diocletian get the empire back on an even keel (301–302). Constantine legalizes Christianity (313) and moves the capital of his empire from Rome to Byzantium, renaming it Constantinople (324). Circa 360, the last Pythia at Delphi gives a final oracle to Julian the Apostate. Theodosius closes the temples of the old gods (391). Honorius withdraws the Roman legions from Britain (410). Geseric and his Vandals sack Rome in 455, and 21 years later, an Ostrogothic king establishes rule over Italy.

Timeline II
Classical Archaeology

1738 .... By order of Charles of Bourbon, king of Naples, the military engineer Roque Joaquín Alcubierre begins the first systematic archaeological excavations at the site of Herculaneum, an ancient city buried during the eruption of Mt. Vesuvius in A.D. 79.

1748 .... Alcubierre extends the Bourbon excavations to Pompeii, where the shallow layers of pumice pellets ultimately allow much of the buried city to be completely uncovered.

1750 .... Swiss military engineer Karl Weber excavates and maps the great Villa of the Papyri in Herculaneum, famous for its library of papyrus scrolls. More than two centuries later, American tycoon J. Paul Getty will attempt to recreate the villa as a museum of ancient art at Malibu in California.

1764 .... Johann Joachim Winckelmann publishes his groundbreaking *History of Ancient Art*, in which he distinguished Greek originals from Roman copies and laid out the four periods of art (corresponding to Archaic, Classical, 4th Century, and Hellenistic/Roman) that still form the basis of art historical chronology.

1766 .... Sir William Hamilton, British envoy to Naples; volcanologist; and collector of ancient vases, coins, and other antiquities, publishes his first collections of vases with lavish engravings by d'Hancarville. He identifies most of the figured vases as Greek, rather than Etruscan or Roman, and champions the study of vases alongside ancient sculpture and architecture.

1803 ....Thomas Bruce (Lord Elgin) removes sculpted marbles from the Parthenon in Athens, including pedimental sculptures and reliefs from the frieze, and ships them to England, where they eventually find their way to the British Museum. The Elgin Marbles have been a source of bitter controversy ever since they were removed from the Acropolis.

1825 ....Faustino Corso publishes *Delle Pietri Antichi*, describing more than 1,000 specimens of ancient marble from Rome and, where possible, tracing the stone back to the quarry from which it had been cut.

1861 ....Giuseppe Fiorelli takes charge of the excavations at Pompeii and initiates the practice of making plaster casts of long-dead Pompeiians from cavities in the volcanic matrix at the site.

1861 ....The emperor Napoleon III of France sponsors the reconstruction and launching of a trireme, along with excavations and reconstructions of the Roman siegeworks at Alesia—both projects marking pioneering efforts in the field of experimental archaeology.

1868 ....Heinrich Schliemann visits Pompeii, tours the excavations, and hears Fiorelli lecture on his discoveries and on the scientific methods used to excavate the buried city.

1871 ....Having informed Heinrich Schliemann of his belief that the tell of Hissarlik was the site of Homer's Troy and, therefore, the city of Priam described in the *Iliad*, British scholar and diplomat Frank Calvert agrees to collaborate with Schliemann in the excavation of the site. In 1873, Schliemann alienates Calvert and the government of

Turkey by smuggling the hoard known as Priam's Treasure out of Turkey, first to Greece, then to Germany.

1875 ....A six-year campaign of excavation begins at Olympia in Greece, site of the ancient Olympic Games, under the direction of German archaeologist Ernst Curtius, who had previously excavated at the site of the Hellenistic city of Pergamon in Turkey and the Assembly Hill (Pnyx) in Athens.

1876 ....Under an agreement that he will pay all costs and turn all finds over to the Greek government, Heinrich Schliemann excavates the late Bronze Age citadel of Mycenae, discovering the Shaft Graves and such treasures as the famous gold Mask of Agamemnon.

1877 ....Italian archaeologist Rodolfo Lanciani begins to survey, excavate, and map ancient structures in the Roman Forum, a project that will eventually embrace Rome's aqueduct system, the port city of Ostia, and Hadrian's villa at Tivoli, and lead to the publication and preservation of many important Roman remains.

1884 ....Greek archaeologist Christos Tsountas attempts the first scientific underwater archaeological survey in history, employing sponge divers to examine the sea floor in the straits of Salamis for remains of the famous sea battle between Greeks and Persians in 480 B.C.

1891 ....French archaeologists begin the decade-long Grande Fouille, or "Big Dig," at Delphi in Greece, uncovering the sanctuary of Apollo, the foundations of the temple that was the site of the famous Delphic Oracle, and masterpieces of art, including the bronze *Charioteer*.

1900 ....British scholar Arthur Evans begins his famous dig at Knossos in north central Crete, site of the palace of King Minos and the legendary labyrinth. The stratigraphic sequence worked out by the field director, archaeologist Duncan MacKenzie, helps to establish a new chronological framework for the Aegean Bronze Age.

1900 ....Greek sponge divers recover important artifacts from an ancient shipwreck at the islet of Antikythera, south of Greece, including the corroded remains of an ancient astronomical computer composed of 39 circular bronze gears of varying sizes, a turntable, and 3 bronze dials. The Antikythera device dates from the 1st century B.C.

1901 ....American archaeologist Harriet Boyd of Smith College excavates at Gournia in eastern Crete, revealing the houses and streets of a working Minoan town that had been abandoned about 1450 B.C. Among Boyd's discoveries was an altar, shrine, and clay statue of a snake-enwreathed mother goddess.

1901 ....Greek archaeologist Christos Tsountas starts excavations at the Neolithic hilltop settlement of Sesklo near the Gulf of Volos in central Greece.

1921 ....Mortimer Wheeler uses his excavations at the Roman fort of Segontium in Wales as a launching platform for his reform of archaeological fieldwork methods, taking as his guide the pioneering but almost forgotten works of General Pitt-Rivers.

1928 .... Russian-American archaeologist and historian Michael Rostovtzeff begins excavations at Dura-Europos on the Euphrates River, where he uncovers remains of a Roman military post, a trading center, and religious centers for Jews, Christians, and followers of Mithras. Rostovtzeff worked his discoveries into his pioneering studies of ancient society and economics.

1932 .... Excavations in the Agora of ancient Athens are undertaken by the American School of Classical Studies in Athens, thus initiating one of the largest, longest-lived, and most productive digs in the field of Classical archaeology.

1939 .... American archaeologist Carl Blegen discovers a late Bronze Age palace at Pylos in southwestern Greece, the so-called Palace of Nestor, having brought the palace's archive room to light on the very first day of digging. Linear B tablets from Pylos helped clinch Ventris's controversial decipherment of the Bronze Age script.

1945 .... American chemist Willard F. Libby initiates a study of radioactive carbon isotopes (carbon-14) that will eventually provide archaeologists with a method for dating ancient artifacts and materials by measuring the amount of radiocarbon that they contain. Libby will receive the Nobel Prize for Chemistry in 1960 for his discovery.

1945 .... Mortimer Wheeler and a team of Indian archaeologists excavate an ancient warehouse containing Roman pottery and other artifacts at Arikamedu in south India.

1947 .... A chance discovery by a Portuguese laborer reveals the immense Roman villa of Torre de Palma in east central Portugal, with a complex of buildings, including barns, stables, smithies, an oil press, bath houses, and an early Christian basilica, as well as extensive mosaic pavements.

1952 ....Jacques Cousteau and a team of divers collaborate with French archaeologist F. Benoit in recovering amphorae and other materials from Hellenistic and Roman shipwrecks at Grand Congloue near Marseilles, using the scuba gear recently developed by Cousteau.

1953 ....English architect Michael Ventris completes his decoding of the Linear B script from late Bronze Age palace sites on Crete and the Greek mainland, proving that the tablets were palace accounting tallies and that the language represented by the Linear B syllabary was Greek.

1953 ....American archaeologist William McDonald and Canadian Richard Hope Simpson begin the Minnesota Messenia expedition—a systematic surface survey of Messenia in southwest Greece, first mapping late Bronze Age sites and later establishing the region's settlement patterns from prehistoric to early modern times. (A similar regional survey is conducted in southern Etruria, Italy, by John Ward Perkins of the British School at Rome.)

1953 ....French archaeologists find the largest Greek bronze *krater* ever discovered, part of the treasures in the tomb of a Celtic queen or princess at Vix in eastern France. The immense vessel for mixing wine with water had a capacity of 250 gallons and attests to the 6th-century wine trade between Greeks and Celts.

1954 ....Emil Kunze locates and excavates the workshop of the ancient sculptor Phidias in the sanctuary at Olympia, Greece, where Phidias created the monumental chryselephantine statue of Zeus that ranked as one of the Seven Wonders of the World.

1954 ....Mortimer Wheeler publishes *Archaeology from the Earth*, an archaeological manifesto that promoted the use of scientific techniques in survey, excavation, recording, and analysis.

1959 ....Italian archaeologists dig at Caesarea Maritima on the coast of Israel, a city of Roman design and construction built during the reign of Herod the Great. Eventually, the excavations will involve the efforts of more than 20 institutions in Israel, the United States, Canada, and other countries and will reveal one of the most ambitious harbor-building projects from the entire ancient world.

1959 ....Italian archaeologists unearth the skeleton of a Greek athlete in an elaborate stone-built tomb at Taranto in southern Italy, permitting a rare opportunity to perform a full battery of anatomical and chemical tests on an ancient Greek of the early 5th century B.C.

1960 ....Led by American archaeologist George Bass, a team of scuba divers and other specialists conducts the first scientific survey and excavation of a shipwreck site at Cape Gelidonya, Turkey. The success of the project leads to the establishment of the Institute of Nautical Archaeology, based at College Station, Texas, and at Bodrum, Turkey.

1963 ....Excavations at Dragonby, Lincolnshire, England, reveal an important Romano-

British village site, later to be excavated by an archaeological team from the University of Nottingham. The site will yield substantial botanical and zoological evidence, permitting archaeologist Jeffrey May to reconstruct changes in the ancient environment brought on by the process of Romanization.

1968 ....Near the harbor of Kyrenia in northern Cyprus, Michael Katzev of the Institute of Nautical Archaeology begins excavation of a 4th-century B.C. wine freighter. Enough of the hull was recovered to permit a full-scale replica of the Kyrenia ship to be built and tested at sea.

1968 ....Subsurface reconnaissance detects the remains of the Classical Greek city of Sybaris in southern Italy, but the overlying sediments are too deep and waterlogged to permit excavation.

1969 ....Greek archaeologist Spyridon Marinatos begins large-scale excavations at the Bronze Age town of Akrotiri on Thera (Santorini), which had been buried by a volcanic eruption in about 1620 B.C. In 1983, Christos Doumas takes over as director of the historic project, which revolutionizes the archaeology of the Cyclades Islands and early Greece.

1971 ....Under the directorship of British archaeologist Barry Cunliffe, a project is launched to excavate the deeply buried Roman West Baths under modern Bath, England, followed by excavations at the Sacred Spring and the temple of Sulis Minerva.

1972 ....An Italian sport diver discovers the bronze statues of two Greek warriors or heroes in shallow water off Riace Marina in Calabria, Italy.

1973 ....At the Roman fort of Vindolanda in northern England, excavators recover a cache of waterlogged documents written in ink on thin wooden tablets, including accounting records and personal letters that record military life on the Roman frontier in the late 1st and early 2nd centuries A.D.

1977 ....Greek archaeologist Manolis Andronikos excavates Tomb II at the royal Macedonian cemetery of Vergina in northern Greece and identifies the occupant as King Philip II, father of Alexander the Great.

1979 ....Edmund Büchner uses historical evidence to locate the remains of the great sundial erected by Augustus in 9 B.C. on the Campus Martius, which had long been concealed beneath the modern buildings of Rome.

1980 ....Italian archaeologists discover hundreds of human skeletons near and under the vaulted concrete docks of ancient Herculaneum, the remains of victims of the eruption of Vesuvius in A.D. 79, thus bringing to light one of the first major collections of human skeletal material from the time of the Roman Empire.

1981 ....Excavations at the Iron Age site of Lefkandi on the island of Euboae (Evvia) in Greece reveal a 10th-century-B.C. long house of a local chieftain, along with elaborate burials and imported goods from Egypt and the Near East—surprising evidence for sophisticated culture in the heart of the Greek Dark Age.

1983 ....Off Uluburun in southern Turkey, American and Turkish archaeologists of the Institute of Nautical Archaeology, led by Cemal Pulak, begin the survey and excavation of an important shipwreck from the late Bronze Age, possibly dating to as early as 1320 B.C. A gold scarab of Queen Nefertiti, the world's oldest known codex or hinged "book," raw glass and ivory, and sections of the massive wooden hull are among the materials recovered from the Uluburun wreck.

1986 ....A banner year for experimental reconstructions of ancient ships in Greece, including the first replica of the Kyrenia ship (*Kyrenia I*) and hypothetical reconstructions of Jason's *Argo* by Tim Severin and of an Athenian trireme, the *Olympias*. The sea trials of these ships were landmarks in experimental archaeology.

1987 ....The site of the Teutoburg Forest battle (A.D. 9) is discovered by British army officer Tony Clunn at Osnabrueck in northwest Germany. Subsequent excavations by German archaeologists locate a mass grave of Roman soldiers killed in the battle.

1992 ....Austrian archaeologists working at Ephesus in Turkey discover a cemetery for gladiators and conduct an interdisciplinary study of the skeletons, the weaponry and modes of killing, and the inscriptions on the grave markers.

1994 ....French archaeologist Jean-Yves Empereur of the Center for Alexandrian Studies begins a project to map and recover stone sculptures, architectural elements, and other antiquities from the ancient harbor of Alexandria, capital of Hellenistic Egypt.

1997 ....Analysis of an ice-core taken from a glacier on Greenland reveals that intensive Roman mining and smelting of lead, mainly from the Rio Tinto mines of southern Spain, created pollution of the atmosphere worldwide in the 1st century A.D.

1999 ....Ten Roman ships with cargoes, plus the skeletons of a man and dog, are found by chance at Pisa in Italy during construction on the site of the ancient harbor, now completely silted up.

2000 ....British archaeologist Hilary Cool publishes an analysis of human remains from a 3rd-century Roman military cemetery at Brougham near Hadrian's Wall and discoveries that two of the graves interpreted as belonging to cavalry officers were the graves of women.

2005 ....Satellite images reveal Roman villas and other previously undetected sites throughout the Classical world.

Glossary

Absolute chronology: A sequence of dates fixed to specific calendar years and based on historical records.

A.D./B.C. dates: These designations indicate the era of a year number or century. Traditionally, *A.D.* was derived from the Latin "*anno domini*" and was written before the year number; the designation could not correctly be ascribed to centuries. In this course, both A.D. and B.C. are used following both annual dates and centuries, with A.D. an abbreviation for "advancing dates" and B.C. an abbreviation for "backward count."

These same eras are sometimes labeled C.E., or Common Era (= A.D.), and B.C.E. (= B.C.). However, that system is *not* universally "common"; the duplication of *C.E.* in *B.C.E.* can create confusion in speaking and in field notes, and the discrepancy in the number of letters (two for C.E., three for B.C.E.) is cumbersome when creating computer programs with coded fields for entering dates.

Adyton: The holy inner sanctum of a Greek temple; literally, the "no entry" chamber.

Aerial reconnaissance: A survey carried out from aircraft or balloons that can reveal features on the ground that are obscured or invisible to people on the surface.

Agora: The open area in the heart of a Greek city, serving as a government, religious, and commercial center.

Alphabet: A script originating among Canaanite peoples in which a couple of dozen signs contrive to represent the sounds of any language. The original alphabet represented only consonants; the Greeks added vowels.

Amber: Golden lumps of fossilized tree resin, highly prized in the Classical world and sometimes imported from as far away as the Baltic.

Amphitheatre: A place of public entertainment in the form of a "double theatre," in which an enclosed circle or oval of tiered seats surrounded a central arena. Modern usage departs from the ancient meaning, by calling any open-air theatre an amphitheatre.

Amphora: A transport container for wine, olive oil, or other comestibles, almost always pottery, with a distinctive pointed foot.

The name derives from the pair of handles on either side of the neck, which allow the pot to be "carried on both sides."

Archaeology: The scientific and humanistic discipline of recovering, analyzing, and interpreting the physical remains of past cultures.

Artifact: Any object made by human agency, as opposed to a *geofact*, made by natural processes.

"Black Athena": A scholarly controversy launched by philologist Martin Bernal, who asserts that the Classical world owed much of its intellectual achievement to cultural borrowings and innovations originating in Egypt and the Near East.

Bronze Age: The middle period in the Old World's three-age system (Stone Age, Bronze Age, Iron Age), when the dominant material used for tools and weapons was bronze—an alloy of nine parts copper and one part tin. The famous Bronze Age civilization of the Mycenaeans began to give way to the Iron Age in about 1200 B.C.

Chronometric chronology: A system of dating based on the measurement of natural processes at the atomic or molecular level, as in radiocarbon dating and thermoluminescence.

Chryselephantine: Made of gold and ivory, as were Phidias's great 5th-century-B.C. sculptures of Athena in the Parthenon at Athens and Zeus at Olympia.

Classical: Derived from the Latin root for "order" (as in modern English *classify*), the term has taken on a life of its own to describe styles or periods that seem to set a pattern for subsequent ages. In this course, it is used of the Greco-Roman culture that arose in the early Iron Age and lasted for about a millennium and a half, down to the collapse of the western Roman Empire.

Crop mark: A variation in the growth of wheat or other field crops, usually only visible through aerial reconnaissance and often indicative of stone walls or other remains below the surface.

Curse tablet: A magical object, usually of lead, on which a secret prayer for harm or destruction was inscribed. The tablet was then deposited in a sacred place or at a spot where it was hoped that the magical spell would take effect.

Dark Age: Modern designation for a period of history in which such civilized attainments as writing, engineering, and sophisticated urban life are reduced or disappear. The Classical world emerged from the Dark Age that followed the collapse of the Bronze Age kingdoms in about 1200 B.C. and was submerged into the Dark Age of early medieval Europe.

Daybooks: The written records that record the excavations and discoveries on an archaeological site; a sort of journal or "site diary." The maintenance of daybooks by Alcubierre and Weber at Herculaneum and Pompeii marked the beginning of archaeology as a discipline.

Dendrochronology: A natural system of dating that can be exact to a specific year, thanks to the unique sequences of annual rings that mark variable rainfall and other conditions during each year of a tree's growth. A dendrochronological sequence must be established region by region; some now extend more than 6,000 years into the past.

Elgin Marbles: The statues and reliefs from 5th-century-B.C. Athens that originally formed part of the pediments, friezes, and metopes of the Parthenon. Their removal from the Parthenon by Lord Elgin, who shipped them to England and ultimately placed them in the British Museum, has been a source of controversy from the first.

Epigraphy: The study of ancient inscriptions.

Etruscan civilization: A sophisticated urban culture of central Italy that preceded and helped shape Roman civilization. Best known from the art in their tombs, the Etruscans spoke a non-Indo-European language that has still not been deciphered.

Experimental archaeology: The field of recreating ancient artifacts or structures and performing trials to test their use, performance, or properties.

Forum: The open area at the heart of a Roman city, equivalent to the Greek *agora*, where governmental, religious, and commercial activities took place.

Fresco: An artistic technique first appearing in the Cycladic and Minoan cultures, in which pigments are applied to plaster while it is still wet or "fresh."

Graffito: Literally "little writing" and more familiar in the plural form, *graffiti*. A graffito is a short piece of informal writing scratched or painted onto a surface that was not originally intended to receive it, such as a house wall or a potsherd.

Ground-penetrating radar: A survey technique in which a box containing a radar transmitter is dragged across a site, and measurements are recorded of the depth at which a hard object (bedrock, a wall, a buried beach) bounces the radar back to the receiver.

House church: The oldest places of Christian worship, found as far apart as Carthage in Tunisia and Dura on the Euphrates, in which the enclosed, courtyard-centered design of the typical Classical home provided a secret place of worship for this banned religion.

Hypocaust: The most typical feature of a Roman bath, composed of close-set stacks of tiles that supported a raised concrete floor and allowed hot air to circulate beneath.

Inhumation: A form of burial in which the entire corpse is buried, as opposed to the more popular rite of *cremation* (burning of the body) or *excarnation* (burial of the disarticulated bones after the flesh has been removed).

Iron Age: An age that is technically still with us, given that most of our tools and weapons are made of steel, but the term is used by Classical archaeologists to designate only the early centuries in which iron-using spread throughout the Mediterranean.

Krater: A large vessel with a wide mouth in which wine was mixed with water before serving at a symposium or banquet.

Latifundia: A Roman villa, farm, or country estate of enormous size, "wide" and "deep" as its name indicates, and generally devoted to commercial mass production of a few varieties of crop or livestock.

Lerici periscope: A reconnaissance device for viewing the contents of buried tombs and sealed chambers before opening them.

Linear B script: The late Bronze Age writing system used at Knossos on Crete and at such sites as Pylos, Mycenae, and Thebes on the Greek mainland. Michael Ventris demonstrated that the Linear B signs represented syllables (consonant plus vowel) and that the language of the tablets was Greek.

Lost-wax casting: A technique for casting bronze and other metals, in which wax that has been encased in a clay matrix is first melted out, then replaced with a flow of molten bronze. The clay core sometimes remains inside the finished piece.

Magnetometer: A device that can measure the degree of magnetism of a buried or submerged object, especially but not exclusively where iron is present. It can also distinguish magnetically charged soil types, such as certain clays.

Minoan civilization: The name coined by Arthur Evans as a label for the advanced Bronze Age culture of Crete, typified by palaces at Knossos and elsewhere and deriving from the name of the mythical Cretan king Minos.

Mithraeum: A subterranean chamber consecrated to the religious rituals of followers of the Eastern god Mithras, a power of light whose triumph over darkness was symbolized in the sacrifice of a bull. This popular religion was widespread throughout the Roman Empire, particularly among soldiers.

Mosaic: A pavement (or, less commonly, a wall or ceiling decoration) in which small square pieces of stone, tile, or glass—*tesserae*—are cemented together. Most mosaics use *tesserae* of different colors to create a pattern or picture.

Mycenaean civilization: The Bronze Age culture that developed on the Greek mainland at such sites as Mycenae, Tiryns, Pylos, Athens, and Thebes, then spread to Knossos and elsewhere. Associated with the legend of the Trojan War, the Mycenaeans established wide trading or colonizing contacts in Sicily and southern Italy, as well as on the Mediterranean coasts of Asia.

Obsidian: A volcanic glass, usually black, that can be traced back to its source and, thus, provides archaeologists with evidence of ancient trade routes.

Oracle: A site where public divination was practiced and where it was believed that one could receive guidance directly from the gods.

Ostrakon: A potsherd and, more specifically, a sherd bearing a graffito or inscription. The casting of votes to exile dangerous citizens in Athens was performed with names written on *ostraka*, hence our word *ostracism*.

Oxhide ingot: A large flat casting of metal—usually copper or bronze—with a pair of projecting handles or "legs" at either end to facilitate carrying. These ingots are important parts of Bronze Age cargoes in the eastern Mediterranean.

Palynology: The study of plant pollens, used in archaeological research to reconstruct the living environment in and around an ancient site or the plant-derived contents that survive as residues in ancient pots and other containers.

Papyrus: The ancestor of modern paper, invented and manufactured in Egypt from the fibrous stems of a river plant and much used throughout the Mediterranean as a medium for written texts and records. Unfortunately, papyrus does not normally survive under humid conditions.

Physical anthropology: The study of human remains, important to archaeology for providing information about demography, health, age at death, and life histories of ancient individuals and populations.

Pompeii premise: A term coined by American archaeologist Lewis Binford to describe the naïve supposition that an archaeological site can reveal a single moment of the past, frozen in time and perfectly preserved.

Pozzolana: A volcanic deposit, occurring naturally in the Bay of Naples and surrounding areas, that can be used in place of sand to create mortar or concrete that will "set up" even underwater.

Radiocarbon dating: A chronometric system developed by Willard Libby that determines the age of an artifact or sample based on the amount of radioactive carbon-14 that it contains. Radiocarbon is found in most living things, but the amount is steadily reduced after death in accordance with a half-life of 5,730 years.

Relative chronology: A chronology based on stratigraphic sequences or typological series that reveals "earlier-than" and "later-than" relationships between structures, layers, or artifacts but does not assign exact dates.

Resistivity meter: A survey technique that identifies buried remains based on their varying ability to transmit (e.g., wet soil) or resist (e.g., stone walls) electrical impulses passing along a row of metal rods set in the ground.

Scuba: An invention by a French team that included Jacques Cousteau, this "self-contained underwater breathing apparatus," with its mouth-held regulator attached to tanks of compressed gas or air, opened up shipwrecks and other submerged sites to archaeological investigation. Because of safety issues involving decompression, scuba is most useful on sites lying in less than 150 feet of water.

Sherd: A broken piece of a pot, tile, brick, or other ceramic object and the most commonly encountered artifact type at most Classical sites. Sherds can reveal the shape and function of the original piece, its place of manufacture, and its date.

Sidescan sonar: A reconnaissance technique for locating anomalies projecting from the sea floor, sidescan sonar relies on echoes bounced back to a receiver from sound waves broadcast obliquely on either side of a research vessel.

Stratigraphy: The recording and reading of layers that have accumulated on an archaeological site.

Syllabary: A writing system, such as Linear B, that uses symbols to record consonant-plus-vowel combinations. Syllabaries require more symbols than alphabets but fewer than hieroglyphic or ideogram-based scripts.

Tell: An artificial hill or mound that is composed of layer upon layer of cities or other human habitations. Tells form in the eastern Mediterranean and the Near East, where prevailingly dry conditions and scarcity of fuel for the baking of bricks encourages construction based on mudbrick, rammed earth, or adobe. The most important tell in the realm of Classical archaeology was Hissarlik, identified with Homer's Troy.

Teredo: Mistakenly called a "ship worm," this marine organism is actually a mollusk that uses its razor-sharp residual shell to bore holes in wood. Thanks to the relentless activity of the teredo, most wooden parts of ancient shipwrecks have been destroyed, except in cases where they were sealed away from attack by an overburden of mud, sand, ballast, or solid cargo.

Thermoluminescence: A chronometric method of dating ceramic objects that have been fired rather than merely dried, this process reheats the sample to firing temperature and measures the amount of energy stored in the clay since the original firing. Thermoluminescence dates tend to have a fairly wide margin of error, and the method is most used by Classical archaeologists to distinguish genuine ancient pottery from fakes.

Thermopolium: A type of sidewalk shop popular in Pompeii, where food, including hot, ready-to-eat food, was sold from pots set in a counter, and patrons could socialize around the counter in the open shop front as at a bar.

Trace elements: Impurities found in ancient stone, metal, clay, and bone that allow chemists to identify the geographical source of the sample.

Trireme: A type of oared ship with a bronze ram, much used in Greek and Roman fleets. Attempts to reconstruct the three-level arrangement of the oars have featured in the field of experimental archaeology since its 19th-century inception. No part of any trireme's wooden hull has yet been recovered by archaeologists.

Villa: In its simplest original sense, a villa was a Roman farm. Large villas were called *latifundiae*. The cluster of buildings on a typical Roman farm included a *villa urbana* for the landowner and his family and *villa rustica* for the workers and the agricultural functions. The term *villa* was later extended to describe private seaside establishments or country retreats for wealthy citizens.

Biographical Notes

Alcubierre, Roque Joaquín (1702–1780). Spanish military engineer who directed the first archaeological campaigns at Herculaneum starting in 1738 and at Pompeii a decade later. He is notable for keeping daybooks and creating the oldest surviving scientific archaeological illustration: a plan and cross-section of the theatre at Herculaneum, indicating different phases of excavation, find spots of various artifacts, and the layering of volcanic deposits on top of the ruins.

Andronikos, Manolis (1919–1992). Greek archaeologist most famous for his excavations at the royal Macedonian cemetery of Vergina. Andronikos also worked on early Iron Age remains at Vergina and other sites in northern Greece.

Bass, George. American archaeologist who, in 1960 at Cape Gelidonya, directed the first excavation of a shipwreck that met fully scientific standards for archaeological fieldwork and publication. He subsequently founded the Institute of Nautical Archaeology.

Blegen, Carl (1887–1971). American archaeologist who discovered and excavated the Bronze Age palace at Pylos in southwestern Greece.

Boyd, Harriet (1871–1945). American archaeologist who excavated the Bronze Age town of Gournia in eastern Crete.

Calvert, Frank (1828–1908). British diplomat and archaeologist who devoted his life to research in the Troad region of northwestern Turkey. His test trenches in the tell at Hissarlik convinced him and, soon after, Heinrich Schliemann, also, that Calvert had found the site of Homer's Troy.

Camp, John M. American archaeologist and director of excavations in the Athenian Agora.

Curtius, Ernst (1814–1896). German archeologist who established important precedents for fieldwork during his excavations at Olympia in Greece.

Dörpfeld, Wilhelm (1853–1940). German archaeologist whose wide-ranging career began at Olympia and included work with Schliemann at Hissarlik.

Elgin, Lord (Thomas Bruce) (1766–1841). British ambassador to Constantinople in 1799, known for his removal of marble statues and reliefs from the Parthenon in Athens to the British Museum in London.

Evans, Sir Arthur (1851–1941). British archaeologist whose excavations at Knossos in Crete spanned 40 years and added the term *Minoan* to the vocabulary of Classical studies.

Fiorelli, Giuseppe (1823–1896). Italian archaeologist who was appointed by Garibaldi as director of excavations at Pompeii. He provided the site with the system of area designations that is still in use and pioneered the use of plaster poured into hollow cavities to recover casts of ancient Pompeiians who had died during the eruption of Vesuvius.

Frost, Honor. British underwater archaeologist who has conducted fieldwork throughout the Mediterranean, from Sicily to Alexandria, and published important studies of ancient stone anchors.

Hamilton, Sir William (1730–1803). British envoy to Naples and a scholar who used his time in Italy to study vulcanology and amass an immense collection of Greek and Etruscan vases.

Hohlfelder, Robert. American underwater archaeologist specializing in Roman harbor construction from Cosa in Italy to Caesarea Maritima; one of his particular interests is in the properties of Roman hydraulic concrete.

Kuniholm, Peter. American archaeologist and founder of the Aegean Dendrochronology Project.

Marinatos, Spyridon (1901–1974). Greek archaeologist known for excavations at the Bronze Age site of Akrotiri on the volcanic island of Santorini (Thera).

Pulak, Cemal. Turkish underwater archaeologist who directed the excavation of the Bronze Age shipwreck at Uluburun.

Schliemann, Heinrich (1822–1890). German tycoon and archaeological enthusiast, famous for his claim to have discovered Homer's city of Troy in the tell at Hissarlik. His explorations and books opened up the field of Bronze Age archaeology in Greece and the Aegean.

Thucydides (c. 460–404 B.C.). Athenian historian of the Peloponnesian War and the first writer to use the term and the concept of *archaeology*.

Tsountas, Christos (1857–1934). Greek archaeologist who conducted pioneering work in the fields of prehistory at Sesklo and underwater survey at Salamis but is best known for his work at Mycenae.

Ventris, Michael (1922–1956). British architect who deciphered the Linear B script of Bronze Age Crete and Greece and determined that the language was Greek.

Ward, Cheryl. American underwater archaeologist and paleobotanist who has done pioneering work in the study of wood and plant remains in ancient wrecks and their cargoes.

Weber, Karl Johann (1712–1764). Swiss military engineer who directed excavations at Herculaneum and Pompeii from 1749 until his death. His plans and reconstructions of the Villa of the Papyri, the House of Julia Felix, and the entire landscape of the Bay of Naples set a high standard for archaeological recording and illustration.

Wheeler, Sir Mortimer (1890–1976). British archaeologist who championed more rigorous methods of fieldwork in a series of excavations at Roman sites in Britain and an ancient warehouse full of Roman pottery in southern India.

Winckelmann, Johann Joachim (1717–1768). Prussian scholar whose publications on the history of Greek and Roman art transformed the field into an academic discipline and established a chronology still followed today.

Bibliography

Essential Reading:

Allen, Susan Hueck. *Finding the Walls of Troy: Frank Calvert and Heinrich Schliemann at Hisarlik.* Berkeley: University of California Press, 1999. The most authoritative study yet written on what happened at Troy and what it has meant to Classical archaeology.

Alsebrook, Mary. *Born to Rebel: The Life of Harriet Boyd Hawes.* Oxford: Oxbow Books, 1992. This biography of the pioneering discoverer of Gournia was written by the archaeologist's daughter.

Amandry, Pierre. *Delphi and Its History.* Athens: Archaeological Guide Editions, 1984. Formerly the director of the French Archaeological School, Amandry has devoted much of his long and eminent career to the study of Delphi. His short and authoritative essays here accompany maps, photos, and reconstruction drawings of both the site and the artifacts in the Delphi Museum.

American School of Classical Studies at Athens, various authors. *Excavations of the Athenian Agora: Picture Books* (series). Athens: American School of Classical Studies, 1959 to present. These two dozen pamphlets cover topics ranging from pots and pans (1959) to women and marbleworkers (2005), with lamps, birds, waterworks, inscriptions, graffiti, horsemanship, coins, Socrates, building methods, and law-court apparatus among the feast of subjects.

Bass, George. *Beneath the Seven Seas.* London: Thames and Hudson, 2005. This worldwide survey includes first-hand accounts of the underwater exacavations of shipwrecks at Cape Gelidonya, Kyrenia, and Uluburun in the eastern Mediterranean.

Berry, Joanne, ed. *Unpeeling Pompeii: Studies of Region I of Pompeii.* Milan: Electa, 1998. In its in-depth stratigraphic study of one sector of Pompeii, this little volume sets a high standard for illustration and presentation of a very complex chronological picture.

Biek, Leo. *Archaeology and the Microscope: The Scientific Examination of Archaeological Evidence.* New York: Praeger, 1963. Do not be put off by the uninformative table of contents. Physical chemist Biek offers stimulating insights into palynology, analysis of waterlogged wood and leather, aerial photography, and scientific dating techniques.

Birley, Anthony. *Hadrian: The Restless Emperor.* London: Routledge, 1997. This biography of the peripatetic emperor emphasizes Hadrian's building projects and is illustrated throughout with Hadrianic coins, medallions, and other artworks.

Boardman, John. *The History of Greek Vases: Potters, Painters and Pictures*. London: Thames and Hudson, 2001. An essential work on a vital aspect of Greek archaeology. The chapters on "Trade," "Greek Vases in Use," and "Tricks of the Trade" would alone be worth the price of the book.

Boatwright, Mary, Daniel Gargola, and Richard Talbert. *The Romans from Village to Empire: A History of Ancient Rome from Earliest Times to Constantine*. This book is recommended to those who prefer a traditional historical narrative to set archaeological discoveries in context. The early chapters on Rome's Italian neighbors are especially rewarding.

Bowman, Alan K. *Life and Letters on the Roman Frontier: Vindolanda and Its People*. London: British Museum Press, 1994. This book, by one of the scholars who worked on the Vindolanda tablets, provides text and translations of 34 important Roman letters, accounting records, and military documents from a fort in northern England.

Broad, William. *The Oracle: The Lost Secrets and Hidden Message of Ancient Delphi*. New York: Penguin, 2006. A study of the geology and history of Delphi and its famous oracle, including an account of the interdisciplinary research conducted at the site since 1996 by geologist Jelle de Boer, archaeologist John Hale, chemist Jeff Chanton, and toxicologist Henry Spiller.

Brown, Peter. *The World of Late Antiquity, AD 150–750*. London: Thames and Hudson, 1971. An extremely influential historical reassessment of the transition between the Classical and medieval worlds, in which the author proposes "Late Antiquity" as a designation for these turbulent centuries.

Bullitt, Orville. *Search for Sybaris*. Philadelphia: Lippincott, 1969. A painfully honest account of an archaeological "failure," this book chronicles the attempts to find the lost city of Sybaris using a barrage of subsurface detection devices. (The site was finally located but judged to be too deep and too waterlogged for excavation.)

Camp, John M. *The Archaeology of Athens*. New Haven: Yale University Press, 2001. This masterly survey embraces archaeological discoveries dating from the Stone Age to the late Roman period, illustrated throughout with great photographs, maps, plans, and colorful reconstruction paintings. Camp goes far beyond familiar Classical monuments to provide a geographical study and includes sections on more than a dozen sites of ancient Attica, from Cape Sounion to Marathon and Eleusis.

————. *The Athenian Agora: Excavations in the Heart of Classical Athens*. London: Thames and Hudson, 1986. A clear and compelling reconstruction of daily life, governmental operations, and commercial activity in the cradle of ancient democracy.

————, and Elizabeth Fisher. *The World of the Ancient Greeks*. London: Thames and Hudson, 2002. An excellent introduction to archaeological sites and discoveries in Greece, this book is co-written by the director of excavations in the Athenian Agora and an authority on Bronze Age pottery.

Chadwick, John. "Linear B," in J. T. Hooker, ed., *Reading the Past: Ancient Writing from Cuneiform to the Alphabet*. London: British Museum Press, 1990. The author collaborated with Michael Ventris on the decipherment of the Linear B script found at Bronze Age palaces on Crete and mainland Greece.

Chamberlain, Andrew. *Interpreting the Past: Human Remains*. London: British Museum Press, 1994. From biomolecular evidence to demographics and from ancient disease to legal ethics, this short handbook covers the field concisely and clearly.

Clunn, Tony. *The Quest for the Lost Roman Legions: Discovering the Varus Battlefield*. New York: Savas Beatie, 2005. Major Clunn used a magnetometer to search for the "Teutoburg Forest" battle site and has written an account that merges archaeology with a novelistic recreation of the Roman campaign in Germany in 9 A.D.

Connolly, Peter, and Hazel Dodge. *The Ancient City: Life in Classical Athens and Rome*. Oxford: Oxford University Press, 1998. This is a book for the ages, and for *all* ages, thanks to Connolly's brilliant and inimitable artistic recreations of ancient architecture, landscapes, and daily life.

Cook, B.F. "Greek Inscriptions," in J. T. Hooker, ed., *Reading the Past: Ancient Writing from Cuneiform to the Alphabet*. London: British Museum Press, 1990. This handbook provides an excellent introduction to Greek inscriptions from the earliest days of the alphabet to the heyday of Hellenic civilization.

Cornell, Tim, and John Matthews. *Atlas of the Roman World*. New York: Facts on File, 1982. This historical and cultural atlas vividly charts the rise of the city of Rome and the spread of Roman power and civilization to an empire stretching from the Atlantic to the Euphrates. The region-by-region survey of the empire is especially useful.

Coulston, Jon, and Hazel Dodge, eds. *Ancient Rome: The Archaeology of the Eternal City*. Oxford: Alden Press 2000. This collection of essays provides a valuable overview of current research on the largest urban center of the Classical world.

Cunliffe, Barry. *Roman Bath Discovered*. London: Routledge, 1984. Through this book, the author and excavator presented the results of decades of fieldwork on one of the most important Roman sites in Britain.

———. *The Extraordinary Voyage of Pytheas the Greek*. New York: Walker Publishing Co., 2002. A distinguished British archaeologist uses the 4th-century-B.C. voyage of Pytheas of Marseilles as a lens for examining links between the Greeks and Atlantic Europe.

Curnow, Trevor. *The Oracles of the Ancient World: A Comprehensive Guide*. London: Duckworth, 2004. A detailed survey of Classical oracles, country by country and site by site, written by a scholar who has visited most of them and can cite both ancient authors and personal experience.

De Camp, L. Sprague. *The Ancient Engineers*. New York: Barnes and Noble, 1960. This wide-ranging volume embraces engineering achievements from aqueducts to war ships and includes four chapters on Greek and Roman engineers.

De Grummond, Nancy T., ed. *An Encyclopedia of the History of Classical Archaeology*. Westwood, CT: Greenwood Press, 1996. A comprehensive and indispensable reference work to the most important figures, sites, and discoveries from the Renaissance to 1994.

De la Bedoyere, Guy. *Roman Villas and the Countryside*. London: Batsford 1993. The author, an expert on Roman pottery, presents a clear and vivid reconstruction of villa life in Roman Britain, including detailed drawings.

Delgado, James, ed. *Encyclopedia of Underwater and Maritime Archaeology*. London: British Museum Press, 1997. In addition to short articles on more than 30 ancient wreck sites, this volume features longer essays on subjects from legal issues to underwater survey and excavation techniques.

Diess, Joseph J. *Herculaneum: Italy's Buried Treasure*. Malibu: J. Paul Getty Museum, 1989. A comprehensive overview of the site where Classical archaeology began, organized building by building, with excellent photographs and plans.

Dyson, Stephen L. *Ancient Marbles to American Shores: Classical Archaeology in the United States*. Philadelphia: University of Pennsylvania Press, 1998. An important historical survey of American scholars and institutions involved in the emergence and growth of Classical archaeology.

Empereur, Jean-Yves. *Alexandria Rediscovered*. Paris: George Braziller, 1998. This illustrated survey was written by one of the most active explorers in the rediscovery of ancient Alexandria.

Fantham, Elaine, et al. *Women in the Classical World: Image and Text*. New York: Oxford University Press, 1995. A comprehensive introduction to the role of women in ancient Greece and Rome and the image that they have left behind in works of literature and art.

Fleming, Stuart. *Vinum: The Story of Roman Wine*. Glen Mills, PA: Art Flair, 2001. This well-illustrated survey ranges from archaeological evidence to considerations of wine's use in medicine and religious rites.

Friedrich, Walter. *Fire in the Sea: The Santorini Volcano, Natural History and the Legend of Atlantis*. Cambridge: Cambridge University Press, 2000. Although written by a geologist, this lavishly produced volume is an indispensable guide to the eruption of Santorini from an archaeological standpoint as well.

Futrell, Alison. *Blood in the Arena: The Spectacle of Roman Power*. Austin: University of Texas Press, 1997. Through painstaking scholarship, Futrell assembles from archaeological evidence and literary clues a convincing overview of Roman blood sports and is able to show connections to the realm of human sacrifice.

Hale, John and Jelle de Boer, Jeff Chanton, and Henry Spiller. "Questioning the Delphic Oracle." *Scientific American*, August 2003. This article, also available online at the "SCIAM" website, recounts the results of an interdisciplinary investigation into the geological origins of the famous Delphic Oracle in Greece.

Hawes, Charles, and Harriet Boyd Hawes. *Crete: The Forerunner of Greece.* New York: Harper, 1909. One of the early attempts to produce a synthesis on Minoan sites and archaeology, this overview by the excavator of Gournia and her husband was written less than a decade after Evans started work at Knossos.

Holum, Kenneth, Robert Hohlfelder, Robert Bull, and Avner Raban. *King Herod's Dream: Caesarea on the Sea.* New York: W.W. Norton, 1988. This multidisciplinary study presents a colorful and scholarly introduction to one of the most important sites created by the Romans, a harbor city for the client kingdom of Judea.

Humphrey, John, et al. *Greek and Roman Technology: A Sourcebook.* London: Routledge, 1998. This grand anthology collects passages from Classical authors on agriculture, mining and quarrying, metallurgy, engineering, hydraulics, crafts, transport, time-keeping, writing, military technology, and ancient attitudes toward labor and innovation, along with short essays and extensive bibliographies.

Jashemski, Wilhelmina, and Frederick Meyer, eds. *The Natural History of Pompeii.* Cambridge: Cambridge University Press, 2002. Jashemski pioneered the study of gardens at Pompeii and, along with Meyer (a botanist), has assembled an extraordinary collection of specialist studies ranging from volcanology and pollen studies to human health and nutrition.

Jenkins, Ian, and Kim Sloan. *Vases and Volcanoes: Sir William Hamilton and His Collection.* London: British Museum Press, 1996. Six illuminating essays precede an illustrated catalogue of an exhibition that did full justice to Hamilton's life and work.

Lambert, Joseph B. *Traces of the Past: Unraveling the Secrets of Archaeology through Chemistry.* Reading, MA: Helix Books, 1997. Aegean obsidian, Greek vases and bronzes, and Roman glass and statuary are among the items considered in this worldwide survey on the applications of chemical analysis to archaeological materials.

Levi, Peter. *Atlas of the Greek World.* New York: Facts on File, 1984. The maps in this historical and cultural atlas are supplemented by short, thoughtful essays and hundreds of images of sites and artifacts.

Lewis, Sian. *The Athenian Woman: An Iconographic Handbook.* London: Routledge, 2003. This volume analyzes women in Athenian vase paintings to draw an in-depth portrait of women's lives in Classical Athens.

Liversidge, Joan. *Everyday Life in the Roman Empire*. London: Batsford, 1976. This authoritative overview, with superb drawings by Eva Wilson, was written by the Hon. Keeper of the Roman Collections in the Museum of Archaeology and Ethnology at Cambridge University.

Lombardi Satriani, Luigi, and Maurizio Paoletti, eds. *Heroes from the Sea*. Rome: Gangemi, 1986. Eight informative and provocative essays examine various aspects of the bronze statues known as the Riace Warriors, from their chance discovery and possible provenance to a humorous look at their impact on Italian popular culture.

MacDonald, William, and John Pinto. *Hadrian's Villa and Its Legacy*. New Haven: Yale University Press, 1995. This beautifully illustrated volume presents a detailed survey of Hadrian's famous villa at Tivoli and a consideration of its lasting influence on art and architecture.

MacKendrick, Paul L. *The Greek Stones Speak: The Story of Archaeology in Greek Lands*. New York, W.W. Norton, 1983. This archaeological tour through the world of the ancient Greeks weaves history, architecture, and major discoveries into a gripping narrative. MacKendrick visits sites from Alexandria in Egypt to Paestum in Italy, but the emphasis rests firmly on Greece and the Aegean.

————. *The Mute Stones Speak: The Story of Archaeology in Italy*. New York: W.W. Norton, 1984. This original volume in MacKendrick's "Speaking Stones" series ultimately led as far afield as *The Dacian Stones Speak*, covering Roman remains in modern Romania. All are great reading and useful reference works.

Maloney, Stephanie, and John Hale. "The Villa of Torre de Palma (Alto Alentejo)." *Journal of Roman Archaeology* 9 (1996). This report covers the first decade of fieldwork at this Roman villa and presents the evidence for determining the dates and functions of buildings in this large rural complex, which includes an early Christian basilica.

Mancinelli, Fabrizio. *The Catacombs of Rome and the Origins of Christianity*. Florence: Scala, 1981. The author, a curator in the Vatican collections, provides an extensively illustrated tour of

Rome's catacombs and the art and artifacts that have been found in them.

Mattusch, Carol. *Classical Bronzes: The Art and Craft of Greek and Roman Statuary*. Ithaca: Cornell University Press, 1996. The author considers the techniques of ancient bronze production and sets statues in the context of the ancient art market.

May, Jeffrey. *Dragonby: Report on Excavations at an Iron Age and Romano-British Settlement in North Lincolnshire.* Oxford: Oxbow Monograph 61, 1996. The two volumes of this report include valuable chapters on reconstructing the ancient environment, including the impact of Romanization on the natural setting of the town.

McGovern, Patrick. *Ancient Wine: The Search for the Origins of Viniculture*. Princeton: Princeton University Press, 2003. The study of Greek wine is here set in the wider context of wine's Near Eastern origins, in a book that does full justice to archaeology, chemistry, and history.

McIntosh, Jane. *The Practical Archaeologist: How We Know What We Know About the Past*. New York: Facts on File, 1986. Through concise presentation and down-to-earth style, the author manages to compress most current fieldwork and lab procedures into this short and effective overview.

Olesen, John, et al. "The Caesarea Ancient Harbour Excavation Project," *Journal of Field Archaeology* 11 (1984). This article is a report on the important discoveries of the 1980–1983 field seasons.

Palyvou, Clairy. *Akrotiri, Thera: An Architecture of Affluence 3,500 Years Old.* Philadelphia: INSTAP Academic Press, 2005. This book takes the reader through the ruins of Akrotiri, house by house and room by room, in the company of an architect who participated in the dig under both Marinatos and Doumas.

Pomeroy, Sarah. *Goddesses, Whores, Wives, and Slaves: Women in Classical Antiquity.* New York: Schocken, 1995. Despite the sensational title, this book is an authoritative work that goes beyond conventional literary sources to include demographic, legal, and medical evidence. The writer has also written a book devoted to the women of Sparta in ancient Greece.

Powell, Barry. *Homer and the Origin of the Greek Alphabet.* Cambridge: Cambridge University Press, 1991. The development of the alphabet in Greece is here tracked through a sequence of archaeological discoveries of early inscriptions, each one meticulously described and interpreted.

Prag, John, and Richard Neave. *Making Faces: Using Forensic and Archaeological Evidence.* College Station: Texas A&M University Press, 1997. The authors are most famous for having brought their combined archaeological and medical expertise to bear on reconstructing the face of King Philip II of Macedon, but their book includes a well-illustrated history of the field and many case studies.

Rook, Tony. *Roman Baths in Britain.* Risborough, UK: Shire Publications, 1992. An excellent introduction to Roman bath technology and architecture in general, with comparisons to the great imperial baths of Rome and good details on lead piping.

Runnels, Curtis, and Priscilla Murray. *Greece before History: An Archaeological Companion and Guide.* Stanford: Stanford University Press, 2001. The authors share their insights and observations on sites ranging in space from Crete to northern Greece and in time from the Paleolithic to the end of the Bronze Age.

Snodgrass, Anthony. *An Archaeology of Greece: The Present State and Future Scope of a Discipline.* Berkeley: University of California Press, 1987. In the course of these Sather Lectures, the author considers everything from Dörpfeld's hunt for the palace of Odysseus on the island of Leukas (!) to Iron Age settlements, the rural landscape, figural scenes in early art, and the discovery of Augustus's sundial in Rome.

Swaddling, Judith. *The Ancient Olympic Games.* Austin: University of Texas Press, 1988. This short work packs in a tremendous amount of information about the events of the ancient Olympics and the site on which they were held.

Taplin, Oliver. *Greek Fire: The Influence of Ancient Greece on the Modern World.* New York: Macmillan, 1990. An enthusiastic essay on the persistence of Greek cultural elements in the modern mainstream.

Thompson, F. Hugh. *The Archaeology of Greek and Roman Slavery.* New York: International Publications Marketing, 2005. An immense work that combines literary evidence with archaeological discoveries, this book serves to emphasize the many gaps in our knowledge of ancient slaves and their lives.

Ulansey, David. *The Origins of the Mithraic Mysteries: Cosmology and Salvation in the Ancient World*. Oxford: Oxford University Press, 1989. The author reconstructs Mithraic religion by combining ancient texts with the evidence of archaeological discoveries—and with a heavy emphasis on iconography.

Valavanis, Panos. *Games and Sanctuaries in Ancient Greece: Olympia, Delphi, Isthmia, Nemea, Athens*. Los Angeles: J. Paul Getty Trust, 2004. A big book on an epic subject, this survey by an archaeologist at the University of Athens focuses on the archaeological remains involving ancient athletic events, along with the monuments that attest to the cult of victorious athletes and the religious dimension of the games.

Wallace-Hadrill, Andrew. *Houses and Society in Pompeii and Herculaneum*. Princeton: Princeton University Press, 1994. This book presents a startlingly new vision of social history and everyday life in these famous cities, based on the author's extensive excavations and researches as director of The British School at Rome.

Ward-Perkins, Bryan. *The Fall of Rome and the End of Civilization*. Oxford: Oxford University Press, 2005. An archaeologist rebuts the currently popular view that the western Roman Empire transformed itself peacefully and without much loss of cultural complexity into medieval Christendom.

Wells, Peter S. *The Battle That Stopped Rome: Emperor Augustus, Arminius, and the Slaughter of the Legions in the Teutoburg Forest*. New York: W.W. Norton, 2003. An American archaeologist combines a report on the archaeological discoveries with a close reading of the ancient historical record to create a detailed reconstruction of a pivotal military disaster.

Westermann, William. *The Slave Systems of Greek and Roman Antiquity*. Philadelphia: American Philosophical Society, 1955. This work concentrates on literary and historical evidence but does offer a broad survey that compares slavery in Greece and Rome.

Wheeler, Mortimer. *Roman Art and Architecture*. London: Thames and Hudson, 1985. This handbook shows Sir Mortimer's familiarity with Roman sites from Britain to India, as well as his genius for synthesizing data from many fields.

White, K. D. *Greek and Roman Technology*. London: Thames and Hudson, 1984. This classic study takes a problem-oriented approach, supplemented with many illuminating line drawings and reconstructions.

Woods, Michael. *In Search of the Trojan War*. Berkeley, University of California Press, 1998. This popular bestseller offers an excellent introduction to the many questions raised by the excavations at Hisarlik (ancient Ilium), and what they tell us about the historical reality behind Homer's epic poem.

Supplementary Reading:

Coles, John. *Archaeology by Experiment*. New York: Scribner's, 1973. The author covers experimental reconstructions and trials involving artifacts from plows to boats and from weapons to musical instruments.

Fagan, Brian. *Time Detectives: How Scientists Use Modern Technology to Unravel the Secrets of the Past*. New York: Touchstone, 1995. The author includes sections on Mortimer Wheeler's excavation techniques, the Uluburun shipwreck, the Vindolanda tablets, and Hadrian's Wall.

Frost, Honor. *Under the Mediterranean: Marine Antiquities*. Englewood Cliffs, NJ: Prentice-Hall, 1963. A fascinating account of early days in underwater archaeology by a diver and scientific artist who worked with both Cousteau and Bass and, ultimately, became an authority on stone anchors.

Greene, Kevin. *The Archaeology of the Roman Economy*. Berkeley: University of California Press, 1991. The author methodically marshals archaeological evidence and statistics from a broad area to reconstruct the Roman economy from its agricultural base to inter-regional trade networks.

Hawkes, Jacquetta. *Adventurer in Archaeology: The Biography of Sir Mortimer Wheeler*. New York: St Martin's, 1982. A life of the great innovator of archaeological field technique; this book was written by an eminent archaeologist who has a keen appreciation for Wheeler's contributions.

Higgins, Michael D., and Reynold Higgins. *A Geological Companion to Greece and the Aegean*. Ithaca: Cornell University Press, 1996. The authors, a geologist and an archaeologist, explored the ancient sites of Greece and the Greek island to create this important handbook, illustrated with many maps and plans.

Hitchens, Christopher, et al. *The Elgin Marbles: Should They Be Returned to Greece?* London: Verso, 1998. A history of the controversy spanning 200 years, this book follows the marbles from the Acropolis to the British Museum and advocates restitution.

King, Anthony. *Archaeology of the Roman Empire.* London: Bison Books, 1982. The author surveys the empire thematically, rather than by period or region, with sections on the army, cities, villas, technology, trade, entertainment, mosaics, religion, and the collapse of the empire.

Koloski-Ostrow, Ann O., ed. *Naked Truths: Women, Sexuality, and Gender in Classical Art and Archaeology.* New York: Routledge, 1997. A wide-ranging collection of essays that reaches well beyond its primary theme of visual representations and gender identity.

Leppmann, Wolfgang. *Winckelmann.* New York: Knopf, 1970. This biography of the great 18th-century art historian offers detailed background information on the intellectual life of Europe during the decades in which the science of archaeology took form.

Medwid, Linda M. *The Makers of Classical Archaeology.* New York: Humanity Books, 2000. Biographical sketches of 119 archaeologists, antiquarians, and art historians, with invaluable details on the education, career, and publications of each.

MacDonald, William L. *The Pantheon: Design, Meaning, and Progeny.* Through vivid firsthand accounts and extensive plans and photographs, the author surveys every part of the best preserved structure from antiquity, from its deeply buried foundations to its soaring concrete dome.

McDonald, William A., and Carol G. Thomas. *Progress into the Past: The Rediscovery of Mycenaean Civilization.* Bloomington: Indiana University Press, 1990. This classic overview includes sections on the career of Heinrich Schliemann and the decipherment of Linear B script by Michael Ventris.

Parslow, Christopher C. *Rediscovering Antiquity: Karl Weber and the Excavation of Herculaneum, Pompeii and Stabiae.* Cambridge: Cambridge University Press, 1995. Weber may get star billing, but Parslow has conducted detailed research into the life of almost every figure involved in the 18th-century excavations. An essential sourcebook.

Runnels, Curtis. *The Archaeology of Heinrich Schliemann: An Annotated Bibliographic Handlist*. Boston: Archaeological Institute of America, 2002. This evaluation of Schliemann's achievements is based on a comprehensive study of all his publications.

Schuetze, Sebastian, and Madeleine Gisler-Huwiler. *The Complete Collection of Antiquities from the Cabinet of Sir William Hamilton*. Cologne: Taschen, 2004. This gigantic, landmark volume includes a lavish reprinting of d'Hancarville's original 18th-century engravings of Hamilton's vases, along with beautifully illustrated modern essays.

Sear, Frank. *Roman Architecture*. Ithaca: Cornell University Press, 1992. From the late republic to the end of the empire, Sear has drawn together examples of buildings that illustrate all aspects of Roman architecture, including valuable information on building techniques, construction materials, and city planning.

Shanks, Michael. *Classical Archaeology of Greece: Experiences of a Discipline*. New York: Routledge, 2000. A personal reflection on the current state of the field, interweaving vivid site and artifact descriptions with thought-provoking observations.

Silverberg, Robert. *Clocks for the Ages: How Scientists Date the Past*. New York: Macmillan, 1971. A handy journalistic compendium, this book offers background to the problems of archaeological dating and detailed accounts of dendrochronology and radiocarbon dating.

Talbert, Richard J. A. *Barrington Atlas of the Greek and Roman World*. Princeton: Princeton University Press, 2000. A monument of scholarship and cartography, this atlas includes both magnificent maps of the entire Classical world and references to ancient and modern sources on the location of sites from Scotland to Sri Lanka.

Throckmorton, Peter, ed. *The Sea Remembers: Shipwrecks and Archaeology*. New York: Weidenfeld and Nicolson, 1987. With sections on "The Ancient Mediterranean" and "From Rome to Byzantium," this book collects essays by underwater archaeologists discussing their own work.

Welsh, Frank. *Building the Trireme*. London: Constable, 1988. This account of the design, construction, and sea trials of the ship *Olympias* was written by a member of the Trireme Trust and provides an engaging personal diary of the project.

Wheeler, Sir Mortimer. *Archaeology from the Earth*. Baltimore: Penguin, 1954. An important manifesto, setting forth a coherent plan and rationale for archaeological fieldwork.

———. *Rome Beyond the Imperial Frontiers*. Baltimore: Penguin, 1954. This study of Roman influence outside the empire reflects Wheeler's own discoveries on Roman sites from Britain to southern India.

Website:

www.arts.cornell.edu\dendro\ This indispensable archaeological resource presents an ongoing record of dendrochronology dates and studies from the entire Aegean area.